THIRD EDITION

SUMMIT 2

ENGLISH FOR TODAY'S WORLD

JOAN SASLOW
ALLEN ASCHER

Summit: English for Today's World Level 2, Third Edition

Pearson, 221 River Street, Hoboken, NJ 07030

Staff credits: The people who made up the *Summit* team representing editorial, production, design, manufacturing, and marketing are Pietro Alongi, Rhea Banker, Peter Benson, Stephanie Bullard, Jennifer Castro, Tracey Munz Cataldo, Rosa Chapinal, Aerin Csigay, Dave Dickey, Gina DiLillo, Christopher Leonowicz, Laurie Neaman, Alison Pei, Sherri Pemberton, Jennifer Raspiller, Mary Rich, Courtney Steers, Katherine Sullivan, and Paula Van Ells.

Cover credit: Tonis Pan/Shutterstock

Text composition: emc design ltd

Library of Congress Cataloging-in-Publication Data

Names: Saslow, Joan M., author. | Ascher, Allen, author.
Title: Summit : English for today's world / Joan Saslow and Allen Ascher.
Description: Third Edition. | White Plains, NY : Pearson Education, [2017]
Identifiers: LCCN 2016017942| ISBN 9780134096070 (book w/ CD) | ISBN 9780134176888 (book w/ CD) | ISBN 013409607X (book w/ CD)
Subjects: LCSH: English language--Textbooks for foreign speakers. | English language--Rhetoric. | English language--Sound recording for foreign speakers.
Classification: LCC PE1128 .S2757 2017 | DDC 428.2/4--dc23
LC record available at https://lccn.loc.gov/2016017942

Photo credits: Original photography Mike Cohen. Page 2 Robert Churchill/Alamy Stock Photo; p. 3 (t) Amble Design/Shutterstock, (b) Maximino gomes/Fotolia; p. 4 (l) YUTAKA/AFLO SPORT/Newscom, (r) FRANCISCO TRUJILLO/NOTIMEX/Newscom; p. 5 (r) Alistair Berg/DigitalVision/Getty Images, (l) blvdone/Fotolia; p. 6 (tr) wavebreakmedia/Shutterstock, (b , 1-4) Monkey Business/Shutterstock, DRB Images/IIC/Getty Images, Andersen Ross/Blend Images/Getty Images, Jupiterimages/Stockbyte/Getty Images (b, 5-8) Tracy Whiteside/Shutterstock, Djomas/Shutterstock, Juanmonino/E+/Getty Images, pressmaster/Fotolia; p. 7 YAY Media AS/Alamy Stock Photo; p. 9 (t) Juniart/Shutterstock, (r) Monkey Business/Fotolia, (l) Stefan Schurr/Shutterstock; p. 13 goodluz/Fotolia; p. 15 Andersen Ross/Stockbyte/Getty Images; p. 17 Kzenon/Fotolia; p. 18 petrunjela/Fotolia; p. 19 Bits and Splits/Fotolia; p. 20 Wavebreak Media Ltd/123RF; p. 21 Zurijeta/Shutterstock; p. 22 (Machal) ROBIN TOWNSEND/EPA/Newscom, (Ka-shing) YONHAP/EPA/Newscom, (Caldicott) Paul Lovelace/REX/Newscom (human rights) tang90246/Fotolia, (smokestacks) Nickolay Khoroshkov/Shutterstock, (refugees) Photo by Antonio Masiello/NurPhoto/REX/Shutterstock, (children in line) Joseph Project - Malawi/Alamy Stock Photo, (school) BSIP/Newscom, (elderly woman and child) Kumar Sriskandan/Alamy Stock Photo; p. 23 demerzel21/Getty Images; p. 26 Drobot Dean/Fotolia; p. 27 ONOKY/Eric Audras/Brand X Pictures/Getty Images, p. 28 (l-r) BMP/Shutterstock, Vladimir Wrangel/Shutterstock, Billion Photos/Shutterstock; p. 29 bertys30/Fotolia; p. 30 (t) Imagewerks/Getty Images, (r) Monkey Business Images/Shutterstock, (l) Racorn/Shutterstock; p. 32 Byron Purvis/AdMedia/Newscom; p. 33 Shariff Che'Lah/123RF; p. 34 Kook Je Newspaper/AP Images; p. 35 (Parks) World History Archive/Alamy Stock Photo, (Khan) Pardis Sabeti, (crocodile) Jeep5d/Fotolia; p. 37 (l-r) Otnaydur/Shutterstock, AVAVA/Fotolia, Andresr/Shutterstock; p. 38 (clockwise) Jade/Blend Images/Getty Images, Andresr/Shutterstock, iofoto/Shutterstock, Monkey Business/Fotolia, nyul/Fotolia, fotogenicstudio/Fotolia, nyul/Fotolia; p. 39 wavebreakmedia/Shutterstock; p. 43 wavebreakmedia/Shutterstock; p. 44 (l) Phil Date/Shutterstock, (r) Jack Hollingsworth/Stockbyte/Getty Images; p. 46 georgerudy/Fotolia; p. 47 gstockstudio/Fotolia, BillionPhotos.com/Fotolia, Mat Hayward/Fotolia, Scott Griessel/Fotolia, Cheryl Savan/Shutterstock, gstockstudio/Fotolia; p. 50 (sand) Douglas Sacha/Moment Open/Getty Images, (caution) jdoms/Fotolia, (bad cat) FotoYakov/Shutterstock, (zipper) memo_frame/Fotolia, (egg) Morrowind/Shutterstock, (corn) Patti McConville/Photographer's Choice/Getty Images, (horse) byIlwill/Vetta/Getty Images, (kitten) pavelmayorov/Shutterstock; p. 51 Tom Merton/Hoxton/Getty Images; p. 52 Rouelle Umali Xinhua News Agency/Newscom; p. 53 DragonImages; p. 54 (l) DW labs Incorporated/Shutterstock, (r) east2/Fotolia; p. 55 (laptop/park) wavebreakmedia/Shutterstock, (baby) Cbarnesphotography/E+/Getty Images, (cartoon) Cartoonresource/Shutterstock; p. 57 Tyler Olson/Fotolia; p. 64 (tl) Kurhan/Fotolia, (tr) Hill Creek Pictures/UpperCut Images/Getty Images, (br) Birkholz/E+/Getty Images , (bl) EMPPhotography/E+/Getty Images; p. 66 Daisy Daisy/Fotolia; p. 68 Tetra Images/Getty Images; p. 69 nakophotography/Fotolia; p. 70 (t) Thinkstock Images/Stockbyte/Getty Images, (m) Petert2/Fotolia, (b) Digital Vision/Photodisc/Getty Images; p. 71 Robin Nelson/ZUMA Press/Newscom; p. 73 Photographyttl/Fotolia; p. 74 (A) Cosid/Shutterstock, (B) Juriah Mosin/Shutterstock, (C) Til Vogt/Shutterstock, (D) Pathdoc/Fotolia, (E) Objowl/Shutterstock; p. 75 Dave/Les Jacobs/Blend Images/Getty Images; p. 77 (t) kupicoo/E+/Getty Images, (m) kupicoo/E+/Getty Images, (b) Monkey Business Images/Shutterstock (diamond) Atiketta Sangasaeng/Shutterstock; p. 80 (l) kubais/Shutterstock, (r) Steven Heap/123RF; p. 84 t_fuji/Fotolia; p. 86 SWP/Fotolia; p. 87 Digitalskillet/E+/Getty Images; p. 88 BillionPhotos.com/Fotolia, Rick Gomez/Blend Images/Getty Images, Huntstock/Getty Images, Scott Griessel/Fotolia, BillionPhotos.com/Fotolia, Istockalypse Elkor/Getty Images, Bst2012/Fotolia, Monkey Business/Fotolia; p. 89 StockLite/Shutterstock; p. 90 VLADGRIN/Shutterstock; p. 91 Nomad_Soul/Fotolia; p. 92 DragonImages/Fotolia; p. 93 Indeed/Getty Images, JackF/Fotolia, Minerva Studio/Fotolia, Felix Mizioznikov/Shutterstock, Jeanette Dietl/Shutterstock, leungchopan/Fotolia; p. 94 (Einstein) akg images/Newscom, (Ramanujan) Nick Higham/Alamy Stock Photo; p. 98 Anibal/Fotolia; p. 99 Michal Krakowiak/Getty Images; p. 100 (Olsen) Carol Francavilla/AP Images, (Jobs) Terry Schmitt/UPI/Newscom, (Gates) Richard Ellis/Alamy Stock Photo; p. 101 (tl) Jun Dangoy/Fotolia, (tr) Patrick/Fotolia, (br) VictorHabbickVisions/Science Photo Library/Getty Images, (bl) Hxdyl/Fotolia; p. 102 (headset) wayne_0216/Fotolia, (finger) Mihaperosa/Fotolia, (atom) Petecek/Fotolia; p. 103 Serge Black/Fotolia; p. 104 (redwoods) Tomasz Zajda/Fotolia, (Milarch) Dusty Christensen/MCT/Newscom, (Tuy) Jeremy_Holden/Photoshot/Newscom; p. 105 Design56/Fotolia, Robraine/Shutterstock; p. 106 Epicurean/Vetta/Getty Images; p. 107 (wedding) Paylessimages/Fotolia, (babies) rSnapshotPhotos/Shutterstock, (wheelchair) Kzenon/Shutterstock; p. 110 (t) Bst2012/Fotolia, (b) XiXinXing/Shutterstock; p. 111 (park backdrop) Trofotodesign/Fotolia; p. 113 Djoronimo/Fotolia; p. 114 (t) StockLite/Shutterstock, (m) Daniel Ingold/Getty Images, (b) LDprod/Shutterstock; p. 115 (l) James Brunker/Alamy Stock Photo, (c) Natalie Behring/Newscom, (tr) Peter Muller/ Cultura/Getty Images, (b) Dean Bertoncelj/Shutterstock; p. 117 Federico Rostangno/Fotolia; p. 118 (l) Dmitrimaruta/Fotolia, (r) Alen-D/Fotolia.

Illustration credits: Aptara pp. 8, 26, 44, 56, 67, 78; Steve Attoe p. 45, 58 (b); Dusan Petricic p. 16, 57, 59; el Primo Ramon p. 10, 14, 31, 58 (t), 62, 82, 119.

Printed in the United States of America

ISBN-10: 0-13-417688-X
ISBN-13: 978-0-13-417688-8
4 18

ISBN-10: 0-13-449891-7 (with MyEnglishLab)
ISBN-13: 978-0-13-449891-1 (with MyEnglishLab)
4 18

pearsonelt.com/summit3e

9 2019

ABOUT THE AUTHORS

Joan Saslow

Joan Saslow has taught in a variety of programs in South America and the United States. She is author or coauthor of a number of widely used courses, some of which are *Ready to Go*, *Workplace Plus*, *Literacy Plus*, and *Top Notch*. She is also author of *English in Context*, a series for reading science and technology. Ms. Saslow was the series director of *True Colors* and *True Voices*. She has participated in the English Language Specialist Program in the U.S. Department of State's Bureau of Educational and Cultural Affairs.

Allen Ascher

Allen Ascher has been a teacher and teacher trainer in China and the United States, as well as academic director of the intensive English program at Hunter College. Mr. Ascher has also been an ELT publisher and was responsible for publication and expansion of numerous well-known courses including *True Colors*, *NorthStar*, the *Longman TOEFL Preparation Series*, and the *Longman Academic Writing Series*. He is coauthor of *Top Notch*, and he wrote the "Teaching Speaking" module of *Teacher Development Interactive*, an online multimedia teacher-training program.

Ms. Saslow and Mr. Ascher are frequent presenters at professional conferences and have been coauthoring courses for teens, adults, and young adults since 2002.

AUTHORS' ACKNOWLEDGMENTS

The authors wish to thank Katherine Klagsbrun for developing the digital Extra Challenge Reading Activities that appear with all reading selections in *Summit 2*.

The authors are indebted to these reviewers, who provided extensive and detailed feedback and suggestions for *Summit*, as well as the hundreds of teachers who completed surveys and participated in focus groups.

Cris Asperti, CEL LEP, São Paulo, Brazil • **Diana Alicia Ávila Martínez**, CUEC, Monterrey, Mexico • **Shannon Brown**, Nagoya University of Foreign Studies, Nagoya, Japan • **Cesar Byrd**, Universidad ETAC Campus Chalco, Mexico City, Mexico • **Maria Claudia Campos de Freitas**, Metalanguage, São Paulo, Brazil • **Alvaro Del Castillo Alba**, CBA, Santa Cruz, Bolivia • **Isidro Castro Galván**, Instituto Teocalli, Monterrey, Mexico • **Melisa Celi**, Idiomas Católica, Lima, Peru • **Carlos Celis**, CEL LEP, São Paulo, Brazil • **Jussara Costa e Silva**, Prize Language School, São Paulo, Brazil • **Inara Couto**, CEL LEP, São Paulo, Brazil • **Gemma Crouch**, ICPNA Chiclayo, Peru • **Ingrid Valverde Diaz del Olmo**, ICPNA Cusco, Peru • **Jacqueline Díaz Esquivel**, PROULEX, Guadalajara, Mexico • **María Eid Ceneviva**, CBA, Cochabamba, Bolivia • **Erika Licia Esteves Silva**, Murphy English, São Paulo, Brazil • **Cristian Garay**, Idiomas Católica, Lima, Peru • **Miguel Angel Guerrero Pozos**, PROULEX, Guadalajara, Mexico • **Anderson Francisco Guimarães Maia**, Centro Cultural Brasil Estados Unidos, Belém, Brazil • **Cesar Guzmán**, CAADI Monterrey, Mexico • **César Iván Hernández Escobedo**, PROULEX, Guadalajara, Mexico • **Robert Hinton**, Nihon University, Tokyo, Japan • **Segundo**

Huanambal Díaz, ICPNA Chiclayo, Peru • **Chandra Víctor Jacobs Sukahai**, Universidad de Valle de México, Monterrey, Mexico • **Yeni Jiménez Torres**, Centro Colombo Americano Bogotá, Colombia • **Simon Lees**, Nagoya University of Foreign Studies, Nagoya, Japan • **Thomas LeViness**, PROULEX, Guadalajara, Mexico • **Amy Lewis**, Waseda University, Tokyo, Japan • **Luz Libia Rey**, Centro Colombo Americano, Bogotá, Colombia • **Diego López**, Idiomas Católica, Lima, Peru • **Junior Lozano**, Idiomas Católica, Lima, Peru • **Tanja McCandie**, Nanzan University, Nagoya, Japan • **Tammy Martínez Nieves**, Universidad Autónoma de Nuevo León, Monterrey, Mexico • **María Teresa Meléndez Mantilla**, ICPNA Chiclayo, Peru • **Mónica Nomberto**, ICPNA Chiclayo, Peru • **Otilia Ojeda**, Monterrey, Mexico • **Juana Palacios**, Idiomas Católica, Lima, Peru • **Giuseppe Paldino Mayorga**, Jellyfish Learning Center, San Cristobal, Ecuador • **Henry Eduardo Pardo Lamprea**, Universidad Militar Nueva Granada, Colombia • **Dario Paredes**, Centro Colombo Americano, Bogotá, Colombia • **Teresa Noemí Parra Alarcón**, Centro Anglo Americano de Cuernavaca, S.C., Cuernavaca, Mexico • **Carlos Eduardo de la Paz Arroyo**, Centro Anglo Americano de Cuernavaca, S.C.,

Cuernavaca, Mexico • **José Luis Pérez Treviño**, Instituto Obispado, Monterrey, Mexico • **Evelize Maria Plácido Florian**, São Paulo, Brazil • **Armida Rivas**, Monterrey, Mexico • **Luis Rodríguez Amau**, ICPNA Chiclayo, Peru • **Fabio Ossaamn Rok Kaku**, Prize Language School, São Paulo, Brazil • **Ana María Román Villareal**, CUEC, Monterrey, Mexico • **Reynaldo Romano C.**, CBA, La Paz, Bolivia • **Francisco Rondón**, Centro Colombo Americano, Bogotá, Colombia • **Peter Russell**, Waseda University, Tokyo, Japan • **Rubena St. Louis**, Universidad Simón Bolivar, Caracas, Venezuela • **Marisol Salazar**, Centro Colombo Americano, Bogotá, Colombia • **Miguel Sierra**, Idiomas Católica, Lima, Peru • **Greg Strong**, Aoyama Gakuin University, Tokyo, Japan • **Gerald Talandis**, Toyama University, Toyama, Japan • **Stephen Thompson**, Nagoya University of Foreign Studies, Nagoya, Japan • **José Luis Urbina Hurtado**, Instituto Tecnológico de León, Mexico • **René F. Valdivia Pereyra**, CBA, Santa Cruz, Bolivia • **Magno Alejandro Vivar Hurtado**, Salesian Polytechnic University, Ecuador • **Belkis Yanes**, Caracas, Venezuela • **Holger Zamora**, ICPNA Cusco, Peru • **Maria Cristina Zanon Costa**, Metalanguage, São Paulo, Brazil • **Kathia Zegarra**, Idiomas Católica, Lima, Peru.

LEARNING OBJECTIVES

UNIT	COMMUNICATION GOALS	VOCABULARY	GRAMMAR
UNIT 1 **Dreams and Goals** PAGE 2	• Ask about someone's background • Discuss career and study plans • Compare your dreams and goals in life • Describe job qualifications	• Job applications • Collocations for career and study plans • Describing dreams and goals **Word Study:** • Collocations with <u>have</u> and <u>get</u> for qualifications	• Simultaneous and sequential past actions: review and expansion • Completed and uncompleted past actions closely related to the present **GRAMMAR BOOSTER** • Describing past actions and events: review • Stative verbs: non-action and action meanings
UNIT 2 **Character and Responsibility** PAGE 14	• Describe the consequences of lying • Express regret and take responsibility • Explore where values come from • Discuss how best to help others	• Taking or avoiding responsibility • Philanthropic work	• Adjective clauses: review and expansion • "Comment" clauses **GRAMMAR BOOSTER** • Adjective clauses: overview • Grammar for Writing: adjective clauses with quantifiers • Grammar for Writing: reduced adjective clauses
UNIT 3 **Fears, Hardships, and Heroism** PAGE 26	• Express frustration, empathy, and encouragement • Describe how fear affects you physically • Discuss overcoming handicaps and hardships • Examine the nature of heroism	• Expressing frustration, empathy, and encouragement • Physical effects of fear **Word Study:** • Using parts of speech	• Clauses with <u>no matter</u> • Using <u>so</u> … (<u>that</u>) or <u>such</u> … (<u>that</u>) to explain results **GRAMMAR BOOSTER** • Embedded questions: review and common errors • Non-count nouns made countable • Nouns used in both countable and uncountable sense
UNIT 4 **Getting Along with Others** PAGE 38	• Discuss how to overcome shortcomings • Acknowledge inconsiderate behavior • Explain how you handle anger • Explore the qualities of friendship	• Shortcomings • Expressing and controlling anger	• Adverb clauses of condition • Cleft sentences: review and expansion **GRAMMAR BOOSTER** • Grammar for Writing: more conjunctions and transitions • Cleft sentences: more on meaning and use
UNIT 5 **Humor** PAGE 50	• Discuss the health benefits of laughter • Respond to something funny • Analyze what makes us laugh • Explore the limits of humor	• Ways to respond to jokes and other funny things • Common types of jokes • Practical jokes	• Indirect speech: backshifts in tense and time expressions • Questions in indirect speech **GRAMMAR BOOSTER** • Imperatives in indirect speech • Changes to pronouns and possessives • <u>Say</u>, <u>tell</u>, and <u>ask</u> • Other reporting verbs

CONVERSATION STRATEGIES	LISTENING / PRONUNCIATION	READING	WRITING
• Use <u>Thanks for asking</u> to express appreciation for someone's interest. • Use <u>Correct me if I'm wrong, but …</u> to tentatively assert what you believe about someone or something. • Say <u>I've given it some thought and …</u> to introduce a thoughtful opinion. • Informally ask for directions by saying <u>Steer me in the right direction</u>. • Say <u>As a matter of fact</u> to present a relevant fact. • Offer assistance with <u>I'd be more than happy to</u>. • Say <u>I really appreciate it</u> to express gratitude.	**Listening Skills:** • Listen to activate vocabulary • Listen for main ideas • Listen to confirm content • Listen for supporting details • Listen to infer **PRONUNCIATION BOOSTER** • Sentence stress and intonation: review	**Texts:** • An application for employment • An article about two famous people • An article about good and bad interview behavior • A job advertisement • A résumé **Skills / strategies:** • Understand idioms and expressions • Confirm information • Apply ideas	**Task:** • Write a traditional cover letter to an employer **Skill:** • A formal cover letter
• Admit having made a mistake by apologizing with <u>I'm really sorry, but …</u> • Confirm that someone agrees to an offer with <u>if that's OK</u>. • Use <u>That's really not necessary</u> to politely turn down an offer. • Take responsibility for a mistake by saying <u>Please accept my apology</u>.	**Listening Skills:** • Listen to infer information • Listen to support an opinion • Listen for main ideas • Listen to classify • Listen to confirm content • Listen for point of view • Listen to summarize • Listen to draw conclusions **PRONUNCIATION BOOSTER** • Emphatic stress and pitch to express emotion	**Texts:** • A survey about taking or avoiding responsibility • An article about lying • A textbook article about the development of values • Dictionary entries • Short biographies **Skills / strategies:** • Understand idioms and expressions • Relate to personal experience • Classify vocabulary using context • Critical thinking	**Task:** • Write a college application essay **Skill:** • Restrictive and non-restrictive adjective clauses
• Ask <u>Is something wrong?</u> to express concern about someone's state of mind. • Ask <u>What's going on?</u> to show interest in the details of someone's problem. • Begin an explanation with <u>Well, basically</u> to characterize a problem in few words. • Say <u>Hang in there</u> to offer support to someone facing a difficulty. • Say <u>Anytime</u> to acknowledge someone's appreciation and minimize what one has done.	**Listening Skills:** • Listen to predict • Listen to activate parts of speech • Listen for details • Listen to retell a story • Listen to summarize **PRONUNCIATION BOOSTER** • Vowel reduction to /ə/	**Texts:** • A self-test about how fearful you are • Interview responses about how fear affects people physically • An article about Marlee Matlin • Profiles of three heroes **Skills / strategies:** • Understand idioms and expressions • Understand meaning from context • Summarize	**Task:** • Write a short report about a dangerous or frightening event **Skill:** • Reducing adverbial clauses
• Introduce an uncomfortable topic with <u>there's something I need to bring up</u>. • Say <u>I didn't realize that</u> to acknowledge a complaint about your behavior. • Use <u>I didn't mean to …</u> to apologize for and summarize someone's complaint. • Say <u>On the contrary</u> to assure someone that you don't feel the way they think you might. • Say <u>I can see your point</u> to acknowledge someone's point of view.	**Listening Skills:** • Listen to activate grammar • Listen to summarize the main idea • Listen to infer information • Listen to draw conclusions **PRONUNCIATION BOOSTER** • Shifting emphatic stress	**Texts:** • Profiles about people's shortcomings • Descriptions of different workshops • An article on friendship **Skills / strategies:** • Understand idioms and expressions • Understand meaning from context • Apply ideas • Relate to personal experience	**Task:** • Write a three-paragraph essay presenting a solution to a common shortcoming **Skill:** • Transitional topic sentences
• Exclaim <u>You've got to see this</u>! to urge someone to look at something. • Introduce a statement with <u>Seriously</u> to insist someone not hesitate to take your suggestion. • Say <u>That's priceless</u> to strongly praise something. • Agree informally with <u>Totally</u>.	**Listening Skills:** • Listen to activate vocabulary • Listen to summarize • Listen to take notes • Listen to apply ideas **PRONUNCIATION BOOSTER** • Intonation of sarcasm	**Texts:** • A self-test about your sense of humor • An article about the health benefits of laughter • An article about the theories of humor • Descriptions of practical jokes **Skills / strategies:** • Understand idioms and expressions • Critical thinking • Classify	**Task:** • Write a true or imaginary story **Skill:** • Writing dialogue

UNIT	COMMUNICATION GOALS	VOCABULARY	GRAMMAR
UNIT 6 **Troubles While Traveling** PAGE 62	• Describe some causes of travel hassles • Express gratitude for a favor while traveling • Discuss staying safe on the Internet • Talk about lost, stolen, or damaged property	• Travel nouns **Word Study:** • Past participles as noun modifiers	• Unreal conditional sentences: continuous forms • Unreal conditional statements with <u>if it weren't for</u> … / <u>if it hadn't been for</u> … **GRAMMAR BOOSTER** • The conditional: summary and extension
UNIT 7 **Mind Over Matter** PAGE 74	• Suggest that someone is being gullible • Examine superstitions for believability • Talk about the power of suggestion • Discuss phobias	• Ways to express disbelief • Expressions with <u>mind</u> **Word Study:** • Noun and adjective forms	• Nouns: indefinite, definite, unique, and generic meaning (review and expansion) • Indirect speech: <u>it</u> + a passive reporting verb **GRAMMAR BOOSTER** • Article usage: summary • Definite article: additional uses • More non-count nouns with both a countable and an uncountable sense • Grammar for Writing: indirect speech with passive reporting verbs
UNIT 8 **Performing at Your Best** PAGE 86	• Discuss your talents and strengths • Suggest ways to boost intelligence • Explain how you produce your best work • Describe what makes someone a "genius"	• Expressions to describe talents and strengths • Adjectives that describe aspects of intelligence	• Using auxiliary <u>do</u> for emphatic stress • The subjunctive **GRAMMAR BOOSTER** • Grammar for Writing: emphatic stress • Infinitives and gerunds in place of the subjunctive
UNIT 9 **What Lies Ahead?** PAGE 98	• Discuss the feasibility of future technologies • Evaluate applications of innovative technologies • Discuss how to protect our future environment • Examine future social and demographic trends	• Innovative technologies • Ways to express a concern about consequences • Describing social and demographic trends	• The passive voice: the future, the future as seen from the past, and the future perfect • The passive voice in unreal conditional sentences **GRAMMAR BOOSTER** • Grammar for Writing: when to use the passive voice
UNIT 10 **An Interconnected World** PAGE 110	• React to news about global issues • Describe the impact of foreign imports • Discuss the pros and cons of globalization • Suggest ways to avoid culture shock	• Phrasal verbs to discuss issues and problems	• Separability of transitive phrasal verbs **GRAMMAR BOOSTER** • Phrasal verbs: expansion

CONVERSATION STRATEGIES	LISTENING / PRONUNCIATION	READING	WRITING
• Ask a stranger for help with <u>I wonder if you could do me a favor</u>. • Agree to offer assistance with <u>How can I help?</u> • Confirm willingness to perform a favor with <u>I'd be happy to</u>. • Introduce a statement of relief with <u>It's a good thing</u>.	**Listening Skills:** • Listen to infer • Listen to activate grammar • Listen for main ideas • Listen to confirm content • Listen to understand meaning from context • Listen for details • Listen to summarize **PRONUNCIATION BOOSTER** • Regular past participle endings • Reduction in perfect modals	**Texts:** • A travel tips contest • Interview responses about travel hassles • An article about the dangers of public Wi-Fi **Skills / strategies:** • Understand idioms and expressions • Understand meaning from context • Paraphrase • Find supporting details	**Task:** • Write an essay comparing and contrasting two means of transportation **Skill:** • A comparison and contrast essay
• Call someone's attention to an outrageous claim with <u>Can you believe this?</u> • Express surprise at someone's gullibility with <u>Oh, come on</u>. • Use <u>That's got to be</u> to underscore a conclusion. • Add <u>I guess</u> to an opinion one isn't sure about. • Express extreme agreement to another's opinion with <u>You can say that again</u>.	**Listening Skills:** • Listen for details • Listen to confirm content • Listen to summarize • Listen to infer **PRONUNCIATION BOOSTER** • Linking sounds	**Texts:** • A website about superstitions • An article about the placebo and nocebo effects **Skills / strategies:** • Understand idioms and expressions • Infer meaning • Draw conclusions • Critical thinking	**Task:** • Write a four-paragraph essay on superstitions **Skill:** • Subject / verb agreement: expansion
• Say <u>Guess what?</u> to introduce exciting news. • Use <u>I can't make up my mind between …</u> to signal indecision. • Use <u>I wouldn't say …</u> to express modesty or doubt. • Support a statement or point of view with <u>I've been told that</u>. • Provide support for someone's decision with <u>I don't think you can go wrong</u>.	**Listening Skills:** • Listen for main ideas • Listen to infer • Listen for supporting details • Listen to draw conclusions **PRONUNCIATION BOOSTER** • Emphatic stress with auxiliary verbs	**Texts:** • A quiz on emotional intelligence • An article on whether intelligence can be increased • An article on staying on target **Skills / strategies:** • Understand idioms and expressions • Apply ideas • Relate to personal experience	**Task:** • Write a three-paragraph essay about the challenges of staying focused **Skill:** • Explaining cause and result
• Use <u>For one thing</u> to introduce an important first argument. • Say <u>Well, if you ask me …</u> to offer an opinion. • Use <u>I mean</u> to clarify what you just said. • Say <u>I see your point</u> to concede the value of someone else's opinion.	**Listening Skills:** • Listen to activate vocabulary • Listen to identify point of view • Listen to confirm content • Listen to infer information • Listen to draw conclusions **PRONUNCIATION BOOSTER** • Reading aloud	**Texts:** • A survey on future predictions • An article on how people in the past envisioned the future • An article on what some people are doing to protect the environment • Dictionary entries **Skills / strategies:** • Understand idioms and expressions • Understand meaning from context • Draw conclusions	**Task:** • Write a four- or five-paragraph essay about the future **Skill:** • The thesis statement in a formal essay
• Begin a statement with <u>Can you believe …</u> to introduce surprising, exciting, or disturbing information. • Use <u>But on the bright side</u> to change a negative topic to something more positive. • Begin a statement with <u>It just goes to show you …</u> to emphasize a point. • Say <u>Well, that's another story</u> to acknowledge a positive or negative change of topic. • Begin a statement with <u>You'd think …</u> to express frustration with a situation.	**Listening Skills:** • Listen to activate vocabulary • Listen to summarize • Listen to confirm information • Listen to understand meaning from context • Listen to draw conclusions **PRONUNCIATION BOOSTER** • Intonation of tag questions	**Texts:** • A quiz on English in today's world • News stories about global issues and problems • People's opinions about foreign imports • An article about the pros and cons of globalization **Skills / strategies:** • Understand idioms and expressions • Understand meaning from context • Identify supporting ideas • Interpret information in a graph	**Task:** • Write a four-paragraph essay to rebut an opposing view about globalization **Skill:** • Rebutting an opposing point of view

What is *Summit?*

Summit is a two-level high-intermediate to advanced communicative course that develops confident, culturally fluent English speakers able to navigate the social, travel, and professional situations they will encounter as they use English in their lives. *Summit* can follow the intermediate level of any communicative series, including the four-level *Top Notch* course.

Summit delivers immediate, demonstrable results in every class session through its proven pedagogy and systematic and intensive recycling of language. Each goal- and achievement-based lesson is tightly correlated to the Can-Do Statements of the Common European Framework of Reference (CEFR). The course is fully benchmarked to the Global Scale of English (GSE).

Each level of *Summit* contains material for 60 to 90 hours of classroom instruction. Its full array of additional print and digital components can extend instruction to 120 hours if desired. Furthermore, the entire *Summit* course can be tailored to blended learning with its integrated online component, *MyEnglishLab. Summit* offers more ready-to-use teacher resources than any other course available today.

NEW This third edition represents a major revision of content and has a greatly increased quantity of exercises, both print and digital. Following are some key new features:

- **Conversation Activator Videos** to build communicative competence
- **Discussion Activator Videos** to increase quality and quantity of expression
- A **Test-Taking Skills Booster** (and **Extra Challenge Reading Activities**) to help students succeed in the reading and listening sections of standardized tests
- An **Understand Idioms and Expressions** section in each unit increases the authenticity of student spoken language

Award-Winning Instructional Design*

Demonstrable confirmation of progress
Every two-page lesson has a clearly stated communication goal and culminates in a guided conversation, free discussion, debate, presentation, role play, or project that achieves the goal. Idea framing and notepadding activities lead students to confident spoken expression.

Cultural fluency
Summit audio familiarizes students with a wide variety of native and non-native accents. Discussion activities reflect the topics people of diverse cultural backgrounds talk about in their social and professional lives.

Explicit vocabulary and grammar
Clear captioned illustrations and dictionary-style presentations, all with audio, take the guesswork out of meaning and ensure comprehensible pronunciation. Grammar is embedded in context and presented explicitly for form, meaning, and use. The unique "Recycle this Language" feature encourages active use of newly learned words and grammar during communication practice.

Active listening syllabus
More than 50 listening tasks at each level of *Summit* develop critical thinking and crucial listening comprehension skills such as listen for details, main ideas, confirmation of content, inference, and understand meaning from context.

Summit is the recipient of the Association of Educational Publishers' Distinguished Achievement Award.

Conversation and Discussion Activators
Memorable conversation models with audio provide appealing natural social language and conversation strategies essential for post-secondary learners. Rigorous Conversation Activator and Discussion Activator activities with video systematically stimulate recycling of social language, ensuring it is not forgotten. A unique Pronunciation Booster provides lessons and interactive practice, with audio, so students can improve their spoken expression.

Systematic writing skills development
Summit teaches the conventions of correct English writing so students will be prepared for standardized tests, academic study, and professional communication. Lessons cover key writing and rhetorical skills such as using parallel structure and avoiding sentence fragments, run-on sentences, and comma splices. Intensive work in paragraph and essay development ensures confident and successful writing.

Reading skills and strategies
Each unit of *Summit* builds critical thinking and key reading skills and strategies such as paraphrasing, drawing conclusions, expressing and supporting an opinion, and activating prior knowledge. Learners develop analytical skills and increase fluency while supporting their answers through speaking.

*We wish you and your students enjoyment and success with **Summit**. We wrote it for you.*
Joan Saslow and Allen Ascher

ActiveTeach

Maximize the impact of your *Summit* lessons. Digital Student's Book pages with access to all audio and video provide an interactive classroom experience that can be used with or without an interactive whiteboard (IWB). It includes a full array of easy-to-access digital and printable features.

For class presentation . . .

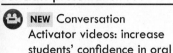 **NEW** Conversation Activator videos: increase students' confidence in oral communication

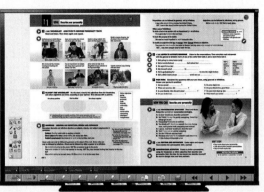

NEW Discussion Activator videos: increase quality and quantity of expression

NEW Extra Grammar Exercises: ensure mastery of grammar

NEW Extra Challenge Reading Activities: help students succeed at standardized proficiency tests.

PLUS

- Interactive Whiteboard tools, including zoom, highlight, links, notes, and more.
- Clickable Audio: instant access to the complete classroom audio program
- *Summit TV* Video Program: fully-revised authentic TV documentaries as well as unscripted on-the-street interviews, featuring a variety of regional and non-native accents

For planning . . .

- A *Methods Handbook* for a communicative classroom
- Detailed timed lesson plans for each two-page lesson
- *Summit TV* teaching notes
- Complete answer keys, audio scripts, and video scripts

For extra support . . .

- Hundreds of extra printable activities, with teaching notes
- *Summit TV* activity worksheets

For assessment . . .

- Ready-made unit and review achievement tests with options to edit, add, or delete items.

Ready-made Summit Web Projects provide authentic application of lesson language.

MyEnglishLab

An optional online learning tool

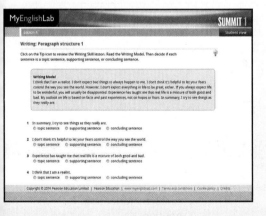

- **NEW** Immediate, meaningful feedback on wrong answers
- **NEW** Remedial grammar exercises
- **NEW** Grammar Coach videos for general reference
- Interactive practice of all material presented in the course
- Grade reports that display performance and time on task
- Auto-graded achievement tests

Workbook

Lesson-by-lesson written exercises to accompany the Student's Book

Full-Course Placement Tests

Choose printable or online version

Classroom Audio Program

- A set of Audio CDs, as an alternative to the clickable audio in ActiveTeach
- Contains a variety of authentic regional and non-native accents to build comprehension of diverse English speakers
- **NEW** The app *Summit Go* allows access anytime, anywhere and lets students practice at their own pace. The entire audio program is also available for students at www.english.com/summit3e.

Teacher's Edition and Lesson Planner

- Detailed interleaved lesson plans, language and culture notes, answer keys, and more
- Also accessible in digital form in ActiveTeach

For more information: www.pearsonelt.com/summit3e

Dreams and Goals

PREVIEW

A FRAME YOUR IDEAS Complete the first section of an application for employment, using real or invented information.

👤 Application for Employment

PERSONAL INFORMATION   date of application [/   /   ]

Name

[   ] [   ] [   ]
　　　　 last 　　　　　　　 middle 　　　　　　　 first

Address 　　　　　　 **City** 　　　 **State / province**　**Country**　**Postal code / zip code**

[   ] [   ] [   ] [   ] [   ]

Contact Information

[   ] [   ] [   ]
　　 home telephone 　　　　　　 cell phone 　　　　　　　 e-mail

Type of position sought 　　　　　　　　　　　　 **Available start date**

[   ] [/   /   ]

CURRENT EMPLOYMENT

Are you currently employed?　**If so, where?**　　　　　**How long have you worked there?**

[   ] [   ]　[   ]　　　　　[   ]
yes 　 no

EDUCATION

	Name	Major field of study	Did you graduate?
High School			
College or University			
Other Education			

SKILLS AND / OR TRAINING: Please list skills and / or training you have had that may contribute to your ability to perform the position you seek:

[   ]

📎 **PREVIOUS EMPLOYMENT HISTORY**
Please attach a list of previous positions and job responsibilities, starting with the most recent. Include the names and addresses of each company.

📎 **STATEMENT OF GOALS**
Please attach a short statement about your short-term and long-term employment goals.

To apply online, go to getajob@jobco.com

B ▶ 1:02 **VOCABULARY**　**JOB APPLICATIONS**　Find and circle these words and phrases in the application. Then listen and repeat.

> employment
> contact information
> position
> start date
> training
> employment history

C ACTIVATE VOCABULARY Look at how each word or phrase from Exercise B is used in the job application. Then on a separate sheet of paper, write a definition or synonym for each one.

D PAIR WORK What are some do's and don'ts for filling out a job application? With a partner, create a list of suggestions to help an applicant complete a job application successfully.

Be neat and spell all words correctly.

E ▶1:03 **SPOTLIGHT** Read and listen to a conversation between two friends discussing career plans. Notice the spotlighted language.

Anne: Well, I finally sent in the applications. Now **it's just wait and see**.

Nina: How many schools did you end up applying to?

Anne: Ten. That's just about every single one within a hundred-mile radius!

Nina: Don't you think **that might be a little overkill**? You shouldn't have any trouble getting in, should you?

Anne: Well, the food industry's so trendy right now, and it's gotten pretty competitive. **I didn't want to take any chances**. This has been a lifelong dream of mine.

Nina: So which one's your first choice? I've read the Taste Institute's pretty good.

Anne: Actually, at first I'd been thinking of going there, but now **I've got my heart set on** the Culinary Center. I've heard it's far superior to the TI.

Nina: The Taste Institute? Really? Aren't chef schools all **six of one, half a dozen of the other**?

Anne: I would have thought so, but it turns out they're not.

Nina: How so?

Anne: Well, the CC's training is more demanding. You've really got to work hard. And their certificate's got a lot more prestige. A CC certificate's a ticket to an interview with all the top restaurants.

Nina: And that's not true with the TI?

Anne: Apparently not. I did a lot of reading, and it seems that the TI's pretty **run-of-the-mill**— nothing wrong with it, but nothing particularly outstanding about it either. **All in all**, the CC's a better bet if I can get in.

Nina: Well, **I'll keep my fingers crossed** for you, Anne. Hope all your dreams come true.

Anne: Thanks! I appreciate that.

F **UNDERSTAND IDIOMS AND EXPRESSIONS** With a partner, paraphrase each of these expressions from Spotlight, saying each one a different way.

1 " … it's just wait and see."

2 " … that might be a little overkill?"

3 "I didn't want to take any chances."

4 "I've got my heart set on … "

5 " … six of one, half a dozen of the other."

6 "run-of-the-mill"

7 "all in all"

8 "I'll keep my fingers crossed … "

G **THINK AND EXPLAIN** Answer the following questions. Explain your answers.

1 Why did Anne apply to so many schools?

2 In your opinion, which of the two reasons Anne gives for preferring the Culinary Center is a better reason? Explain.

3 What does Nina mean when she says, "Hope all your dreams come true"?

SPEAKING Which factors are the most important to you in choosing a job or career? Rate each of the following on a scale of 1 to 5, with 1 being the most important. Then compare charts with a partner, explaining your ratings to each other.

The training period for the job is short.		The job has lots of prestige.	
There's not too much competition in the field.		The field is trendy right now.	
The work is interesting and fun.		The job doesn't require a lot of overtime work.	
The pay is good.		The field contributes something important to the world.	
The people in this field are interesting.			

GOAL Ask about someone's background

A ▶ 1:04 **GRAMMAR SPOTLIGHT** Read about two famous people. Notice the spotlighted grammar.

Kohei Uchimura

Kohei Uchimura is considered by some to be the greatest gymnast of all time. He **began** gymnastics very early in life. When Uchimura **joined** Japan's national team at the age of eighteen in 2007, he **had** already **been practicing** gymnastics for fifteen years. And since then, he **has competed** in world-class events year after year and **has won** many prizes and honors. Uchimura trains hard and consistently beats almost all his competition. Although Uchimura **had** already **won** many competitions before the 2012 Olympics, he **had** a close call there and **fell** as he **was dismounting** from the pommel horse. In spite of this, his team **managed** to win the silver medal, so the event **went** into his "win" record anyway. Uchimura has continued to win prize after prize ever since. Uchimura is renowned for the intensity of his concentration during practice. Surprisingly, however, for a world-class athlete, he is known to be pretty relaxed and has a normal life outside of the gym. He's been married since 2012, and he and his wife **had** their first child in 2013.

Singer, songwriter, and actress Lila Downs, whose mother was from Mexico and whose father was from the United States, **grew up** in both countries. She **had learned** to sing as a child and **had performed** with traditional mariachi bands before she **had** any formal training. She **attended** the Institute of Arts in Oaxaca and **studied** classical voice at the University of Minnesota. During the time Downs **was living** in the United States, she **became** more and more interested in the diverse cultural heritage of Mexico. To help support pride in those cultures, Downs **learned** and **incorporated** a variety of indigenous Mexican languages into her songs. One of Downs's other passions is social justice, and the lyrics of some of her songs focus on the stories of workers who **migrated** from rural Mexico to the U.S. Downs has won many prizes, including a Grammy and a Latin Grammy. She and her husband **had been trying** for many years to have a baby, and in 2010, they **adopted** a son. The family travels together on Downs's international singing tours.

Lila Downs

B **DISCUSSION** Is it necessary to have formal training to be an elite athlete or a world-class singer? Support your opinion with reasons and examples.

GRAMMAR BOOSTER p. 128
Describing past actions and events: review

DIGITAL
INDUCTIVE
ACTIVITY

C **GRAMMAR** SIMULTANEOUS AND SEQUENTIAL PAST ACTIONS: REVIEW AND EXPANSION

Review: completed past actions: the simple past tense and the past perfect
The simple past tense describes actions completed in the past, whether or not a specific time is mentioned. Context or time expressions can indicate whether the actions were simultaneous (at the same time) or sequential (one before the other).

> **When** Uchimura **entered** the stadium, the gymnastics event **began**. (= simultaneous completed actions)

> Downs **studied** voice in the U.S. **in the years before** she **moved** back to Mexico. (= sequential completed actions)

The simple past tense and the past perfect can be used to describe two sequential completed past actions. However, in informal spoken English it's common to avoid the past perfect and use the simple past tense for both actions, especially when context clarifies the order of occurrence.

> Before Uchimura **competed** in the 2012 Olympics, he **had won** several world championships.

Review: simultaneous actions in progress: the past continuous
A statement in the past continuous describes an action that was in progress at a time—or during a period of time—in the past.

> Lila Downs **was** already **singing** while I **was looking** for my seat.

> **Remember:** The present perfect can also describe completed past actions.
> Uchimura has competed in world-class events year after year.

> **Remember:** To describe an action that was completed during an action in progress, use the simple past tense.
> Lila met her future husband, Paul, when [or while] she was working in Oaxaca.

Expansion: sequential continuing and completed past actions: the past perfect continuous and the simple past tense
The past perfect continuous can be used to focus on the fact that one past action was already in progress before another one occurred. (It often emphasizes the duration of the action.) Form the past perfect continuous with had been and a present participle. Describe the completed action with the simple past tense.

> By the time Downs **moved** to the United States with her parents, she **had been performing** with mariachis for several years.

> How long **had** Uchimura **been training** before he **was asked** to join the Japan National Team?

D ▶ 1:05 **UNDERSTAND THE GRAMMAR** Listen to the conversations and circle the letter of the correct summary of the events. Listen again if necessary.

1	**a** They continued filming after he got on the bus.	**b** The bus arrived after the filming was finished.
2	**a** Lisa had been thinking of buying the sweater that she left on the table.	**b** The other girl bought the sweater before Lisa had a chance to try it on.
3	**a** Diane was texting and driving at the same time.	**b** Diane had stopped driving before she texted.

E **GRAMMAR PRACTICE** Complete the statements with the past perfect or past perfect continuous.

1 My brother (had already won / had already been winning) the swim meet when the diving competition began.

2 The house was completely dark when I got home because the family (had gone / had been going) to bed.

3 The audience (had stood / had been standing) in line for hours to buy tickets when they canceled the concert.

4 The women's tennis team (had practiced / had been practicing) on a grass court four times before today's event started.

5 My friend (had already seen / had already been seeing) Lila Downs in concert, so we decided not to go.

NOW YOU CAN   Ask about someone's background

A **FRAME YOUR IDEAS** Complete the questionnaire about your background.

Where were you born? _____   How long have you been living at your current address? _____

Where had you been living before you moved to your current address? _____

If you are married, when did you get married? _____   Where were you living then? _____

If you have children, what are their names and ages? _____

If you have a career, what is it? _____

How long have you been studying English? _____

If you divided your life into three periods, how would you describe each one?

1. _____

2. _____

3. _____

B **DISCUSSION ACTIVATOR** Get to know a classmate's background. Use the questionnaire as an interview guide. Use the simple past tense, the past perfect, the past continuous, and the past perfect continuous in your questions and answers to clarify events in the past. Say as much as you can.

> Where were you living when you got married?

OPTIONAL WRITING Write a one-page biography of your partner, using the information from your Discussion Activator. Put the biographies together in a notebook or post them on a class blog. Include pictures of the classmates.

Lisa Lee

Lisa has been living in Templeton Towers since February. Before that, she had been living with her family in Easton. She got married in January…

5

LESSON 2

GOAL Discuss career and study plans

DIGITAL STRATEGIES **A** ▶ 1:06 **VOCABULARY** COLLOCATIONS FOR CAREER AND STUDY PLANS Read and listen. Then listen again and repeat.

---

decide on a course of study or a career

Jonathan decided on a career as a veterinarian because he's interested in medicine and loves animals.

> I started out in art, but **I'm switching** to graphic design.

take up something you're interested in

Lida is so impressed by the latest animated films that she's decided to take up computer graphics.

switch to a new course of study or a career

Magdalena started out in cultural anthropology but soon switched to medicine.

apply for a job or a position in a company

Gary is interested in environmental conservation, so he's applied for a job at the Wildlife Center.

be accepted to / into / by a school or a program

Only two students from our class were accepted to medical school this year.

apply to a school or program of study

I hope it's not too late to apply to dental school. I don't want to wait another year.

be rejected by a school or a program

Iris couldn't believe she had been rejected by the Wright College of Music, but luckily she was accepted elsewhere.

sign up for a course or an activity

Nora needs math for engineering school, but she hasn't used it since secondary school, so she's signed up for a refresher course.

enroll in a school or program

Matt has been accepted into flight school, but he won't enroll in the program until next year.

B ▶ 1:07 **LISTEN TO ACTIVATE VOCABULARY** Listen to the conversations. Then listen again. After each conversation, complete the statement with the Vocabulary. Use each collocation only once.

1 She has .... engineering school.

2 She has .... a career in music.

3 He has .... meditation.

4 She has .... two graduate programs.

5 He has .... teaching math.

6 She has .... a position in a medical lab.

C **VOCABULARY PRACTICE** Complete each person's statement, using the Vocabulary. There may be more than one way to answer correctly.

1 I've just .... graduate school!

2 I've been an English teacher all my life, but I've decided to .... teaching French!

3 It may take me years, but my lifelong dream has been to be an architect. I'm going to .... architecture school this year.

4 I retired a few years ago, but I'm bored, so I've just .... law school. My kids think I'm crazy.

5 When I finish school I want to be a conductor, so I've .... the music program at my university.

6 I've just had a baby, but I'm .... an evening program at the college. I want to study graphic design.

7 I want to ride a motorcycle, but my mom and dad won't even let me .... lessons!

8 I'm really a nervous person, but I've .... yoga and it really helps calm me down.

D **GRAMMAR** COMPLETED AND UNCOMPLETED PAST ACTIONS CLOSELY RELATED TO THE PRESENT

You can use the present perfect for recently completed actions. The adverbs just, recently, and lately often accompany these statements. (Note: Lately is rarely used in affirmative statements.)

She's **just been accepted** into a top-notch business school.
Have you **looked** at the program requirements **lately**? They**'ve changed**.

The present perfect continuous can describe an action or event that began in the recent past (and continues in the present and is therefore uncompleted). You can use recently and lately.

We**'ve been filling** out a lot of applications **recently**.

However, the following adverbs are used only with the present perfect, not the present perfect continuous, because they signal a completed action: ever, never, before, already, yet, still (with negative), so far, once, twice, (three) times.

Have you **ever** considered applying to graduate school? I **never** have.
I **still** haven't signed up for lifeguard training.

> **Be careful!**
> Use the simple past tense, not the present perfect, to talk about actions completed at a specific time in the past.
> She applied for a position at the Science Institute last week.
> NOT She has applied for the position at the Science Institute last week.

> **Remember:** Don't use the present perfect continuous with these stative verbs: be, believe, hate, have (for possession), know, like, love, own, seem, understand.
> DON'T SAY I've been knowing him for a year.

> **GRAMMAR BOOSTER** p. 128
> Stative verbs: non-action and action meanings

E **GRAMMAR PRACTICE** Circle the correct verb phrase to complete each statement.

1 In 2016, I (have enrolled in / enrolled in) the computer graphics program.

2 I still (haven't been receiving / haven't received) an acceptance letter.

3 No one (saw / has seen) Mike lately.

4 We (haven't been signing up / haven't signed up) for the professional development course yet.

5 The class (has started / started) at 9:00 sharp.

6 Lately, she's (been getting / got) ready to apply for that new position.

F **GRAMMAR PRACTICE** On a separate sheet of paper, write five questions to ask someone about his or her career or education plans. Use the present perfect, the simple past tense, and appropriate adverbs.

> **PRONUNCIATION BOOSTER** p. 143
> Sentence stress and intonation: review

NOW YOU CAN   Discuss career and study plans

A ▶1:08 **CONVERSATION SPOTLIGHT** Read and listen. Notice the spotlighted conversation strategies.

A: So, Vanessa, have you decided on a career yet?
B: **Thanks for asking.** Actually, I've been thinking of taking up social work.
A: Social work. That's interesting. **Correct me if I'm wrong,** but weren't you a biology major?
B: Yes, that's right. But **I've given it some thought and** decided science just isn't for me.
A: So how can I help?
B: Well, I'd like to enroll in a good graduate program. I was hoping you could **steer me in the right direction.**
A: **As a matter of fact** we have a great program right here. **I'd be more than happy to** write you a recommendation.
B: That's super! **I really appreciate it.**

B ▶1:09 **RHYTHM AND INTONATION** Listen again and repeat. Then practice the conversation with a partner.

C **CONVERSATION ACTIVATOR** Create a similar conversation, using the questions you wrote in Exercise F. Start like this: *So, have you decided on …* Be sure to change roles and then partners.

DON'T STOP!
• Discuss your background and interests.
• Say as much as you can.

7

GOAL Compare your dreams and goals in life

A ▶1:10 **LISTENING WARM-UP** **VOCABULARY** **DESCRIBING DREAMS AND GOALS** Read and listen to what the people are saying. Then listen again and repeat the verb phrases and adjectives.

I'm fulfilling my lifelong dream to be an archaeologist. I'm in a graduate program and expect to get my degree in three years.

I know the goal I've set is ambitious, but I don't think it's unrealistic.

My husband will be working from home for the next three years so we can share the housekeeping and childcare responsibilities 50-50.

Verb phrases
fulfill a dream
set a goal
work towards / pursue a goal
put [something] off
share responsibilities

Adjectives	
ambitious	modest
achievable	unachievable
realistic	unrealistic

My wife put off her studies and worked to support us while I was studying. Now it's my turn to support her as she pursues her goal.

If we have a common goal and work towards it, anything's achievable. Hey, the sky's the limit for us!

B **ACTIVATE THE VOCABULARY** Complete each statement, using a word or phrase from the Vocabulary.

1 One way a husband and wife can .... is by each one doing half of the household chores.

2 Sometimes a goal requires too much work and it becomes ....

3 When you finally achieve what you've wanted all your life, you have ....

4 .... is an adjective that means almost the same thing as "challenging."

5 Sometimes people .... working towards their own goals for a while in order to help a spouse pursue his or her own goals for now.

6 The first step in achieving something is to ....

C ▶1:11 **LISTEN FOR MAIN IDEAS** Listen. Complete each statement, choosing the correct word or phrase.

1 Dan stays home because he (lost his job / wants to stay home).

2 Sarah is the primary (breadwinner / caregiver) in the family.

3 Sarah's lifelong dream was to be (a stay-at-home mom / a surgeon).

4 The number of (mothers / fathers) who choose to stay home to take care of the children is increasing.

5 Dan and Sarah have decided to lead a (traditional / nontraditional) lifestyle.

D ▶1:12 **LISTEN TO CONFIRM CONTENT** Write a checkmark next to the topics that were discussed. Write an X next to the topics that weren't. Listen again to check your answers.

☐ the definition of a stay-at-home dad

☐ the number of stay-at-home dads in the U.S.

☐ the kind of work Dan did before the children were born

☐ the ages of Dan and Sarah's children

☐ the sexes of Dan and Sarah's children

☐ the number of years it took for Sarah to complete her degree

LISTEN FOR SUPPORTING DETAILS On a separate sheet of paper, answer each question. Explain your answers with details from what Dan said. Listen again if necessary.

1 Is Dan happy with his lifestyle choice? How do you know?

> ❝ He's happy because he's doing what he always wanted to do. ❞

2 Why does Dan think comments about his life choices are sexist?

3 What's Dan's opinion of women who become the primary breadwinner of the family?

4 Why does Dan think it's good for his children to observe the roles he and Sarah have taken?

5 Why would the person who sent the tweet be against his son's deciding to be a stay-at-home dad?

6 How do you know Dan doesn't like the terms *housewife* and *househusband*?

7 What's Dan's hope for the next generation?

F **DISCUSSION** Discuss the following questions. Express and support your opinions.

1 Should any careers or parental / household roles be limited to people of one sex or the other? Be specific and support your opinion with reasons.

2 Why do people have a double standard for men and women? Is there any good reason to have one?

3 Will Dan and Sarah's children benefit or be harmed by their parents' reversal of roles. In what ways?

4 Are men or women naturally more ambitious in their careers? If you think they are, why do you think that is?

5 Do you think Dan and Sarah fulfilled their dreams and goals? If so, explain how.

NOW YOU CAN | Compare your dreams and goals in life

A **FRAME YOUR IDEAS** Complete the chart with your own dreams and goals. If you need more space, continue on a separate sheet of paper.

Goals I've set	What I have done to achieve them
to get married and have three children	I've signed up for an online dating site.

	Goals I've set	What I have done to achieve them
for my family		
for my career		
other		

RECYCLE THIS LANGUAGE	
· decide on	· be rejected by
· take up	· a breadwinner
· apply for / to	· a caregiver
· sign up for	· sexist
· switch to	· traditional
· be accepted to / into / by	· have a double standard

B **DISCUSSION** Share and compare goals with your partner. Use the Vocabulary from page 8.

DIGITAL SPEAKING BOOSTER

9

GOAL Describe job qualifications

A **READING WARM-UP** How qualified are you for the job you want—now or in the future? Explain.

B ▶ 1:13 **READING** Read the article about good and bad interview behavior. In your opinion, which suggestion is the most important?

DIGITAL STRATEGIES

🔺 JOB BUILDER

Home   About   Advice & tips   Build a career   Search 🔍

The Successful Job Interview

Charlotte Watson

OK. So you've sent in an application and a résumé for that dream job you saw advertised. The employer thinks you might be a good candidate, and you've landed an interview. You already know it's important to dress right, offer a firm handshake, and maintain eye contact, but do you know that other aspects of your behavior can make the difference between getting that job or not?

Being late to a job interview is almost always a disqualifier. Most candidates are on their best behavior for their interview, so being late is a major red flag for employers. Since punctuality is expected in any kind of work setting, arriving late makes your future employer think you'll be late for work if you get the job. If you are late for your interview, it's important to provide an airtight detailed excuse, explaining why your lateness was unavoidable. Apologize and reassure the interviewer that this isn't habitual behavior on your part.

Another thing that can get an interviewee off on the wrong foot is being overly informal or too familiar.

Even though the person who interviews you might be friendly or dressed informally, don't take this as permission to be inappropriately casual. If an interviewer wants to be addressed by his or her first name, he or she will invite you to do that. If not, be sure to stick with last names and titles.

Remember that employers want to know that you are interested in the job and will be a motivated employee. A candidate who hasn't taken the time to learn something about the company or the position being offered appears unmotivated and willing to take anything that comes along. Even if you are sure you already know everything you need to know about the job or the company, prepare two or three relevant questions for the interviewer of the position. And listen with obvious interest to the answers, following up with thoughtful questions that demonstrate that you have been listening.

So before your next job interview, check out the list of do's and don'ts and follow the suggestions. They'll take you a long way towards getting that dream job!

Top Ten Do's and Don'ts for Your Job Interview

Do	Don't
Arrive on time.	Be too familiar.
Stay on topic when answering questions.	Talk too much.
Ask questions.	Seem desperate to get the job.
Listen.	Criticize your current employer.
Be modest, yet positive about yourself.	Brag about yourself.

C **CONFIRM INFORMATION** Write a checkmark for the ideas that Charlotte Watson expressed in the article. Then, for the statements that don't reflect what she said, work with a partner to clarify what she <u>did</u> say.

☐ **1** Employers expect employees to be punctual on the job.

☐ **2** You shouldn't ask the employer questions during a job interview because it might indicate that you don't know anything about the company.

☐ **3** It's important for job candidates to express interest in the company offering the job.

☐ **4** Employers should dress informally when they interview job candidates.

☐ **5** It's better not to explain why you are late for an interview.

D APPLY IDEAS Read more things Ms. Bates said in her interview. With a partner, explain whether she followed Watson's suggestions.

1 "I'd say I'm kind of a people person and a pretty good listener. My colleagues often come to me when they need advice and support."

2 "Correct me if I'm wrong, Ian—you're married, right?"

3 "I really can't stand my supervisor. He's not fair. If I don't get this job, I'll be very depressed!"

4 "I make even better presentations than my boss. You would be lucky to have me in this job."

5 "What is the biggest challenge the company sees itself facing in the next year?"

6 "Let me tell you what my teacher did when I was still a child. My mother was visiting and the teacher showed her my artwork, which she said was the best in the class. And since this job entails creating presentations at meetings, I thought that information would indicate that this has been a lifelong interest of mine and something that I have developed a lot of skills in."

E DISCUSSION Explain the reason for each of the do's and dont's on the list in the article.

❝ If you criticize your current employer, the interviewer could think you're not a loyal employee and might say bad things about his or her company too. ❞

F ▶1:14 **WORD STUDY** COLLOCATIONS WITH <u>HAVE</u> AND <u>GET</u> FOR QUALIFICATIONS
Read and listen to the collocations, paying attention to <u>have</u>, <u>get</u>, and the prepositions. Repeat.

have experience	get experience in
have experience with	get training in
have experience in	get a degree / certificate in
have training in	get certified in

G PERSONALIZE THE VOCABULARY On a separate sheet of paper, write statements about your qualifications, using at least four of the collocations.

I've had some training in IT and gotten some experience in managing technical staff ...

NOW YOU CAN Describe job qualifications

A FRAME YOUR IDEAS Read the job ad and Ben Breeden's résumé. With a partner, make notes describing his qualifications for this job. Use the collocations from Word Study.

Wilton Hotel, Miami FLORIDA, USA

Seeks Assistant Manager to work at front desk and in office. Must possess good people skills and knowledge of the hotel industry. The Wilton Hotel has many guests and workers from Latin America so ability to speak Spanish and Portuguese fluently a must.

B ROLE PLAY In pairs, role-play a job interview between Ben Breeden and the hiring manager of the Wilton Hotel. Follow Charlotte Watson's suggestions.

OPTIONAL WRITING Write your own one-page résumé. Include your employment history, education and / or training. Use Breeden's résumé as a model, or select a template from an online résumé-building website.

Ben Breeden

102 Shanley Avenue
Newtown, FL 32793

+1 555 776 9833
ben.breeden@blue.net

Objective
To use my background and experience in a managerial position in the hotel industry

Experience
July 2016 to the present
  Corporate sales associate, Holiday House Hotel, Newtown, FL

August 2015 to June 2016
  Event planning assistant, Holiday House Hotel, Newtown, FL

September 2013 to June 2015
  Part-time salesclerk, Pennyworth's Department Store, Newtown, FL

Education
Comstock School of Hotel Management, Comstock, GA
  Certificate in Hotel Management (June 2015)

University of Central Florida, Hyperion, FL
  B.S. in Communication with major in Spanish and Portuguese (June 2014)

A WRITING SKILL   Study the rules.

The purpose of a cover letter is to acquaint an employer with you and to express interest in a position. If a job ad provides instructions about what to include in your cover letter, be sure to follow the directions carefully. If you don't, you may not receive a response. The letter can be sent in traditional paper form by mail, or as an e-mail.

Traditional paper form

Follow the style used for other formal letters. Use good quality paper and be neat. Proofread your letter carefully to be sure there are no spelling mistakes or typographical errors. Try to limit the letter to one page. Include your résumé on a separate sheet of paper in the same envelope.

E-mail form

Use formal e-mail style, addressing the recipient with his or her title and last name followed by a colon. Make paragraphs easy to read by separating them with a blank line space. Do not attach your cover letter to your e-mail. Make the e-mail the actual cover letter so the recipient can see the information upon opening the e-mail. Attach your résumé to your e-mail.

Here are some suggestions:

· Tell the employer why you are writing (in response to an ad, as a general expression of interest in working at that company or institution, etc.).
· Say why you think you would be a good candidate for the (or a) position; i.e., briefly state your qualifications.
· Tell the employer how to contact you for follow-up or to schedule an interview.
· Do not include too much information about your life.

WRITING MODEL

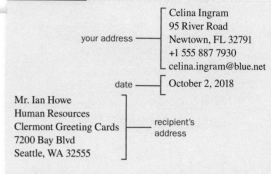

your address — Celina Ingram
95 River Road
Newtown, FL 32791
+1 555 887 7930
celina.ingram@blue.net

date — October 2, 2018

Mr. Ian Howe
Human Resources
Clermont Greeting Cards — recipient's address
7200 Bay Blvd
Seattle, WA 32555

Dear Mr. Howe, — salutation

I am writing in response to your advertisement on giantjob.com for the executive administrative assistant position at the Clermont Card Company in Seattle.

I have often bought Clermont greeting cards because of their positive messages and nice graphics, which is why I would be proud to work there. In addition, I believe I would be a good candidate because of my successful experience as an administrative assistant at Pinkerton Greeting Cards.

I have attached my résumé and the names and contact information of two managers here at Pinkerton who have offered to provide a recommendation.

If you agree that my experience and other qualifications make me a good candidate, please contact me at the address or e-mail address above. As I will be moving to Seattle in two weeks, please contact me at my e-mail address after October 15.

I look forward to hearing from you.

Cordially, — complimentary close

Celina Ingram — signature

Celina Ingram — typewritten name

attachment — indicates another document included in the same envelope

B PRACTICE   Read the e-mail cover letter. On a separate sheet of paper, rewrite it, correcting errors in style and formality.

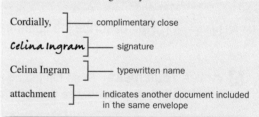

Subject:

Hi, Bill—Just wanted u 2 know Im intersted in that great advertising copy writer job I saw listed in the want ads ☺. I think I'm the rite person 4 u. Here's why: I am 26 years old and graduated from Meecham College with a major in english. I have been working at Poco Cola in the advertising department for five years I am ready to move to a new company. My résumé is attached so you can see my qualifications. If you are interested in discussing the job, please e-mail me at the address above to set up an interview. –Jon

DIGITAL WRITING PROCESS

C APPLY THE WRITING SKILL   On a separate sheet of paper, write a formal cover letter to an employer, expressing interest in a job. Create a job title that interests you and use the name of a real or a fictitious employer. Use real or invented information.

SELF-CHECK

☐ Does my letter have any spelling, punctuation, or typographical errors?

☐ Did I use formal letter writing conventions?

☐ Did I tell the employer the purpose of my letter?

☐ Did I say why I think I would be a good candidate?

☐ Did I tell the employer how to contact me for follow-up?

A ▶ 1:15 **Listen to the conversations. Then read the questions in the chart and listen again. Complete the chart after each conversation.**

What is his or her dream in life?	Is he or she confident about achieving his or her goal?	
1	☐ yes	☐ no
2	☐ yes	☐ no
3	☐ yes	☐ no
4	☐ yes	☐ no

B **Complete the statements with the correct prepositions.**

1 She has always wanted to take .... the piano and has enrolled .... a program that teaches the basics of music to adults.

2 Anyone applying .... a job in the newspaper business should have training .... journalism.

3 He has decided .... a career as a chef and has been accepted .... a top-notch cooking school in Peru.

4 Her experience .... the diplomatic service and her degree .... international relations make her an excellent candidate for a position at the U.N.

5 After being rejected .... two accounting firms for a summer internship, he decided to switch .... a different major at his university.

6 Before she applied .... law school, she signed up .... speed reading.

C **Match each word or phrase with its definition. Then, on a separate sheet of paper, use each one in a statement about your own plans and goals.**

...... **1** achievable   **a** capable of being reached

...... **2** ambitious   **b** decide what one wants to do and work towards it

...... **3** work towards a goal **c** divide necessary work between two or more people so neither one has to do it all

...... **4** put off   **d** postpone

...... **5** unrealistic   **e** requiring a lot of work

...... **6** share responsibilities **f** unreasonably hard and thus unlikely to be achieved

D **Complete each information question, using the past perfect continuous.**

1 (how long / you / work on) .... that project before you changed jobs?

2 (where / they / study) .... before they moved to Europe?

3 (which program / she / apply for) .... when she decided to change majors?

4 (what professor / you / study with) .... when they closed the university?

5 (how long / they / look) .... at résumés before they saw yours?

TEST-TAKING SKILLS BOOSTER p. 151

Web Project: Careers
www.english.com/summit3e

UNIT

2

COMMUNICATION GOALS
1 Describe the consequences of lying
2 Express regret and take responsibility
3 Explore where values come from
4 Discuss how best to help others

Character and Responsibility

PREVIEW

A **FRAME YOUR IDEAS** Look at the pictures. Then answer the questions in the survey. Check what you would do in each situation.

Taking
responsibility...
or avoiding it

IS IT HARD FOR YOU TO ACCEPT RESPONSIBILITY?

What would you do if you ...	A	B	C	Other
made a serious mistake at work or school?	☐	☐	☐	☐
forgot to finish an assignment at work or school?	☐	☐	☐	☐
broke or lost something you had borrowed?	☐	☐	☐	☐
were late for an appointment?	☐	☐	☐	☐
were stopped for exceeding the speed limit?	☐	☐	☐	☐
damaged someone's car while parking, but no one saw you?	☐	☐	☐	☐
hadn't kept a promise you made to a friend or relative?	☐	☐	☐	☐
forgot a friend's birthday?	☐	☐	☐	☐
were caught telling a lie?	☐	☐	☐	☐

Sorry. It was my fault!

It was the cat's fault!

A I would admit making a mistake.

B I would shift the blame to someo or something els

Sorry, I'm going to be late. The traffic is just terrible!

8:30

C I would make up an excuse.

B ▶1:16 **VOCABULARY** TAKING OR AVOIDING RESPONSIBILITY
Listen and repeat.

- admit making a mistake
- make up an excuse
- shift the blame
- keep a promise
- tell a lie / tell the truth

C **PAIR WORK** Compare and explain your responses to the survey.

D **DISCUSSION** Are there ever good reasons *not* to be truthful? Is it ever a better idea to make up an excuse or shift the blame to someone else? Explain your answers and give examples.

E ▶ **1:17** **SPOTLIGHT** Read and listen to a conversation between a father and his teenage son. Notice the spotlighted language.

Jason: Dad … I think I messed up big time today.

Dad: What happened?

Jason: Well, you know how teachers always like to put up students' artwork on the walls? So Joey and I noticed this really weird drawing of a horse.

Dad: So what? You didn't like it. That's not a crime.

Jason: True. But that's not all.

Dad: Uh-oh.

Jason: See, Mr. Rogg had to step out for a bit. And Joey—you know how he's always fooling around—he starts **making fun of** the drawing, acting like he's the horse.

Dad: And I suppose the class loved that?

Jason: Totally. Everyone was cracking up. Anyway, I **couldn't help myself.** I started joking around, too, and I guess we just kind of **got carried away**.

Dad: Don't tell me the kid who drew it was in that class!

Jason: No one realized it until she got up and ran out.

Dad: Wow. Her feelings must have really been hurt.

Jason: **That's not the worst of it.** She came back with Mr. Rogg and she was crying, which made me feel awful. I could just kick myself! I wish I'd told Joey to **cut it out**.

Dad: Well, it's never too late to apologize. If I were you, I'd **own up to** what you did and tell her how bad you feel. Take responsibility for **letting things get out of hand**. Maybe later you could **make it up to her** by buying her lunch.

Jason: You're probably right.

Dad: And it wouldn't hurt to talk to Mr. Rogg afterward … just so he knows you did the right thing.

F **UNDERSTANDING IDIOMS AND EXPRESSIONS 1** Find two spotlighted expressions that mean someone allowed his or her behavior to go too far.

G **UNDERSTANDING IDIOMS AND EXPRESSIONS 2** Complete the statements.

1 "Making fun of something" means …… .

2 "Couldn't help myself" means …… .

3 "That's not the worst of it" means …… .

4 "Cut it out" means …… .

5 "Own up to something" means …… .

6 "Make it up to someone" means …… .

a admit you did it and take responsibility for it.

b "Stop doing that!"

c do something nice for someone you have wronged.

d joking about it in order to criticize it.

e wasn't able to stop doing [something].

f there's even more negative information.

H **DISCUSSION** Discuss the questions.

1 Whose responsibility was it to prevent what happened in the art class—Joey's, Jason's, Mr. Rogg's, or the girl's? Explain.

2 In what way could Joey, Jason, Mr. Rogg, or the girl have handled the situation differently?

SPEAKING **PAIR WORK** Tell a partner about a situation in which someone's feelings were accidentally hurt. How was the situation resolved? Use the Vocabulary from page 14 and expressions from Spotlight.

GOAL Describe the consequences of lying

A ▶1:18 **GRAMMAR SPOTLIGHT** Read the article. Notice the spotlighted grammar.

"Telling the Truth? It's Not So Easy!

I REALLY LIKE YOUR NEW HAIRCUT.

The honest truth? We *all* tell lies. In a psychological study, 147 participants were asked to keep a diary of the lies they told over the course of a week. Researchers found that:

- Participants told lies to about 30 percent of the people **with whom they interacted**.

- There wasn't a single day **when the participants didn't tell at least one lie**.

In fact, we live in a world **where we are often punished for telling the truth and rewarded for lying**. For example, we tell our boss we got stuck in traffic instead of admitting that we overslept. Making up an excuse keeps us out of trouble.

Here's another common situation **in which we often tell lies**: we pretend to like something to avoid hurting others. For example, we say we love a friend's gift when in fact we don't like it.

Some researchers argue that lying may in fact be good for us socially because it protects the feelings of the people **with whom we interact**. Interestingly, they note that the people **whose profession require the most social contacts**—for example, store clerks, salespeople, politicians, and journalists—tell the most lies.

The truth is, everyone tells "white lies" to avoid hurting others. Sometime **when you're ready**, try keeping a diary for a week and see how long you can go without telling a single lie!

B **APPLY IDEAS** With a partner, brainstorm one or more additional situations in which people would be likely to tell a lie, according to the article. Explain why.

C **EXPRESS AND SUPPORT AN OPINION** Do you agree that "lying may in fact be good for us socially because it protects the feelings of the people with whom we interact"? Explain, using examples from your life if possible.

D **PAIR WORK** How truthful are you? Write an X on the continuum. Explain your choice to your partner, giving examples from your experience.

◄ NEVER TRUTHFUL   SOMETIMES TRUTHFUL   ALWAYS TRUTHFUL ►

E **RELATE TO PERSONAL EXPERIENCE** Discuss and then make a list of times in your life when you …

- made an excuse to avoid getting in trouble.
- told a lie to avoid hurting someone else's feelings.
- were punished or got in trouble after telling the truth.
- were rewarded for telling a lie.

> **GRAMMAR BOOSTER** p. 129
> · Adjective clauses: overview
> · Adjective clauses with quantifiers

DIGITAL INDUCTIVE ACTIVITY

F **GRAMMAR** ADJECTIVE CLAUSES: REVIEW AND EXPANSION

Remember: An adjective clause gives more information about a noun. The relative pronouns who, whom, and that introduce adjective clauses about people. The relative pronouns that and which introduce adjective clauses about things.

> The participants **who kept a diary** recorded that they told lies every day. (who = the participants)
> White lies are some of the most common lies **that people tell**. (that = the most common lies)

Use when, where, and whose to introduce adjective clauses about time, location, and possession.

> **Time:** There has never been a time **when** some form of lying wasn't a part of everyday life.
> **Location:** There's no place in the world **where** people are completely honest all the time.
> **Possession:** People **whose** jobs require frequent social contact have the most opportunity to lie.

In formal English, when a relative pronoun is the object of a preposition, the preposition appears at the beginning of the clause. In informal English, the preposition usually appears at the end.

The participants lied to many of the people **with whom** they interacted. (formal)
The participants lied to many of the people **who** they interacted **with**. (informal)

It's a question **to which** most people don't give a truthful answer. (formal)
It's a question **which** most people don't give a truthful answer **to**. (informal)

Be careful!
Use <u>whom</u>, not <u>who</u>, directly after a preposition.
... **with whom** they interacted.
NOT ~~with who~~ they interacted.
Use <u>which</u>, not <u>that</u>, directly after a preposition.
... **to which** most people don't give a truthful answer.
NOT ~~to that~~ most people don't give a truthful answer.

G UNDERSTAND THE GRAMMAR With a partner, study the adjective clauses in Grammar Spotlight on page 16 and answer the questions.

1 Which adjective clause is about possession? Which is about location? Which are about time?

2 Which three are objects of a preposition? On a separate sheet of paper, rewrite those sentences in informal English.

H GRAMMAR PRACTICE Complete the sentences with one of the relative pronouns from the box. (Do not add any prepositions.)

who	whom
which	whose
where	when

1 The workplace is the place .... people tend to tell the most lies.

2 People .... lies are discovered lose the trust of their friends and colleagues.

3 The people with .... I work are trustworthy.

4 People .... break their promises cannot be trusted.

5 There are situations in .... it's impossible to tell the truth.

6 There are moments .... being honest can cause you problems.

7 The people to .... I never lie are the people .... are really close to me.

8 There are times .... I lie to avoid getting into trouble and times .... I lie to avoid hurting others.

9 Telling the truth is an action for .... there is sometimes no reward.

10 The people .... lies were recorded said they would tell about 75 percent of those lies again.

NOW YOU CAN Describe the consequences of lying

A NOTEPADDING With a partner, write examples for each category.

Situations in which we shouldn't tell lies	Situations in which telling a lie is the best solution

B ACTIVATE THE GRAMMAR On a separate sheet of paper, describe the consequences of lying in the situations on your notepad. Use adjective clauses.

> Lying to someone who is a good friend is wrong.
> You could destroy the friendship that way.

C DISCUSSION ACTIVATOR Discuss the consequences of lying. Explain further by providing examples. Say as much as you can.

17

GOAL Express regret and take responsibility

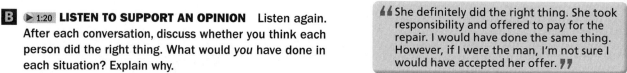

A ▶ 1:19 **LISTEN TO INFER INFORMATION** Listen to the conversations. Then listen again and choose the expression that best describes each person's behavior.

1 She ...... the damage.
  a took responsibility for   **b** avoided taking responsibility for

2 He ...... the damage.
  a took responsibility for   **b** avoided taking responsibility for

3 He ....
  a admitted making a mistake   **b** shifted the blame to someone else

4 She ....
  a admitted making a mistake   **b** made up an excuse

5 She ...... for being late.
  a took responsibility   **b** made up an excuse

6 She ...... for losing the scarf.
  a took responsibility   **b** made up an excuse

B ▶ 1:20 **LISTEN TO SUPPORT AN OPINION** Listen again. After each conversation, discuss whether you think each person did the right thing. What would *you* have done in each situation? Explain why.

> ❝ She definitely did the right thing. She took responsibility and offered to pay for the repair. I would have done the same thing. However, if I were the man, I'm not sure I would have accepted her offer. ❞

DIGITAL
INDUCTIVE
ACTIVITY

C **GRAMMAR** "COMMENT" CLAUSES

An adjective clause beginning with <u>which</u> can be used to modify—or comment on— an independent clause.

  He broke his sister's camera, **which made him feel terrible**.
  She blamed Paul for causing the accident, **which was totally unfair**.
  I had avoided taking responsibility, **which was embarrassing**, so I just
    made up an excuse.

Comment clauses are non-restrictive—that is, they provide additional information that is not essential to the meaning of the sentence. Use a comma before a comment clause and after it if something else follows.

Be careful!
You cannot use <u>that</u> in place of <u>which</u> in a comment clause:
  She always borrows Bob's tablet, **which** really bugs him.
  NOT She always borrows Bob's tablet, ~~that~~ really bugs him.

> **GRAMMAR BOOSTER** p. 130
> Reduced adjective clauses

DIGITAL
MORE
EXERCISES

D **GRAMMAR PRACTICE** Write sentences that include comment clauses with <u>which</u>.

Example: Mark is going to replace my camera. (It's really thoughtful of him.)
  ...Mark is going to replace my camera, which is really thoughtful of him...

1 Lena insists on paying for the tickets I gave her. (It's just unnecessary.)
  ....

2 Mona never returned the book I lent her. (It really bothers me.)
  ....

3 Apparently, replacing Nancy's ring would cost an arm and a leg. (It's just ridiculous.)
  ....

4 I offered to pay for dinner. (It was the right thing to do, in my opinion.)
  ....

5 Gerry crossed the street in the middle of the block. (It's against the law and dangerous.)
  ....
  ....

> **PRONUNCIATION BOOSTER** p. 144
> Emphatic stress and pitch to express emotion

A ▶ 1:21 **CONVERSATION SPOTLIGHT** Read and listen. Notice the spotlighted conversation strategies.

A: Tim, you know that tablet you lent me? Well, **I'm really sorry, but** I have some bad news. I broke it.

B: Oh, no. How did that happen?

A: Well, I tripped and dropped it, which was completely my fault. I feel awful about it.

B: Are you sure it can't be fixed?

A: Pretty sure. I took it to the store, and they said it wouldn't be worth it. I'm going to get you a new one, **if that's OK.**

B: **That's really not necessary.** I was just about to get a new one anyway.

A: No, I insist. It's no problem. And **please accept my apology.**

> ▶ 1:23 **Ways to express regret**
> I feel awful (about it).
> I feel (just) terrible.
> I'm so sorry.

B ▶ 1:22 **RHYTHM AND INTONATION** Listen again and repeat. Then practice the conversation with a partner.

C **NOTEPADDING** Choose two situations from the survey on page 14 that have actually happened in your life. Make notes about what happened and what you said and did. Use "comment" clauses when possible.

> **Situation 1:** I forgot a friend's birthday, which was embarrassing.

Situation 1:	Situation 2:
What I said:	What I said:
What I did:	What I did:

D **CONVERSATION ACTIVATOR** Create a conversation similar to the one in Exercise A. Start like this: *I'm afraid I have some bad news ...* Be sure to change roles and then partners.

RECYCLE THIS LANGUAGE	
· messed up big time	· tell a lie
· got carried away	· shift the blame to someone else
· let things get out of hand	· take responsibility
· admit making a mistake	· avoid taking responsibility
· make up an excuse	· So what?
· tell the truth	· That's not the worst of it.

E **DISCUSSION** Choose one of the situations you wrote about on your notepad. Tell your classmates about what happened and details about what you said and did. Then say whether or not you're satisfied with the outcome and why.

DON'T STOP!
- Continue to negotiate how you'll make up for what happened.
- Say as much as you can.

GOAL Explore where values come from

A READING WARM-UP Where do you think people learn the difference between right and wrong? What are the most important lessons children need to learn?

B ▶ 1:24 READING Read the article. Which influences do you think are the most important?

THE DEVELOPMENT OF VALUES

We all live by a set of principles or beliefs that guide our actions and help us distinguish between what is morally acceptable or unacceptable. But where do our values come from? In fact, they develop throughout our lives and originate from a variety of sources. Here are some key influences:

PARENTS From earliest childhood, most of us learn a sense of right and wrong from our parents. When they tell us children's stories, we learn simple morals—life lessons about the consequences of good and bad behavior. Our parents correct us when we make mistakes. More importantly, we learn from our parents' actions. Children see everything. They observe how their parents relate to each other and handle social situations, and they always notice whether their parents are truthful or not.

PEERS From childhood through adulthood, our everyday conversations with our friends, classmates, colleagues, neighbors, and acquaintances play a role in developing our moral outlook. We are strongly affected by the views of our peers. We naturally "categorize" the people we know or who we hear about on the news—for instance, who is unfriendly, who is generous, which politicians or celebrities are honest.

RELIGION AND CULTURE Many people attribute their moral principles to their religious upbringing. Religion can provide a clear set of guidelines to live by that make it easier to distinguish between right and wrong. All the world's religions offer values that can move us away from being self-centered toward helping others. The dominant values of the group, community, or culture we grow up in are also a powerful influence on our own worldview. For example, more importance may be placed on conforming to society than on the individual, which affects the choices we make in life.

INSTITUTIONS We also pick up values from the code of ethics promoted by our school, profession, or company. Some schools take a public stand against students' bullying their classmates, which sets a clear principle for how students should behave. A corporation might establish a mission statement for all its employees to follow. In such cases, the company expects employees to make its values part of their personal values.

LIFE EVENTS Significant life events, such as the death of a loved one, a divorce, an accident, or an illness, can shape our sense of ethics. Perhaps a loved one falls gravely ill. Having to take care of a sick relative teaches us about setting priorities and the value of selflessness. A sudden financial loss may force us to re-examine and rethink what is important to us. We might be the victim of a major accident or a natural disaster. Surviving such an event teaches us about the miracle and fragility of life and helps us see—and appreciate—each day differently from the way we did before the event.

Sometimes we face an ethical dilemma in which we have to choose between two opposing values. For example, a close friend may ask us to tell a lie in order to avoid his or her getting in trouble, which presents us with a conflict. While we believe it's important to protect the ones we love, our values also may place great importance on remaining truthful. It's the combined lessons we have learned throughout our lives that help us make the right (or wrong) choices.

C RELATE TO PERSONAL EXPERIENCE Complete the chart. Identify one or more values you learned from each of the influences mentioned in the Reading.

Your parents
They taught me to work hard.

Your parents	Your school, profession, or company
Your peers	Your life events
Your religion or culture	Other

D **CLASSIFY VOCABULARY USING CONTEXT** Cross out the one word that doesn't belong with the other three in each group of words. Explain your answers, based on how the words are used in the article.

1 values   events   beliefs   guidelines
2 peers   acquaintances   celebrities   colleagues
3 a situation a divorce   an accident   a life event
4 ethics   priorities   morals   principles
5 moral   ethical   right   self-centered

E **CRITICAL THINKING** Read each quote from the article and discuss the questions.

1 "[Children] observe how their parents relate to each other and handle social situations, and they always notice whether their parents are truthful or not."

How do you think children develop values from their observations?

2 "A sudden financial loss may force us to re-examine and rethink what is important to us."

In what ways could a financial loss affect our values?

3 "Sometimes we face an ethical dilemma in which we have to choose between two opposing values."

In addition to the one mentioned in the article, what are some other examples of ethical dilemmas?

DIGITAL
EXTRA
CHALLENGE

NOW YOU CAN Explore where values come from

A **FRAME YOUR IDEAS** Where do you think your values mostly come from?
Rank the following influences in the order of importance in your life, from 1 to 10, with 1 being the most important. Include an "other" if necessary.

my mother		my colleagues or classmates		my culture
my father		my teachers		a life event
other relatives		my school or job		other:
my friends		my religion		

B **PAIR WORK** Take turns explaining the most important influences on the development of your own values. Provide specific examples. Refer to the chart you completed in Exercise C on page 20. Ask your partner questions.

❝The religious teaching I got as a child was, I think, the strongest influence on me. Those are the guidelines that help me remember the difference between right and wrong. ❞

❝When I was just a kid, my dad got very sick and he couldn't work. We all had to help take care of my dad. My mom and my oldest sister both worked, so it was a lot harder for both of them. It made me realize how important family is. ❞

GOAL Discuss how best to help others

A ▶ 1:25 **VOCABULARY** **PHILANTHROPIC WORK** Read and listen. Then listen again and repeat.

do•nor /ˈdoʊnər/ *n.* a person or organization that gives money for a specific cause or charity ALSO **do•na•tion** *n.* *A number of donors have chosen to make their contributions privately. They prefer not to have their names associated with their donations.*

phi•lan•thro•pist /fɪˈlænθrəpɪst/ *n.* a wealthy person who donates a significant amount of his or her money, time, and / or reputation to charitable causes ALSO **phi•lan•thro•py** *n.*, **phi•lan•thro•pic** *adj.* *A number of celebrities have gotten deeply involved in philanthropy. As philanthropists, they have become almost as famous for their philanthropic work as for their work as actors, singers, and athletes.*

hu•man•i•tar•i•an /hyuˌmænəˈtɛriən/ *n.* a person who is dedicated to improving people's living conditions and treatment by others ALSO **hu•man•i•tar•i•an** *adj.*, **hu•man•i•tar•i•an•ism** *n.* *Many celebrities choose to make humanitarianism an important part of their lives. In some cases, they discover that humanitarian work takes up even more of their time—that being a humanitarian can be a full-time job.*

ac•tiv•ist /ˈæktəvɪst/ *n.* a person who works hard for social or political change, often as a member of a social or political organization ALSO **ac•tiv•ism** *n.* *His activism has often gotten him into trouble. As a political activist, he comes into conflict with those who do not share his views.*

B **ACTIVATE THE VOCABULARY** Read the biographies. Use the Vocabulary to write a sentence about each person and his or her work.

Graça Machel

Graça Machel, the widow of two presidents of two countries—Mozambique and South Africa—is known for her work protecting the rights of child refugees. She currently works to improve children's health.

Li Ka-shing

Hong Kong businessman Li Ka-shing is considered to be the wealthiest man in Asia. A number of universities have benefited from the numerous multi-million dollar contributions from his Li Ka-shing Foundation.

Helen Caldicott

In an effort to protect the environment for the future, Australian physician Helen Caldicott has worked for decades to oppose the use and spread of nuclear weapons and the use of nuclear power.

C **LISTENING WARM-UP** When someone achieves wealth and fame, do you think it's that person's responsibility to donate time and money to help others? Explain your point of view.

D ▶ 1:26 **LISTEN FOR MAIN IDEAS** Listen to Part 1 of a report on celebrity philanthropic work. Choose the best title for it.

☐ **1** Many celebrities try to change the world.

☐ **2** Two celebrities try to make a difference.

☐ **3** Jolie and Bono are highly successful in their chosen careers.

☐ **4** Philanthropic work teaches celebrities new skills.

human rights

defending human rights

protecting the environment

improving literacy

helping refugees

fighting hunger

eliminating poverty

E ▶1:27 **LISTEN TO CLASSIFY** Read the following philanthropic activities. Listen to Part 1 again and write J for Jolie's activities and B for Bono's, according to the report.

1 ...... donates money to build schools.

2 ...... organizes events to raise money.

3 ...... works to protect wildlife.

4 ...... gets world leaders to work together.

5 ...... works to improve medical care.

6 ...... works with the United Nations.

F ▶1:28 **LISTEN TO CONFIRM CONTENT** Listen to Part 1 again. Cross out the reasons for celebrity philanthropy that are NOT mentioned.

1 to develop new skills

2 to get attention from the media

3 to satisfy a desire to help end human suffering

4 to show gratitude for one's success

5 to increase one's fame and wealth

6 to change how one is seen by others

7 to address one's concerns about the future

G ▶1:29 **LISTEN FOR POINT OF VIEW** Now listen to Part 2. Which statement best represents the speaker's point of view? Explain your answer.

☐ 1 Celebrity philanthropists are only interested in their own fame and getting "photo ops."

☐ 2 While the criticism may have some truth, Jolie's and Bono's philanthropy has been mainly positive.

☐ 3 Despite their good work, Jolie's and Bono's philanthropy deserves a lot of criticism.

H ▶1:30 **LISTEN TO SUMMARIZE** Listen to Part 2 again. With a partner, write at least five criticisms of celebrity philanthropists from the report on a separate sheet of paper.

I **SUPPORT AN OPINION** Do celebrities make good philanthropists? Explain. Use information from the report or about other celebrity philanthropists you are aware of.

NOW YOU CAN Discuss how best to help others

A **FRAME YOUR IDEAS** Which three of the issues in the photos on page 22 do you think most urgently need attention? Write them on the notepad and write one activity that would help for each one.

1.	2.	3.

B **DISCUSSION** Discuss the best activities for solving one of the problems on your notepad.

> 🙶 I feel strongly about helping children, so I think it's crucial to provide good schools and ... 🙷

OPTIONAL WRITING Do rich and famous people have a responsibility to donate fame and money to help others? Write at least two paragraphs, supporting your point of view.

A **WRITING SKILL** Study the rules.

Restrictive adjective clauses

A restrictive adjective clause provides *essential information* necessary to identify the noun or pronoun it modifies. Do not use commas.

The person **who borrowed my camera yesterday** just told me she had broken it.
She replaced the camera lens **that she had broken the day before**.
The friend **whose phone I lost** insisted I didn't need to replace it.
The hotel in the town **where we stayed last weekend** offered to give us a refund.

Non-restrictive adjective clauses

A non-restrictive adjective clause provides *additional information* that is not necessary to identify the noun or pronoun it modifies. Use commas before and after, except at the end of a sentence, when the adjective clause ends with a period.

Lara, **who works in my office,** told me she broke the camera that she had borrowed.

The Aimes Hotel, **where we always get a room in July,** offered to give us a refund.

She replaced the tablet, **which made her very happy.**

My laptop, **which was always crashing when I really needed it,** finally died.

> **Be careful!**
> Use punctuation that supports your intended meaning.
> The laptop **which I bought last week** is great. (Differentiates this laptop from others: essential)
> The laptop, **which I bought last week**, is great. (An additional comment about the laptop: not essential)

B **PRACTICE** Read the college application essay, in which the writer describes a life lesson. Correct punctuation errors with adjective clauses. Add three commas and delete three.

C **PRACTICE** Decide if the adjective clause provides essential or additional information. Write a checkmark if the punctuation is correct. Make corrections if it is a non-restrictive clause.

- ☐ **1** His grandparents are the ones who taught him the most about right and wrong.
- ☐ **2** My cousin who was always truthful about everything told my aunt she was wrong.
- ☐ **3** I told a lie that I have regretted for more than ten years.
- ☐ **4** Her favorite vase which her mother had given her had been broken.
- ☐ **5** We found out that Megan was going to join us which was great.

What I Learned from My First Job

While working at my first job which was at a clothing store, I had a co-worker who got me into a lot of trouble. When the manager counted the money in the cash register, it had come up short. The co-worker had taken some of the money, so she shifted the blame to me. I insisted that I wasn't responsible, but the manager who didn't know me fired me immediately.

Ten years later, I got a phone call, that really surprised me. It was from the woman, who had blamed me for taking the money. She called me to apologize for what she had done. Apparently it had been bothering her for a long time.

This incident taught me an important lesson. Sometimes when people tell a lie, they hurt themselves more than the other person. While I had completely forgotten about the incident, it was my former co-worker, who felt badly about it for all those years.

DIGITAL WRITING PROCESS **D** **APPLY THE WRITING SKILL** On a separate sheet of paper, write a college application essay in which you describe an experience that taught you a life lesson or that shaped your values. Provide details by including at least three adjective clauses to add essential and additional information.

> **SELF-CHECK**
> ☐ Did I include at least three adjective clauses?
> ☐ Did I distinguish between essential and additional information?
> ☐ Did I use commas correctly in non-restrictive adjective clauses?

A ▶ 1:31 Listen to each conversation. Then listen again and complete the statements.

Conversation 1

1 The man is thinking about ....

a shifting the blame   **b** taking responsibility   **c** telling the truth

2 The woman suggests ....

a shifting the blame   **b** making up an excuse   **c** telling the truth

Conversation 2

3 The woman has decided to ....

a shift the blame   **b** make up an excuse   **c** take responsibility

B Complete the sentences with phrases from the box. Use each phrase only once.

| shift the blame | admit making a mistake | tell the truth | make up an excuse | take responsibility |

1 If Matt makes a mistake, he tries to .... to other people in his office so he won't get in trouble with his boss.

2 Dan forgot to prepare his report for the sales meeting, so he decided to .... He told his boss that his computer deleted the file.

3 Alice borrowed Susan's umbrella, but she forgot it on the train. She wanted to take responsibility, but she didn't want to .... , so she just replaced it and didn't say anything to Susan about it.

4 Jane doesn't .... when she does something wrong. Either she makes up an excuse or she doesn't tell the truth about what happened.

5 I really believe that in some situations it's better not to .... , especially when you are protecting someone's feelings. For example, if my grandmother spent all day cooking dinner, but it tasted terrible, I would still tell her it was delicious.

C Complete the paragraph with the relative pronouns from the box.

> Nora Richards, with .... I worked for five years, was a person .... (1)   (2)
> could never get her work done on time. I still remember the time ....she asked me to (3)
> help her write a long report .... was due the next day! The report, on .... (4)   (5)
> she had been working for an entire month, was needed for a business deal with a very important
>
> client. The deal, about .... Nora talked all the time (instead of writing the report), fell through, (6)
> and Nora was fired. There are situations in .... you simply have to meet your deadlines. Nora (7)
> was one of those people .... fails to understand that the office is a place .... , as the (8)   (9)
> saying says, "Actions speak louder than words."

| who |
| which |
| that |
| whom |
| where |
| when |

D On a separate sheet of paper, complete each statement with your own comment clause, using <u>which</u>. Don't forget to use a comma.

Example: Some celebrity philanthropists only care about publicity, ...*which I think is a shame*... .

1 Angelina Jolie has received many awards for her philanthropic work... .

2 Most people tell lies to avoid hurting people's feelings... .

3 My brother took responsibility for his mistake... .

4 I made up an excuse for being late to work... .

TEST-TAKING SKILLS BOOSTER p. 152

Web Project: Celebrity Philanthropists
www.english.com/summit3e

3 Fears, Hardships, and Heroism

PREVIEW

A **FRAME YOUR IDEAS** Take the self-test. Total your responses.

How chicken are you?

Rate the situations below, according to how scary they are to you, from 1 to 3, with 1 being not scary at all, 2 being somewhat scary, and 3 being very scary.

getting stuck in an elevator		walking outside during a bad storm	
seeing a bee on your arm		standing near the edge of a cliff	
driving in bad weather		going to the dentist	
eating in an unclean restaurant		walking down a dark street at night	
riding a horse		experiencing turbulence during a flight	
smelling smoke in a building		getting an injection from a doctor or nurse	
being a passenger in a speeding car		seeing a snake in your garden	
taking a roller-coaster ride		being in a place undergoing an epidemic	

YOUR CHICKEN SCORE
TOTAL YOUR SCORE

16–26
You're cool and collected. Nothing freaks you out.

27–37
You're just cautious.

38–48
You're a total chicken! You're probably afraid of your own shadow.

B **PAIR WORK** Compare self-tests with a partner. Are you both afraid of the same things? Which of you is more chicken?

C **GROUP WORK** How chicken is your class? Calculate the average score for each situation in your class. Which situation is the most frightening to everyone?

D ▶ 2:02 **SPOTLIGHT**   Read and listen to two friends discuss a problem.
Notice the spotlighted language.

> **Luiz:** Hey, Michel. Anything wrong? You look like you've lost your best friend.
> **Michel:** No. Nothing like that. I'm just **in hot water** with Emilie.
> **Luiz:** Emilie? But the two of you were so lovey-dovey when I saw you at the restaurant on Sunday. What's up?
> **Michel:** Well, Sunday was her birthday, and we'd been planning to get engaged on her birthday, but I guess I **got cold feet**. I just don't think I'm ready to make that kind of commitment yet. In any case, she's really upset. She feels like I **pulled the rug out from under her**.
> **Luiz:** Well, I can imagine that must have been really disappointing for her. Don't you feel like you're in love anymore? Or is there someone else?
> **Michel:** No. Definitely not. I love her **with all my heart**, but no matter how much I tell myself she's the only one for me, I **just can't take the plunge**. I don't know what's wrong with me. Maybe it's some kind of psychological problem.
> **Luiz:** I wouldn't **jump to that conclusion**. Marriage is **a big deal**, Michel. And it's forever. Most people find that scary.
> **Michel:** I think that's what **freaks me out** about it. Every time I think of proposing, I panic. I feel so guilty that I don't even want to see her right now.
> **Luiz:** Well, **it's not the end of the world**. Sounds like you just **have a minor case of the jitters**.
> **Michel:** You think so?
> **Luiz:** **Mark my words**. She'll wait for you. **Just chill** for a while until you're ready, OK?

E **UNDERSTAND IDIOMS AND EXPRESSIONS**   Choose the best way to complete each statement.

1 If you're "in hot water," you're ....
  a in trouble   **b** excited

2 When you "get cold feet," you ....
  a decide to do something as you had planned
  b decide not to do something as you had planned

3 If Emilie feels like Michel "pulled the rug out from under her," she feels that ....
  a he didn't do what he had promised
  b he was disappointed with her

4 If you do something "with all your heart," you do it ....
  a unwillingly   **b** with 100% commitment

5 When Michel said "I just can't take the plunge," he meant he ....
  a couldn't go through with proposing
  b didn't want to marry her

6 When Luiz says "I wouldn't jump to that conclusion," he's suggesting that Michel's reasoning is probably ....
  a right   **b** not right

7 Something that's "a big deal" is ....
  a full of advantages   **b** of great importance

8 If something "freaks you out," it ....
  a scares you   **b** excites you

9 If something "isn't the end of the world," it's ....
  a not a big deal   **b** not good

10 When Luiz says "Sounds like you just have a minor case of the jitters," he means ....
  a Michel is just nervous
  b Michel should take his doubt seriously

11 When you say "Mark my words," you want someone to ....
  a remember your prediction later
  b wait for you later

12 When Luiz tells Michel to "just chill," he's suggesting that Michel ....
  a do something right away
  b wait

SPEAKING   **SUMMARIZE AND PERSONALIZE**   First, summarize Michel's problem and say what you would do in his situation. Speculate about what will happen next. Then, discuss what scares you more: fears of physical harm such as the ones in the self-test, or emotional fears such as the ones Michel is experiencing. Explain your reasons, using examples from your life.

A ▶2:03 **VOCABULARY** EXPRESSING FRUSTRATION, EMPATHY, AND ENCOURAGEMENT
Read and listen. Then listen again and repeat.

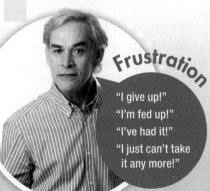

Frustration

"I give up!"
"I'm fed up!"
"I've had it!"
"I just can't take it any more!"

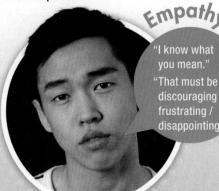

Empathy

"I know what you mean."
"That must be discouraging / frustrating / disappointing."

Encouragement

"Don't let it get you down."
"Don't give up!"
"Hang in there!"

B ▶2:04 **LISTEN TO PREDICT** Listen to the conversations. Then choose what the other person will probably say next.

1 **a** That must be frustrating. **b** I just can't take it anymore.
2 **a** I give up! **b** I know what you mean.
3 **a** I've had it! **b** Well, don't give up.
4 **a** I'm really fed up! **b** Don't let it get you down.
5 **a** Hang in there. **b** I just can't take it any more!

> **GRAMMAR BOOSTER** p. 131
> Embedded questions: review and common errors

C **GRAMMAR** CLAUSES WITH <u>NO MATTER</u>

Use <u>no matter</u> + a noun clause beginning with a question word to express frustration (that no amount of anything, for example *effort*, can make something change). Use a comma before or after clauses with <u>no matter</u>.

No matter how careful I am, I always forget something!
No matter what they said, he didn't believe them.
No matter what time we check in, we always have to wait for a room.
No one answers, **no matter when we call.**
They can't understand her, **no matter how slowly she speaks.**

> **Be careful!**
> Use normal, not inverted, word order in the noun clause and don't use an auxiliary verb.
> No matter **who you ask**, no one can give you directions.
> NOT No matter ~~who do you ask,~~ ...

D **GRAMMAR PRACTICE** Mark correct sentences with a checkmark. Mark incorrect sentences with an X. Correct the incorrect sentences.

☒ **1** No matter how much do I encourage my sister, she won't take a plane anywhere.
  ...No matter how much I encourage my sister, she won't take a plane anywhere.........

☐ **2** Eric couldn't find his folder, no matter how hard did he look.
  ....

☐ **3** No matter how late Phil stays up, he still gets up for his exercise class.
  ....

☐ **4** They were unable to find a gas station, no matter how many people did they ask.
  ....

☐ **5** No matter how many cups of coffee I drink, I sleep like a baby.
  ....

☐ **6** No matter when do I go to bed, I always get up tired.
  ....

E **PAIR WORK** Complete the conversations with your own ideas, using the Vocabulary from page 28. Then read your conversations with a partner.

1 A: .... ! No matter how little I eat, ...

   B: ....

2 A: .... ! No matter what I tell my supervisor at work, ...

   B: ....

3 A: .... ! I can't find my keys, ...

   B: ....

4 A: .... ! Mary is always late, ...

   B: ....

> **PRONUNCIATION BOOSTER** p. 145
>
> Vowel reduction to /ə/

NOW YOU CAN Express frustration, empathy, and encouragement

A ▶ 2:05 **CONVERSATION SPOTLIGHT** Read and listen. Notice the spotlighted conversation strategies.

A: Hey, Nina. You look upset. **Is something wrong?**

B: Actually, I've been having a bit of trouble at work.

A: I'm sorry to hear that. **What's going on?**

B: **Well, basically,** no matter how well I do something, my boss never gives me credit.

A: That must be frustrating.

B: It is. I'm feeling really fed up.

A: I totally understand. **Hang in there,** though, OK?

B: Thanks for the encouragement! I appreciate it.

A: **Anytime.**

B ▶ 2:06 **RHYTHM AND INTONATION** Listen again and repeat. Then practice the conversation with a partner.

C **NOTEPADDING** Write statements on the notepad describing problems. Use no matter.

D **CONVERSATION ACTIVATOR** Create a conversation similar to the one in Exercise A. Start like this: *You look upset. Is something wrong?* Use one of the problems from your notepad. Be sure to change roles and then partners.

DON'T STOP!

• Ask for more details about the problem.
• Offer specific advice.
• Say as much as you can.

RECYCLE THIS LANGUAGE
• No way!
• Don't freak out.
• Just chill.
• It's not the end of the world.
• Wish me luck!
• Mark my words.

with a relationship: with my boyfriend. No matter how many times I ask him, he won't be friendly to my friends.

at home:

at work:

at school:

with money:

with a relationship:

with my health:

GOAL Describe how fear affects you physically

A ▶ 2:07 **GRAMMAR SPOTLIGHT** Read how fear affects people physically. Notice the spotlighted grammar.

Q: What happens to you when you get really scared? What situations usually cause this reaction?

The worst thing for me is that I get sweaty palms and my hands shake. The first time I met my fiancée's parents, we were at a nice restaurant and my hands were shaking **so badly that** I avoided even picking up my glass. I was afraid they would think I had some kind of disease. I wish I could control this, but I can't. It's so embarrassing!

Kenji Yaegashi, 28   Nagoya, Japan

I get **such terrible palpitations that** it feels like my heart's going to jump right out of my chest. And when things are really bad, I can actually lose my voice. Fortunately, this only happens when I'm really panicked, like the time I was on a flight and the landing gear got stuck. I tried to pretend I was cool and collected, but the truth is I was terrified.

Having to speak English on the phone! I know it's crazy because I speak pretty well. But there's just something about it that makes me panic. It's **so bad that** when I know I have to make a call in English, I get **such awful butterflies in my stomach that** I think I'm going to get sick. Silly, I know, but true. But actually, once I start talking the butterflies go away.

Isil Farat, 24   Izmir, Turkey

Jorge Pardo, 32   Cuenca, Ecuador

B **RELATE TO PERSONAL EXPERIENCE** Which situation described in the Grammar Spotlight do you identify with most? Explain, providing examples from your own life.

> **GRAMMAR BOOSTER** p. 132
> Count and non-count nouns:
> · Non-count nouns made countable
> · Nouns used in countable and uncountable sense

C **GRAMMAR** USING <u>SO</u> ... (<u>THAT</u>) OR <u>SUCH</u> ... (<u>THAT</u>) TO EXPLAIN RESULTS

Use <u>so</u> to intensify an adjective or an adverb to explain the result of an extreme situation. <u>That</u> is optional. Don't use a comma.

extreme situation	result
It was **so stormy**	**(that)** I was afraid to get on the plane.
She left **so quickly**	**(that)** she forgot her umbrella.

If the adjective is followed directly by a noun, use <u>such</u>, not <u>so</u>.

I was wearing **such uncomfortable shoes (that)** I could hardly walk.
I made **such salty soup (that)** no one could eat it.
She had **such a bad accident (that)** she never drove again.

If the noun is preceded by <u>many</u>, <u>much</u>, <u>few</u>, or <u>little</u>, use <u>so</u>.

There will be **so many people** there **(that)** we won't be able to find each other.
There was **so much lightning (that)** all the passengers on the plane were terrified.
We ate **so few meals** out last month **(that)** we saved a lot of money.
There's **so little ice** on the road **(that)** I think it's safe to drive.

> **Be careful!**
> Always use <u>a</u> or <u>an</u> with a singular count noun following <u>such</u>.
>   She had **such a bad accident** that she never drove again.
>   NOT She had ~~so bad accident~~ that she never drove again.

> **Remember:** Use <u>many</u> and <u>few</u> with count nouns. Use <u>much</u> and <u>little</u> with non-count nouns.
>   He had **so many tickets** that he lost his driver's license.
>   NOT He had ~~so much tickets~~ that he lost his driver's license.

D GRAMMAR PRACTICE On a separate sheet of paper, combine the statements, using <u>so</u> ... (<u>that</u>) or <u>such</u> ... (<u>that</u>).

> *The fire was so terrible that the building was totally destroyed.*

1 The fire was terrible. The building was totally destroyed.
2 There are usually many accidents. We don't travel on holiday weekends.
3 The games end late. We prefer to watch them on TV.
4 The insects are awful after dark. Most people prefer to stay inside in the evening.
5 Traffic in this region has become a bad problem. Lots of people are taking public transportation.
6 It was a stormy day. We postponed our picnic.

E GRAMMAR PRACTICE Complete each statement with <u>much</u>, <u>little</u>, <u>many</u>, or <u>few</u>.

1 They cancelled so .... flights that we won't be able to get there tonight.
2 There's always so .... trouble when the weather is bad that we don't travel in winter.
3 So .... people ate at that restaurant that they had to close it.
4 There were so .... seats left on the train that my friends and I couldn't sit together.
5 There was so .... time to get to the shelter that we just stayed in our basement.

F ▶ 2:08 **VOCABULARY** **PHYSICAL EFFECTS OF FEAR** Read and listen. Then listen again and repeat.

My hands shake.

I get palpitations.

I get sweaty palms.

I get butterflies in my stomach.

G ACTIVATE THE VOCABULARY Find and underline the Vocabulary and other physical effects of fear in the Grammar Spotlight. Paraphrase the situation that caused the physical effect for each of the three people, using the Vocabulary in your description.

> ❝ Jorge Pardo was so scared that he got palpitations and he lost his voice. ❞

NOW YOU CAN | Describe how fear affects you physically

A NOTEPADDING Choose a time when you were so scared that it affected you physically. Write notes about it on the notepad. Use the grammar and Vocabulary from page 30.

B DISCUSSION ACTIVATOR Discuss the situations on your notepads. Tell each other your stories, asking for more information and details. Idea: Tell the class about what happened to your partner. Say as much as you can.

> **RECYCLE THIS LANGUAGE**
> · No matter ...
> · Did you freak out?
> · It wasn't the end of the world.

OPTIONAL WRITING Write your partner's story. Use sequencing expressions (<u>first</u>, <u>next</u>, <u>after that</u>, etc.) to clarify the order of events in his or her story.

> **What I was afraid of:**
>
> **How it affected me physically:**
>
> **Write one statement with <u>so</u> or <u>such</u> ... (<u>that</u>).**
>
> **What finally happened?**

GOAL Discuss overcoming handicaps and hardships

 A **READING WARM-UP** What are some physical handicaps people face? What are some other hardships that might limit people's ability to succeed?

 B ▶ 2:09 **READING** Read about Marlee Matlin. If you had to choose one adjective to describe her, what would it be?

THE COURAGE TO BE
WHO SHE IS

Marlee Matlin, the only deaf performer ever to win the Oscar for Best Actress in a Leading Role, is also known worldwide as a stage and TV actor, an author, and as a spokesperson for people with hearing disabilities. Through her work and her books she has devoted her life to encouraging children and adults with hearing loss to live normal lives with normal expectations.

Born with normal hearing, Marlee suffered permanent hearing loss at 18 months from an illness with a high fever. As she approached school age, her parents were advised to send her to a specialized boarding school far from home. However, her parents felt that Marlee would be deprived of the parental contact and love essential to normal development if she didn't live at home. So instead, they put her in a public mainstream school that had both hearing and deaf students, which built her confidence to participate in activities with hearing students. At school, Marlee learned sign language, though she was encouraged to use her voice, too.

Throughout her childhood, Marlee's parents did everything they could to give her the same life she would have had if she had had normal hearing. Her family even helped Marlee develop a sense of humor about herself so she wouldn't be ashamed of her handicap. When others wondered about the strange way she pronounced some words (because she had learned to say them without ever having *heard* them), her brother would say she had an accent because she was from a foreign country, which made both of them laugh.

At seven, her parents enrolled her in a summer camp with both hearing and deaf children, and there she learned to use her hands to "sign" the lyrics of songs as the other children sang. Her campmates loved this, and their applause gave Marlee her first taste of the joy of performing.

To encourage her, when Marlee returned home from camp, her mother enrolled her in an afterschool children's theater program (now called the International Center on Deafness and the Arts, or ICODA), where children prepared some performances in sign language and others in spoken English.

Matlin continued performing when she was in college. At one performance, the popular TV actor Henry Winkler was in the audience. Matlin approached him and said she wanted to be a famous actor like him. Winkler, who suffers from dyslexia (a reading disorder that causes difficulty in reading despite normal intelligence), empathized with Matlin and encouraged her, telling her she could be anything she wanted and not to let anything stand in her way. Winkler became a longtime mentor and friend to Matlin, helping her as she pursued her acting career.

Matlin's life hasn't been without controversy or criticism. When presenting an Oscar, she spoke the nominees' names instead of signing them, causing some deaf people to complain she was suggesting *they* should speak instead of signing. To comfort Matlin, African-American actor Whoopi Goldberg told her that once she had worn blue contact lenses just for fun and was criticized for trying to "appear white." Goldberg told Matlin not to worry about what others say and just be herself.

Matlin has never let her handicap stand in her way and has continued to surpass the expectations the public has of people who can't hear. When she competed in TV's *Dancing with the Stars*, people were incredulous: How could she dance if she couldn't hear the music?

The key to Matlin's success may, in part, lie in the support and help others have given her—support that has enabled Matlin to be who she is, no matter what others may believe or say.

Marlee Matlin has never let her handicap stand in her way.

C **UNDERSTAND MEANING FROM CONTEXT**   Match the words and phrases from the article with these definitions. Then, with a partner, write sentences using the terms.

1 a person who represents and speaks for a group of people

2 a system of communication using hand gestures

3 a physical or mental disability or a condition that can limit a person's ability to function normally

4 an advisor from whom someone receives support and encouragement

5 strong differences of opinion, especially between groups of people

> mentor
> spokesperson
> handicap
> conflicts
> sign language

D **SUMMARIZE**   In the chart, summarize how these people and institutions contributed to Matlin's development and success. Then compare summaries with your classmates.

	Ways in which they helped Matlin
Her parents	
Her school	
Her brother	
Her summer camp	
Henry Winkler	
Whoopi Goldberg	

E **DISCUSSION**   Discuss the following questions.

1 How do you think a person can learn to speak without ever hearing others speak?

DIGITAL
EXTRA
CHALLENGE

2 In your opinion, what are some general factors that contribute to the success of people who have handicaps or other problems that could limit their success in life?

NOW YOU CAN   Discuss overcoming handicaps and hardships

A **FRAME YOUR IDEAS**   Choose a historical figure, a fictional character, or someone you know who overcame or has overcome a handicap or other hardship. Write discussion notes.

IDEAS: Some types of hardships
• a physical or mental handicap
• racial, ethnic, or sexual discrimination
• a natural disaster
• political instability or war
• poverty, lack of education or family support

Name:

Summary of handicap or hardship:

Factors that helped him or her overcome it:

Achievements:

She has overcome her handicap by playing tennis in a wheelchair.

DIGITAL
SPEAKING
BOOSTER

B **DISCUSSION**   Compare information. What similarities do the people share? Explain.

33

A ▶ 2:10 **LISTENING WARM-UP   WORD STUDY   USING PARTS OF SPEECH**   Study the forms of these words related to bravery and heroism, according to the part of speech. (Check meaning of any unfamiliar words in a dictionary.) Read and listen. Then listen again and repeat.

adjective	adverb	noun
brave	bravely	bravery
confident	confidently	confidence
courageous	courageously	courage
fearless	fearlessly	fearlessness
heroic	heroically	heroism
willing	willingly	willingness

 B ▶ 2:11 **LISTEN TO ACTIVATE PARTS OF SPEECH**   Listen to a TV news magazine story. Use a word from the Word Study chart in the correct part of speech to complete each statement. Some items have more than one possible answer.

1 Seol's decision to go back to the plane wreckage was extremely ....

2 Although aware that the airplane could explode at any moment, Seol .... returned to the plane again and again to rescue wounded passengers.

3 Seol's .... to risk his life to save others was extraordinary.

4 The story suggests that anyone, even an apparently ordinary person, is capable of .... acts.

5 Most people don't have the .... to act in the way Seol Ik Soo did.

Rescue personnel look for victims in the wreckage of an airliner.

C ▶ 2:12 **LISTEN FOR DETAILS**   Listen to the story again. Complete each statement.

1 Seol carried ...... passengers out of the plane.

   a three   **b** more than three

2 During the rescue, Seol felt as if the passengers were very ....

   a heavy   **b** light

3 Seol used a ...... to make bandages.

   a belt   **b** shirt

4 ...... he took passengers out of the plane, he realized that there was blood on his face.

   a Before   **b** After

5 Before the crash, ... thought of Seol as a hero.

   a no one had ever   **b** everyone had always

D ▶ 2:13 **LISTEN TO RETELL A STORY**   Listen to the story again. Retell the story in writing, including the important details and using at least three of the words from the Word Study chart. Exchange stories with a partner and suggest details your partner may have left out.

NOW YOU CAN   Examine the nature of heroism

A **NOTEPADDING**   Frame your ideas. With a partner, discuss and write your own description of the behavior that makes someone a hero. Use words from the Word Study chart and other phrases.

A hero is someone who …

RECYCLE THIS LANGUAGE
- hangs in there
- doesn't give up
- doesn't freak out
- No matter what happens

B **DISCUSSION**   Read the three profiles. Which person's behavior comes closest to the description you wrote in Exercise A. Explain and discuss with a partner.

DAILY NEWS

ROSA PARKS

Rosa Parks on the Montgomery bus.

In 1955, Rosa Parks got on a city bus in Montgomery, a city in the southern U.S., and sat down in a seat near the front. In those days, buses in Montgomery were racially segregated, and the front 10 seats were permanently reserved for white passengers. The driver told her to move to the back, but Parks refused. The driver then called the police, and she was arrested and taken to jail. Rosa Parks's act of defiance took great courage because of the brutality and injustice African Americans faced at that time in the South of the U.S. Her arrest became a rallying point, and the African-American community organized a bus boycott that lasted 381 days, during which no African American rode a city bus in Montgomery. Parks's action had a powerful economic impact on the bus company, which was forced to change its policy. Ultimately through the efforts of the community, racial segregation of public buses was made illegal.

Dr. Sheikh Umar Khan

In 2014, an Ebola epidemic raged in three African countries—Guinea, Liberia, and Sierra Leone. This frightening viral disease, for which there was no prevention or treatment, typically killed a devastating 60% to 90% of those infected. Dr. Sheikh Umar Khan, already hailed as a medical hero in his native Sierra Leone for having saved hundreds of lives during 10 years of battling Lassa fever, a disease similar to Ebola, rushed in to care for more than 100 Ebola patients. Dr. Khan knew better than anyone else that the people at greatest risk were health care workers. In spite of taking precautions, Dr. Khan and three of the nurses who worked with him died of the virus within three days of each other.

Dr. Sheikh Umar Khan

Alicia Sorohan

On October 11, while camping in Queensland, Australia, Alicia Sorohan awoke to the sound of someone screaming. Rushing out of her tent, she came across her friend Mike Kerr in the mouth of a 4.2-meter saltwater crocodile. The 60-year-old grandmother immediately jumped on the back of the giant crocodile, which dropped Kerr and attacked her, biting her in the face and arm. When shot and killed by another member of the group, the crocodile had Sorohan's arm in its mouth and was dragging her into the water. Sorohan and Kerr both survived the incident though both had serious injuries. Family members of the victims, in shock after the horrible attack, said that Sorohan's speedy response had been astonishing. "She deserves an award of some kind," said Wayne Clancy, her son-in-law.

a giant saltwater crocodile

C **DEBATE**   From pages 34 and 35, choose the person you consider to be the most heroic. Meet with two or three other classmates, each of whom has chosen someone different. Have a debate about which of the persons is the most heroic. Decide among yourselves or among the other students in the class who won the debate.

A **WRITING SKILL** Study the rules.

Reducing adverbial clauses to adverbial phrases

Adverbial clauses can be reduced to adverbial phrases when the subject of the independent clause and the adverbial clause are the same. Reduced adverbial phrases are more common in writing than in speaking.

Adverbial clauses	→	Reduced to adverbial phrases
When I fell off my bike, I hurt my back.	→	**Falling off my bike,** I hurt my back.
When we were eating, we got a call.	→	**When eating** (or **Eating**), we got a call.
We saw a bear **while we were hiking**.	→	We saw a bear **while hiking**.
Before I left, I sent my parents a letter.	→	**Before leaving,** I sent my parents a letter.
After I had shared my news, I felt better.	→	**After having shared my news,** I felt better.

Be careful!
When the subjects of the adverbial clause and the independent clause are different, the clause can't be reduced.
Before **she** saw the crocodile, **it** attacked.
DON'T SAY ~~Before seeing the crocodile~~, it attacked.

Punctuation
Use a comma after a clause or phrase when it comes first.
Before I left, I sent my parents a letter. / I sent my parents a letter **before I left.**

B **PRACTICE** Read the short news report to the right of a frightening event. Underline the reduced adverbial phrases and, on a separate sheet of paper, rewrite the sentences with them, changing the phrases to clauses.

C **PRACTICE** On a separate sheet of paper, rewrite each of the following sentences, reducing adverbial clauses to adverbial phrases when possible. If the sentence can't be reduced, explain why not.

1 When she was waking up, Alicia Sorohan heard a scream.

2 While Dr. Khan was trying to save his patients, several nurses on his staff came down with Ebola.

3 When she refused to move to the back seats on the bus, Rosa Parks was arrested.

4 Before she went to the drama program, Marlee Matlin hadn't ever performed in a play.

5 Seol realized that he was covered in blood after he had exited the plane several times.

WRITING MODEL

May 5—While camping yesterday, the Evans family was surprised by some frightening neighbors: a bear cub and its mother. Twin 5-year-olds Paul and Marcy were delighted because the young animal reminded them of the cute creatures in their picture books and on TV. Their father, on the other hand, wasn't as charmed because he knew that approaching a bear cub was dangerous since an adult bear is usually nearby.

Luckily for the family, Mr. Evans was already awake and getting breakfast ready when he heard the bear. As he posted later on Facebook: "While getting the milk out of our camping bag, I heard a rustling noise behind me. I turned around and saw a bear cub trying to open the garbage can. I knew I had to think fast."

Hearing his kids coming out of the tent, Mr. Evans quickly pushed them back inside to prevent them from approaching the bear to play with it. At that moment, a large adult female, probably the cub's mother, came by and led the cub away. The Evanses' camping day continued peacefully after that.

D **APPLY THE WRITING SKILL** Write a short report about a dangerous or frightening event, using the Writing Model for support. Write at least two paragraphs and tell the story in the order that the events occurred. The event can be real or fictional. Use at least three adverbial clauses and phrases to clarify time relationships.

SELF-CHECK
☐ Did I write two or more paragraphs?
☐ Does my report tell the story in the order that the events occurred?
☐ Did I use at least three adverbial clauses or reduced adverbial phrases to clarify time relationships?

A ▶ 2:14 Listen to each person. Then listen again to summarize each person's reason for being frustrated. Write statements with <u>no matter</u>.

 Felix Tan

....
....
....

 Robert Reston

....
....
....

Eva García

....
....
....

B Complete each statement with <u>no matter</u> and <u>who</u>, <u>whom</u>, <u>when</u>, <u>what time</u>, <u>what</u>, <u>where</u>, or <u>how</u>.

1 I always get up at seven in the morning, ... I go to bed.

2 My daughter won't go to bed early, ... many times I tell her to.

3 .... the weather is like, we're going!

4 .... few calories you eat, it's hard to lose weight.

5 No one knew which gate the train was leaving from, ... we asked.

6 .... you leave from, the trip still takes two hours.

C Complete each statement with the correct word.

1 The thunder was (so / such) loud that we couldn't sleep.

2 The kids ate (so much / such many) candy that they got sick.

3 There was (so / such) bad turbulence that the passengers couldn't leave their seats.

4 The store has (so many / so much) brands of painkillers that I don't know which to buy.

5 Lyn is having (so / such a) good time at the party that she doesn't want to go home.

6 He learned Italian (so / such) quickly that he took the exam after only two months.

D Replace each underlined word with a word that has a similar meaning and the correct part of speech.

1 Many people don't think they are <u>courageous</u> until they are faced with an emergency.

   a fearlessly   **b** brave   **c** heroism

2 Few people are <u>fearless</u> enough to fight an adult bear.

   a courageous   **b** confidence   **c** willing

3 <u>Bravery</u>, especially in dangerous situations, is a rare quality.

   a Courageous   **b** Heroism   **c** Heroically

E On a separate sheet of paper, create a two-line conversation for each pair of expressions. Use <u>no matter</u> and your own ideas.

1 I'm fed up. / Hang in there.

2 I just can't take it anymore. / Don't let it get you down.

3 I've had it. / That must be discouraging.

4 I give up. / Don't let it get you down.

5 I'm fed up. / I know what you mean.

> A: I'm fed up. No matter how much exercise I do, I still look like a weakling!
>
> B: Hang in there. It takes time to see results.

TEST-TAKING SKILLS BOOSTER p. 153

Web Project: Heroes
www.english.com/summit3e

4

Getting Along with Others

COMMUNICATION GOALS

1 Discuss how to overcome shortcomings
2 Acknowledge inconsiderate behavior
3 Explain how you handle anger
4 Explore the qualities of friendship

A FRAME YOUR IDEAS Read about some common shortcomings. Rate each person according to the scale:

A = Sounds just like me!
B = Sounds a bit like me.
C = Doesn't sound like me at all!

What's your biggest shortcoming?

Martin ☐
"I wish I weren't so disorganized. My bedroom's always a mess. I can't remember where I've put anything. The way I'm doing things is just not working for me."

Lena ☐
"You know what my problem is? I'm a procrastinator! I'm always putting things off and waiting till the last minute to do things. Then I go into a panic worrying about whether or not I'll be able to finish on time."

Ricardo ☐
"I admit I'm a bit oversensitive. I tend to overreact to things people say to me—I think I'm being criticized when people are just trying to help. It really doesn't take much to get me upset about stuff."

Paul ☐
"I'm sure I'm too hot-tempered. I get angry way too easily. It doesn't take much to set me off. But I've been trying to change that."

Sophie ☐
"I know I'm too negative. I'm always focusing on the bad rather than the good. And I'm way too critical of others. My husband, though, is just the opposite!"

Jean ☐
"My husband says I'm too controlling— and he's probably right. I complain when he doesn't do things *my* way. I'm sure it drives him crazy!"

Trevor ☐
"My biggest shortcoming is that I'm a perfectionist. No matter what I do, I'm not satisfied. I just don't think it's good enough. My attitude really gets in my way."

B ▶2:15 **VOCABULARY** **SHORTCOMINGS** Listen and repeat.

be disorganized	be negative
be a procrastinator	be controlling
be oversensitive	be a perfectionist
be hot-tempered	

C PAIR WORK Tell your partner how you are—or aren't—like the people in Exercise A. What are your biggest shortcomings?

> ❝One of my biggest shortcomings is that I'm a perfectionist. I'd like to invite friends for dinner at my house, but I never do—because I don't think I cook well enough. ❞

D DISCUSSION Discuss these questions.

1 Do any of the people above sound like someone you know? In what ways?
2 Can you think of any other common shortcomings people have? What are they?

E ▶ 2:16 **SPOTLIGHT** Read and listen to a conversation between two colleagues. Notice the spotlighted language.

ENGLISH FOR TODAY'S WORLD
Understand a variety of accents.
Mike = American English (standard)
Jaya = Hindi

Mike: Wait till you hear this … Sam **lost his cool** again at the status meeting!

Jaya: Oh, please. He's always angry about something. So what **set him off** this time?

Mike: You know how Rob always waits till the last minute to do the sales report? Well, Sam **made a big issue out of** it. When Rob tried to defend himself, Sam **told him off**—in front of *everyone*.

Jaya: That's awful! You know, even if Rob starts things late, he always finishes on time. I don't see what the big deal is.

Mike: But you know Sam. If there's anything he hates, it's procrastination. I'm sure he wanted to make an example out of Rob.

Jaya: Well, it sounds like he went overboard. He could have just **brought it up** privately with Rob after the meeting.

Mike: Good point. But, all things considered, Rob **took it pretty well**. He knows Sam's just hot-tempered.

Jaya: If only he'd just stop and think first before having one of his outbursts! Instead, everyone always has to **walk on eggshells** wondering who's going to be next.

Mike: I agree. Between you and me, I think Sam's been under a lot of pressure lately from *his* boss. But that's no excuse to **take it out on** someone else.

Jaya: That's right. It must have been hard for everyone at the meeting to just **pick up the pieces** afterwards and go on as if nothing had happened. I'll bet it was really awkward.

Mike: Totally. But it's Sam who should feel awkward. What bothers me the most is that he has no clue how he affects other people.

F **UNDERSTAND IDIOMS AND EXPRESSIONS** Find these expressions in Spotlight. Complete each statement.

1 If you "lose your cool," you …… .
   a get angry   **b** are worried

2 If something "sets you off," it …… .
   a makes you angry   **b** relaxes you

3 If someone "makes a big issue out of" something, he or she …… it.
   a enjoys talking about
   b calls too much attention to

4 If you "tell someone off," you are expressing your …… to that person about his or her behavior.
   a anger   **b** appreciation

5 If something bothers you and you "bring it up" with someone, you want to …… .
   a discuss it   **b** avoid discussing it

6 If someone gets angry at you and you "take it well," you are …… by it.
   a not very affected   **b** very affected

7 If you "walk on eggshells," you …… make someone angry.
   a try to   **b** are careful not to

8 If you feel stressed and "take it out on" a friend, you might need to apologize to that person for …… .
   a being stressed   **b** acting angry

9 If you try to "pick up the pieces" after an argument, you try to …… .
   a re-establish a friendly atmosphere
   b understand someone's point of view

G **THINK AND EXPLAIN** With a partner, discuss the questions and explain your answers.

1 Why does Jaya think the other people at the meeting must have felt uncomfortable?

2 Why do you think Rob wasn't upset about the situation?

SPEAKING **GROUP WORK** Which of the shortcomings from page 38 do you think cause the greatest problems for people? Discuss the consequences.

❝ In my opinion, being hot-tempered causes the most problems. Once you've gone overboard, it's hard to pick up the pieces. ❞

A ▶2:17 **GRAMMAR SPOTLIGHT** Read about the workshops. Notice the spotlighted grammar.

SELF-HELP
FOR THE SELF-CRITICAL
Practical workshops to help you reach your goals

1 GET ORGANIZED NOW
Tired of being so disorganized? Is it hard to find things **even if you've filed them away properly?** Have papers been piling up on your desk **whether or not you've had time to go through them?** Take the bull by the horns and discover how getting organized can help you increase your productivity today.

2 STOP TRYING TO CONTROL OTHERS
Do you drive people crazy by constantly supervising what they are doing? Does this sound like you: **"Only if things are done my way** will things get done right!" Let's face it—something's got to change. **Otherwise**, no one's ever going to want to work with you! Letting go of control is easier than you think.

3 END NEGATIVE THINKING NOW
Is your negative attitude interfering with your goals in life? Achieving your goals will be possible **only if you make a decision to change your outlook today.** This workshop will move you from the negative to the positive on a journey that will change your life.

4 SAY GOOD-BYE TO PROCRASTINATION
Have you been putting off till tomorrow what you could have done today? **Unless you're the type who says "I'll never change,"** you too can learn to stop procrastinating today. Learn easy strategies for using your time more efficiently than ever.

B PAIR WORK Do you think people can really overcome their shortcomings? Why or why not? Which of the workshops would you personally find the most useful? Explain.

DIGITAL INDUCTIVE ACTIVITY

C GRAMMAR ADVERB CLAUSES OF CONDITION

Use even if or whether or not in an adverb clause to express the fact that no matter what the condition, there is no way to affect or change an event or situation.

Even if I have plenty of time to finish a project, I still wait till the last minute to begin.
 (= No matter what, I wait till the last minute.)
She would have been late for the meeting **even if she had set her alarm**.
 (= No matter what, she would have been late.)
Whether or not anyone says anything to her about it, Kyla's desk is always a disorganized mess.
 (= No matter what, her desk is always a mess.)
We would have been uncomfortable at the meeting **whether or not he had lost his cool**.
 (= No matter what, we would have been uncomfortable.)

Use only if to express the fact that a certain condition is necessary in order for something to happen or to be true. If the adverb clause comes first, invert the subject and verb (or auxiliary) in the independent clause and do not use a comma.

Nina will be happy at her job **only if she learns to say no to her boss.** OR
Only if Nina learns to say no to her boss **will she** be happy at her job.

Use unless to express the consequence of an action or lack of action. (Note: unless = if ... not)

Unless he writes himself a note, he'll forget to pay his bills.
 (= If he doesn't write himself a note, he will forget to pay his bills.)
We told him we wouldn't come to the meeting **unless he apologized for his outburst**.
 (= We told him we wouldn't come to the meeting if he didn't apologize.)

Note: You can also use the transition word Otherwise at the beginning of a sentence to express the consequences of an action or a lack of action.

He needs to write himself a note. **Otherwise**, he'll forget to pay his bills.
I always set my alarm for 7:00 A.M. on weekdays. **Otherwise**, I'm late for school.

Remember: The unreal conditional with if only expresses a wish for a particular condition (or a strong regret).
 If only I were more organized, I'd get a lot more done.
 (= I wish I were OR I regret that I'm not)

GRAMMAR BOOSTER p. 133
More conjunctions and transitions

D UNDERSTAND THE GRAMMAR Choose the statement with the same meaning.

1 I find it difficult to remember my appointments unless I put a reminder on my smart phone.
   a If I don't put a reminder on my smart phone, I find it difficult to remember my appointments.
   b If I don't put a reminder on my smart phone, I don't find it difficult to remember my appointments.

2 Even if she tries not to be controlling, her friends still think she is.
   a Her friends find her to be controlling, no matter what she does.
   b Her friends find her to be controlling unless she tries not to be.

3 Only if he takes a workshop about procrastination will Martin stop putting things off.
   a Unless Martin takes a workshop, he won't stop putting things off.
   b Whether or not Martin takes a workshop, he won't stop putting things off.

4 Whether or not you apologize, some people always have a hard time picking up the
   pieces after you tell them off.
   a It's always difficult to pick up the pieces after being told off, even if you receive an apology.
   b It's never difficult to pick up the pieces after being told off if you receive an apology.

5 You should try not to overreact when your manager criticizes your work. Otherwise,
   you might lose your job.
   a Unless you try to stop overreacting to your manager's criticisms, you might lose your job.
   b No matter how you react to your manager's criticisms, you might lose your job.

E GRAMMAR PRACTICE Circle the correct way to complete each statement.

1 (Whether or not / Unless) Bob is oversensitive, his friends still like him.

2 (Only if / Unless) Sal overreacts again at the meeting, I won't mention his
   negative attitude.

3 Katia loses her cool with her kids (only if / if only) she's had a bad day at work.

4 Carl's colleagues enjoy working with him (even if / unless) he's a bit hot-tempered.

5 (If only / Unless) she really goes overboard, I don't care that much if my wife tells me off.

6 (Only if / Even if) she puts something off to the last minute does Stacey worry about what
   her boss will think.

> **PRONUNCIATION BOOSTER** p. 145
> Shifting emphatic stress

NOW YOU CAN Discuss how to overcome shortcomings

A NOTEPADDING Look at page 38 again and choose three of the people's shortcomings.
On your notepad, suggest how to overcome each shortcoming.

What is the shortcoming?	Your suggestions for how to overcome it
1. Ricardo is oversensitive.	try not to overreact
	remember that most people just want to be helpful

What is the shortcoming?	Your suggestions for how to overcome it
1.	
2.	
3.	

B DISCUSSION ACTIVATOR Discuss the shortcomings on your
notepads and other ways you think someone could overcome them.
Use adverb clauses of condition. Say as much as you can.

> 〝 Whether or not you have a good
> reason to be angry, you should try
> not to take it out on someone else. 〞

LESSON 2

GOAL Acknowledge inconsiderate behavior

A **GRAMMAR** CLEFT SENTENCES: REVIEW AND EXPANSION

Cleft sentences with <u>What</u>

Remember: A cleft sentence emphasizes an action or a result. You can form a cleft sentence using a noun clause with <u>What</u> as the subject + a form of <u>be</u>. Be sure the form of <u>be</u> agrees with its complement.

What bothers me is getting interrupted when I'm speaking.
What surprised me were the many "thank you" e-mails I received.

Cleft sentences with <u>What</u> often have a subject complement that is a noun clause. If so, always use a singular form of <u>be</u>.

What bothered me the most was **(that) you didn't even apologize**.
What was surprising was **(that) she had completely cleaned up her desk**.
What I mean is **(that) I wish I hadn't lost my cool**.
What I'm trying to say is **(that) I'm really sorry**.

> **GRAMMAR BOOSTER** p. 134
>
> Cleft sentences: more on meaning and use

Cleft sentences with <u>It</u>

A cleft sentence with the impersonal <u>It</u> emphasizes a noun or noun phrase. Use a noun clause with <u>who</u> or <u>that</u>.

Valerie decided to have a talk with her boss. ⟶ **It was Valerie who** decided to have a talk with her boss.
Jack's outbursts make people uncomfortable. ⟶ **It's Jack's outbursts that** make people uncomfortable.

B **NOTICE THE GRAMMAR** Look at Spotlight on page 39.
Find and underline two types of cleft sentences in the last paragraph.

C ▶2:18 **LISTEN TO ACTIVATE GRAMMAR** Listen to the conversations.
Then listen again and complete each statement.

1 It was her ...... that he wanted to bring up.
   a missing the meeting   **b** not finishing the project

2 What bothered him was that Simon ....
   a lost his cool   **b** refused to apologize

3 It was his ...... that made her decide to talk with him.
   a apologizing for his mistake   **b** interrupting her meeting

4 What's surprising to him is that the two women ....
   a are such good friends   **b** had such a bad argument

5 It was his ...... that upset her.
   a constant criticism   **b** refusing to listen to her

D **GRAMMAR PRACTICE** Combine each pair of sentences by writing a cleft sentence with <u>What</u> and a noun clause subject complement.

Example: People tell me I'm too controlling. That has always surprised me.
...*What has always surprised me is that people tell me I'm too controlling.*...........

1 My boss always criticizes me. That makes me kind of angry.

   ....

2 Most people tell lies to protect the ones they love. That fascinates me.

   ....

3 Gary actually has a hard time saying no to people. That's surprising.

   ....

4 My manager and I get along really well. That's nice.

....

5 It's been great working with you. That's what I've always wanted to tell you.

....

6 I wish you would try to control your anger. That's what I mean.

....

E **GRAMMAR PRACTICE**   Write cleft sentences with <u>It</u>, emphasizing the underlined noun phrase.

Example: <u>The way she talks to people</u> is so offensive.
...<u>It's the way she talks to people that's so offensive.</u>...

1 <u>Nancy's negative attitude</u> prevents her from accepting any suggestions.

....

2 <u>The final workshop</u> can give you some ideas for getting more organized.

....

3 <u>Bill's being so hot-tempered</u> makes me want to avoid him.

....

4 <u>The way you spoke to me this morning</u> hurt my feelings.

....

5 <u>His lying about what happened</u> was so surprising.

....

NOW YOU CAN   Acknowledge inconsiderate behavior

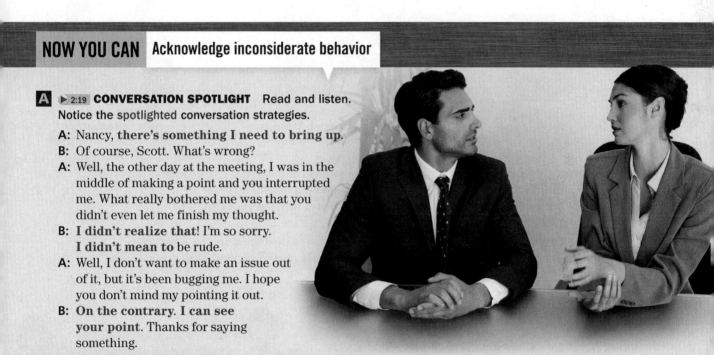

A ▶ 2:19 **CONVERSATION SPOTLIGHT**   Read and listen.
Notice the spotlighted conversation strategies.

A: Nancy, **there's something I need to bring up.**
B: Of course, Scott. What's wrong?
A: Well, the other day at the meeting, I was in the middle of making a point and you interrupted me. What really bothered me was that you didn't even let me finish my thought.
B: **I didn't realize that!** I'm so sorry. **I didn't mean to** be rude.
A: Well, I don't want to make an issue out of it, but it's been bugging me. I hope you don't mind my pointing it out.
B: **On the contrary. I can see your point.** Thanks for saying something.

B ▶ 2:20 **RHYTHM AND INTONATION**   Listen again and repeat.
Then practice the conversation with a partner.

C **CONVERSATION ACTIVATOR**   Create a similar conversation, acknowledging someone's criticism. Start like this: *There's something I need to bring up.* Be sure to change roles and then partners.

DIGITAL VIDEO
DIGITAL SPEAKING BOOSTER

Some possible problems
being late
missing a meeting
losing one's cool
being too critical
not apologizing

DON'T STOP!
• Explain the problem in greater detail and how you felt about it.
• Offer to make up for it.
• Say as much as you can.

DIGITAL STRATEGIES **A** ▶ 2:21 **LISTENING WARM-UP** **VOCABULARY** **EXPRESSING AND CONTROLLING ANGER**
Read and listen. Then listen again and repeat.

"I lost my temper."

- lose one's temper
- have a fit
- hit the roof
- go ballistic
- blow one's top

got really angry

"When I'm angry about something, I prefer to just hold it in."

hold it in / **keep it inside**
avoid expressing your feelings

"When I lose my cool, I take a deep breath and try to calm down."

calm down become quieter and more relaxed

"When someone tells me off, I just let it go."

let it go / **shrug it off** decide not to be bothered by something

"Running helps me let off steam when I'm feeling angry about something."

let off steam get rid of your anger in a way that does not harm anyone; for example, by doing something active

"When I'm upset about something, venting about it with a friend usually calms me down."

vent talk with someone you trust in order to express your anger at someone else

B **PERSONALIZE THE VOCABULARY** Use the expressions to tell about a time when you controlled your anger or lost control of it. What do you usually do to let off steam? Is there someone in particular who you can vent to when you're angry?

DIGITAL STRATEGIES **C** ▶ 2:22 **LISTEN TO SUMMARIZE THE MAIN IDEA** Listen to the interviews. On a separate sheet of paper, write a summary in one or two sentences about the purpose of the interview.

D ▶ 2:23 **LISTEN TO INFER INFORMATION** Listen again and check the correct statements.

	Joseph would …	Celina would …
1 If he or she were angry with his or her boss …	☐ make an issue out of it. ☐ say what's on his mind. ☐ hold his feelings in.	☐ let off steam. ☐ say what's on her mind. ☐ hold her feelings in.
2 If he or she were angry with a friend or colleague …	☐ take it out on someone else. ☐ probably just shrug it off. ☐ probably lose his temper.	☐ take it out on someone else. ☐ probably just shrug it off. ☐ probably not hold it in.
3 If he or she were angry with a complete stranger …	☐ probably let it go. ☐ probably lose his temper. ☐ take it out on someone else.	☐ probably let it go. ☐ probably say what's on her mind. ☐ take it out on someone else.

NOW YOU CAN   Explain how you handle anger

A **FRAME YOUR IDEAS**   Discuss each situation with a partner. How similar is your behavior to your partner's? Describe how you would express or control your anger. Use the Vocabulary in your discussion.

Situation	How would you handle your anger?
1 A friend arrives really late to meet you for a movie.	
2 You tell a friend something in confidence and he or she doesn't keep it a secret.	
 **3** A classmate or colleague says bad things about you to people you know.	
4 Someone tells you off in front of a group of other people.	
 **5** Another driver cuts you off while you are driving.	
6 Someone borrows something from you and doesn't return it.	
7 Your next-door neighbor always plays very loud music and has noisy late-night parties.	
8 (your own idea)	

B **DISCUSSION**   Do you act the same way when you get angry with someone you know as you do with a stranger? Explain.

OPTIONAL WRITING   Write a true story about something that made you angry. What happened? How did you respond? Use the Vocabulary.

RECYCLE THIS LANGUAGE

- lose one's cool
- set someone off
- make a big issue out of something
- tell someone off
- take it out on someone
- mess up big time
- take it [well / badly]
- Even if …
- Whether or not …
- Only if …
- Unless …
- Otherwise, …

45

LESSON 4

GOAL Explore the qualities of friendship

A **READING WARM-UP** How do friendships among men differ from friendships among women? How are they similar?

DIGITAL STRATEGIES **B** ▶ 2:24 **READING** Read the article. Which qualities of friendship do you think are the most important?

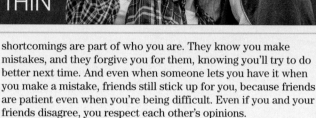

FRIENDS THROUGH THICK AND THIN

What makes friendships stand the test of time? We interviewed 100 men and women, and here is what they had to say:

1. Friends share the good times

You build great memories together. There's nothing like having a friend around to enjoy the best moments of your life with you—graduation, your first rock concert, watching the World Cup, your wedding, and so on. You probably share a similar sense of humor and you can count on your friends to laugh at your jokes—even when they're dumb jokes. Most importantly, good friends aren't jealous of your successes. On the contrary, they cheer you on, which contributes to your achievement. Good friends want only the best for you. Otherwise, what's the point?

2. Friends are there when times are tough

Like the song says, friendship is "like a bridge over troubled water." You can always count on your friends' support when you really need a helping hand. You shouldn't even have to ask. When you're feeling down or are upset about something, friends know what makes you tick—whether or not you want to talk about it. They are thoughtful when it comes to your well-being, and they will accommodate your needs, particularly when you need it the most.

3. Friends don't judge each other

We need our friends to be dependable—through thick and thin. Your friends accept you as you are, and they don't constantly try to change you. And they roll with the punches. They get it that inside you're a good person with flaws, and that those

shortcomings are part of who you are. They know you make mistakes, and they forgive you for them, knowing you'll try to do better next time. And even when someone lets you have it when you make a mistake, friends still stick up for you, because friends are patient even when you're being difficult. Even if you and your friends disagree, you respect each other's opinions.

4. Friends are trustworthy

You need your friends to be totally loyal. Above all, you need to know that your secrets are safe with them. If there's a problem between you, a friend will come to you first and not gossip about you with others. We can always count on our friends to be honest with us when others aren't. We can trust them to stick by us no matter what. Friends don't keep things bottled up inside—if there's a problem, they work things out and move on.

Are there differences between what men and women expect in their friends? Among our interviewees, husbands claimed to understand what made their wives' female friendships tick, but many wives admitted that they wondered what in the world their husbands and their male friends saw in each other. According to the women, the quality of interaction between women friends was crucial to the longevity of their friendships. They valued being able to talk about their problems and feelings. However, for the men, it was mutual acceptance—being able to simply hang out together with no judgment. One man offered this view, "Female friends prefer to face each other, while male friends do things side by side." Nevertheless, it shouldn't be all that surprising that the men and women generally agreed that *all* truly good friends stick by each other through thick and thin.

C **UNDERSTAND MEANING FROM CONTEXT** Find the words and expressions in the article. Use the context of the article to complete each statement.

1 When a friendship can "stand the test of time," it ...... as people change and get older.
  a continues   **b** becomes more difficult

2 When you "count on people" to do something, you ....
  a worry whether they will do it   **b** feel sure they will do it

3 When someone "cheers you on," he or she is ...... of your efforts.
  a supportive   **b** critical

4 When "times are tough," things are ....
  a going well   **b** difficult

5 When you know what "makes someone tick," you understand ....
  a how he or she thinks and responds to things   **b** that he or she likes you

6 When people are friends "through thick and thin," their friendship ....
  a can survive good times and bad times   **b** may be in trouble

7 When someone "lets you have it," he or she ....
  a is being very critical   **b** is being very supportive

8 When someone "sticks up for you," he or she ....
   a defends you against criticism   **b** criticizes you honestly

9 When friends "stick by you," they ....
   a are always loyal to you   **b** tell you off

10 When someone "keeps things bottled up inside," he or she ...... to talk about uncomfortable feelings such as anger.
   a is willing   **b** isn't willing

D **APPLY IDEAS**   Discuss what a good friend would do in response to each situation, waccording to the information in the article. Explain your answers.

1 You get a new job at twice your current salary.

> ❝ It says a true friend cheers you on when times are good. So I think a good friend would be happy for me and want to celebrate. ❞

2 You tell your friend a really dumb joke.

3 You're unhappy about something, but you haven't told anyone about it yet.

4 You lose your temper with your friend.

5 A colleague criticizes you when you're not around.

6 You and your friend have a disagreement.

E **RELATE TO PERSONAL EXPERIENCE**   Work in pairs. Using the four qualities of a good friendship in the article as examples, share personal examples of your friendships that illustrate each quality.

DIGITAL
EXTRA
CHALLENGE

NOW YOU CAN   Explore the qualities of friendship

A **FRAME YOUR IDEAS**   Read each statement and write A, B, or C. Then, with a partner, compare and explain your responses.

> ❝ That's not the kind of friend I am. Remember what the article said? Good friends aren't jealous of your successes. ❞

A = That's not the kind of friend I am.
B = Sometimes I'm a bit like that.
C = I have to admit that sounds a lot like me.

"My friend Carla just got engaged last week. I can't figure it out. I'm so much more popular than she is." ☐

"I was really disappointed when my friend Tom didn't invite me over to watch the World Cup. I guess I just won't invite him anywhere either." ☐

"My friend Trevor is really feeling down right now because he split up with his girlfriend. He's kind of getting on my nerves. I wish he'd just stop talking about it." ☐

"My friend Harriet told me about the problems she's been having with her husband. I only told my neighbor Cynthia about it, but no one else." ☐

"Laura's a good friend, but I think her clothes are really out of style. It's kind of embarrassing to be seen with her. She'd be so much prettier if she took my suggestions." ☐

"My friend Nick is always late for everything. Today was the last straw— if he can't change his habits, he can go find *another* friend." ☐

B **DISCUSSION**   How would you rate your friendships in general? All things considered, in what ways would you say you're a good friend to *your* friends? Explain your answers and give examples.

How I'd generally rate my friends

poor   average   excellent

How I'd rate myself as a friend

poor   average   excellent

47

WRITING · Transitional topic sentences

A WRITING SKILL Study the rules.

> **Remember:** Transition words and subordinating conjunctions link ideas within and between sentences.
>
> They can also be used in a paragraph's topic sentence to connect the paragraph to the one that precedes it.
>
> The following words and phrases can be used as transitions to announce the content of a new paragraph:
>
> **To add information**
>
> > **Furthermore**, it's very convenient.
> >
> > **Moreover**, it's very convenient.
> >
> > **More importantly**, it's very convenient.
>
> **To contrast information**
>
> > **Even though** it's convenient, it's not for everyone.
> >
> > **Although** it's convenient, it's not for everyone.
> >
> > **Despite the fact that** it's convenient, it's not for everyone.
> >
> > **Nevertheless**, it's not for everyone.
> >
> > **On the other hand**, it's not for everyone.
> >
> > **However**, it's not for everyone.

WRITING MODEL

For an effective solution to procrastination I suggest using the daily calendar on your smartphone. It can be used to break up the steps essential to completing a larger task into smaller tasks. That way it is easier to keep things moving forward. It also allows you to check off the smaller tasks as they are finished, which motivates you by providing a feeling of accomplishment.

Furthermore, using a smartphone calendar is not really all that difficult. You can use the calendar that's already installed, or you can download an app for that purpose. Instructions are easily available online, and they are usually very clear.

Nevertheless, using a smartphone calendar does take some getting used to. It may require some time to learn how to use it, but the calendar will make your work easier. Without a calendar, it is far too easy to simply forget about what needs to be done. With one, it is easy to keep track of your progress. If your teacher or manager asks questions, you have a record you can refer to. This increases your confidence. I believe the calendar is one of the best ways to convert procrastination into effective organization.

B PRACTICE Rewrite these transitional topic sentences from the Writing Model, using other words and phrases to announce the content of the new paragraph. (Note: You may have to make other changes in the sentence.)

Furthermore, using a smartphone calendar is not really all that difficult.

1 More importantly, ...

2 Moreover, ...

Nevertheless, using a smartphone calendar does take some getting used to.

3 Even though ....

4 Although ....

5 Despite the fact that ....

6 On the other hand, ...

7 However, ...

C APPLY THE WRITING SKILL Write a three-paragraph essay presenting a solution to a common shortcoming. In paragraph one, introduce the solution. Use transitional topic sentences to link the content of the second and third paragraphs.

SELF-CHECK

☐ Does the first paragraph have a topic sentence?

☐ Do the paragraphs that follow have transitional topic sentences?

☐ Does each transitional topic sentence clearly link to previous content?

A ▶ 2:25   Listen to three people describe their shortcomings. Then listen again and complete the chart. Listen a third time if necessary to check your answers.

	What is the shortcoming?	What solution did the person find?	Did it work?
1			
2			
3			

B Complete each statement with one of the lettered choices. (You will not use all the choices.)

1 Claire overreacts and takes things personally when her friends make suggestions. She ....

2 Bob is always losing his cool over things that aren't important. He ....

3 Laura usually misses her deadlines because she doesn't get started on her assignments right away. She ....

4 Nick is always worrying about every little detail. He hates making mistakes. He ....

a is a perfectionist.

b is negative.

c tends to procrastinate.

d is oversensitive.

e is hot-tempered.

C Complete each statement about the situations in which people express or control their anger.

1 People sometimes hold their feelings in when ....
....

2 People usually only tell someone off when ....
....

3 Most people lose their tempers only when ....
....

D Complete each statement logically and correctly with one of the lettered choices.

1 Even if I know a project is important, ...

2 Unless I know that a project is not important, ...

3 Only if I know that a project is not important ....

4 If only I had known that the project was important, ...

5 I wish I'd known that the project was so important. ......

a Otherwise, I wouldn't have waited till the last minute to get started.

b I never wait till the last minute to get started.

c will I wait till the last minute to get started.

d I still wait till the last minute to get started.

e I wouldn't have waited till the last minute to get started.

E On a separate sheet of paper, rewrite each sentence as a cleft sentence with <u>What</u>. Follow the example.

1 It's the way she criticizes new employees that's so offensive.

> What's so offensive is the way she criticizes new employees.

2 It's maintaining a positive attitude that changes negative thinking.

3 It's fear of failure that causes people to put things off.

4 It's his being so hot-tempered that makes people feel like they're walking on eggshells.

5 It's her ability to organize that makes her so successful.

TEST-TAKING SKILLS BOOSTER p. 154

Web Project: Anger Management
www.english.com/summit3e

COMMUNICATION GOALS
1 Discuss the health benefits of laughter
2 Respond to something funny
3 Analyze what makes us laugh
4 Explore the limits of humor

PREVIEW

A FRAME YOUR IDEAS Take the humor self-test to analyze your sense of humor.

HUMOR SELF-TEST

Rate how funny you think each images is, from 1 to 5, with 1 being not funny at all and 5 being extremely funny.

1 YOUR RATING: 1 2 3 4 5 NOT FUNNY VERY FUNNY
2 YOUR RATING: 1 2 3 4 5 NOT FUNNY VERY FUNNY
3 YOUR RATING: 1 2 3 4 5 NOT FUNNY VERY FUNNY
4 YOUR RATING: 1 2 3 4 5 NOT FUNNY VERY FUNNY
7 YOUR RATING: 1 2 3 4 5 NOT FUNNY VERY FUNNY
5 YOUR RATING: 1 2 3 4 5 NOT FUNNY VERY FUNNY
6 YOUR RATING: 1 2 3 4 5 NOT FUNNY VERY FUNNY
8 YOUR RATING: 1 2 3 4 5 NOT FUNNY VERY FUNNY

CAUTION CHILDREN TEXTING

ID NO. 1278 DATE 20150315 BAD CAT

B PAIR WORK Discuss your funniest and least funny choices with a partner. Explain why you find some of the images funny and other ones not funny. Do you have the same sense of humor?

> **"** I don't like the picture of the boy with the head to his side. I find it kind of scary— even a bit creepy. I gave it a 1. **"**

C DISCUSSION Do a class survey. Which image did your classmates find the funniest? Which did they find the least funny? What were the reasons?

D ▶ 3:02 **SPOTLIGHT** Read and listen to a conversation about an embarrassing social situation. Notice the spotlighted language.

ENGLISH FOR TODAY'S WORLD
Understand a variety of accents.
Sylvie = French
David = American English (standard)

Sylvie: Oh, David, I can't tell you how mortified I am.

David: What on earth happened?

Sylvie: So, last night I told this funny joke French people tell about Americans: How do you know someone's an American? He asks for ketchup for his peanut butter sandwich. Well, **it went over like a lead balloon.** *No one laughed.* **I made a total fool of myself.**

David: Oh, Sylvie! That must have been awful!

Sylvie: The thing is I don't know why they took it personally. The joke wasn't about *them*! They were pretty sophisticated. We were even eating French food!

David: Well, you couldn't have known this, but it's definitely uncool to make fun of a particular nationality, an ethnic group, a religion … **It just isn't done.**

Sylvie: You mean you guys are that politically correct?

David: You could say that. And the fact that you're French probably didn't help. We Americans can get a bit intimidated by the French, but don't quote me on that.

Sylvie: **I don't get it.** Why are people here so sensitive? In France, we can't get enough jokes about ourselves.

David: I'm surmising the French are thicker-skinned than Americans …

Sylvie: You can say that again. Ethnic jokes— even ones about ourselves—are just **par for the course** there. You know, I don't think I can ever face those people again.

David: You know what, Sylvie? We Americans make jokes about ourselves, too. It's just less funny when it comes from an outsider. **Don't take it so hard.**

Sylvie: **Easier said than done!**

E **UNDERSTAND IDIOMS AND EXPRESSIONS** Complete the statements with spotlighted language.

1 If you want to say that someone's advice isn't easy to follow, you can say " ...."

2 Another way to say that no one liked your joke is " ...."

3 When you want to say you just don't understand something, you can say " ...."

4 When you want to suggest that something isn't at all unusual, you can say it's " ...."

5 When you want to suggest that most people consider something rude or inappropriate, you can say " ...."

6 If you do something stupid or silly that causes other people to laugh at you, you feel embarrassed and say " ...."

7 If you want to suggest that someone is reacting too strongly to something, you can tell him or her " ...."

F **THINK AND EXPLAIN** Can a joke about your own nationality or ethnic group ever be funny? Or are those jokes always "politically incorrect" or even offensive? Explain.

SPEAKING **PAIR WORK** Check the things you find funny. Discuss why certain things make people laugh. What other things make you laugh?

☐ Cute video clips about animals and babies	☐ People embarrassing themselves by using the wrong word or expression
☐ Physical "slapstick" humor in TV shows and movies	☐ Stories or pictures of people making fools of themselves
☐ Jokes making fun of men or jokes making fun of women	☐ Your own idea:

❝ Even though some ethnic jokes can be funny, I think we probably shouldn't tell them. They can end up insulting people. ❞

GOAL Discuss the health benefits of laughter

A ▶ 3:03 **GRAMMAR SPOTLIGHT** Read the article about the health benefits of laughter. Notice the spotlighted grammar.

A laughter therapy group

LAUGH YOUR WAY TO HEALTH?

CAN SOMETHING AS SIMPLE AS LAUGHTER CURE DISEASE?

The concept is actually not new. Sixteenth-century humanist educator Richard Mulcaster **said** that because laughter **produced** warmth in the body, it **might be** a good remedy for colds. Other scientists of his time **noted** that laughter **increased** the rate of breathing, **boosted** muscle tone, and **exercised** the body's internal organs. They **claimed** that those effects **were** beneficial to people suffering from colds too. So although many physicians and medical researchers had long **thought** that laughter **could be** helpful, scientific studies had been inconclusive. Then, in his classic 1956 book *The Stress of Life*, Hungarian scientist Hans Selye **wrote**, based on extensive research, that he **had proved** that biological stress **has** negative effects on health. This laid the foundation for the theory that the absence of stress could have positive effects.

Later, in 1976, American editor Norman Cousins—a non-scientist—**reported** in the *New England Journal of Medicine* that laughter **had helped** cure him of a painful life-threatening chronic disease. His article captured the attention of the medical profession and some doctors began considering using laughter as therapy. Then in his 1979 bestseller, *Anatomy of an Illness*, Cousins **wrote** that he **had been** so sick that the only thing he could do was lie in bed. Cousins **theorized** that, based on Selye's research, because the stress of negative emotions **could cause** illness, positive emotions **should be able to exert** a healing effect. So he spent his time watching funny movies and he asked his friends to tell him lots of funny jokes.

Although no one **can state** definitively that laughter **cured** Norman Cousins, the concept of laughter therapy has gained popular acceptance, notably in Madan Kataria's laughter yoga movement practiced by thousands of people worldwide. In this popular activity, large groups of people sit together and force themselves to laugh until the laughter becomes contagious and real.

B **CRITICAL THINKING** Do you think it's possible that Norman Cousins was cured by laughter? Can you think of any other explanation for his recovery? In what ways do you think positive and negative emotions can affect our health?

DIGITAL
INDUCTIVE
ACTIVITY

C **GRAMMAR** INDIRECT SPEECH: BACKSHIFTS IN TENSE AND TIME EXPRESSIONS

In indirect speech, when the reporting verb is in a past form, the verb form in the noun clause (the indirect speech) usually "shifts back" to preserve meaning. Compare the verb forms in direct and indirect speech.

Some common reporting verbs		
admit	insist	theorize
claim	note	think
complain	report	write
continue	state	

Direct speech	Indirect speech
Dr. Ames wrote, "Negative emotions **are** harmful and **cause** illness."	Dr. Ames wrote (that) negative emotions **were** harmful and **caused** illness.
He continued, "But Cousins **hasn't proved** anything."	He continued (that) Cousins **hadn't proved** anything.
Cousins said, "Laughter **cured** me."	Cousins said (that) laughter **had cured** him.
We wrote, "He **isn't practicing** laughter yoga."	We wrote (that) he **wasn't practicing** laughter yoga.
She claimed, "We **were telling** the truth."	She claimed (that) they **had been telling** the truth.
Doctors admitted, "We**'ve learned** from Cousins's article.	Doctors admitted (that) they **had learned** from Cousins's article.
He told her, "I**'ll check** to see how you**'re feeling** later."	He told her (that) he **would check** to see how she **was feeling** later.
Pam told us, "I **can't understand** what **happened**."	Pam told us (that) she **couldn't understand** what **had happened**.
He told me, "You **have to see** this funny movie."	He told me (that) I **had to see** that funny movie.
The nurse told the little girl, "You **must rest**."	The nurse told the little girl (that) she **had to rest**.

Exceptions

When a reporting verb is in the simple past tense, backshifting is optional when the statement refers to something just said, something that's still true, or a scientific or general truth.

Tom just called. He said that the director **is** (OR **was**) leaving. [something just said]
Ann told me that she **needs** (OR **needed**) to renew her passport. [something still true]
He noted that the Earth **is** (OR **was**) the fifth largest planet in the solar system. [a scientific or general truth]

Do not make changes to present or perfect forms of the modals <u>should</u>, <u>could</u>, <u>may</u>, <u>might</u>, <u>would</u>, and <u>ought to</u> when converting to indirect speech.

Expressions of time and place: backshifts in indirect speech

now	→	**then**	this year	→	**that year**
today	→	**that day**	last week	→	**the week before**
tomorrow	→	**the next day**	next month	→	**the following month**
yesterday	→	**the day before**	here	→	**there**

Mark told me, "Judy was here yesterday." → Mark told me Judy had been **there the day before.**

> **GRAMMAR BOOSTER** p. 135
> Indirect speech: review and expansion
> · Imperatives in indirect speech
> · Changes to pronouns and possessives
> · <u>Say</u>, <u>tell</u>, and <u>ask</u>
> · Other reporting verbs

 D **GRAMMAR PRACTICE** On a separate sheet of paper, rewrite the sentences in indirect speech. If the sentence can be written both with and without backshifting, write it both ways.

1 Ms. Barr stated, "I want you to finish your essays for the next class."

2 Last week I told my husband, "This has been the best vacation we've ever taken."

3 My friend Amy said, "I have never seen such exciting paintings before."

4 In his lecture, Dr. White explained, "The earth rotates around the sun."

E **PAIR WORK** With a partner, take turns restating each of the following in indirect speech.

1 Pain researchers reported, "Laughter may help some patients."

2 They said, "Our new study will begin here next week."

3 The doctors said, "We've recommended laughter yoga to cure his pain."

4 The patient told everyone, "I definitely feel better from the laughter yoga."

F **GRAMMAR PRACTICE** On a separate sheet of paper, write what the people actually said, using direct speech.

1 Ellen told me she had read an article about laughter yoga in the New Yorker magazine.

2 She claimed she believed laughter yoga could be helpful.

3 I said I never would have known that.

4 The nurse told me that she had been using laughter therapy with certain patients.

NOW YOU CAN Discuss the health benefits of laughter

A **NOTEPADDING** Complete the statements, based on the article. Then use that information as support in the Discussion Activator.

Richard Mulcaster and other scientists have said that

Much later, Hans Selye wrote that

Norman Cousins claimed that

 B **DISCUSSION ACTIVATOR** Do you believe laughter can be "good medicine"? How could you apply the ideas in the article to help heal a sick friend or family member? If you were very sick, how might you use laughter therapy to get better? Support your opinion with ideas from the article, using indirect speech if you are reporting what someone said. Say as much as you can.

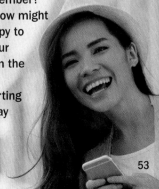

GOAL Respond to something funny

A ▶ 3:04 **VOCABULARY** WAYS TO RESPOND TO JOKES AND OTHER FUNNY THINGS
Read and listen. Then listen again and repeat.

If you think it's funny:

That's so funny!

That's hilarious!

That's hysterical!

That's too much!

If you don't understand what's funny about it:

I don't get it.

That went over my head.

ALSO: That's ridiculous / silly / offensive*

* Be careful! These can be rude and hurt the joke-teller's feelings.

B ▶ 3:05 **LISTEN TO ACTIVATE VOCABULARY** Listen to six conversations. After each one, check <u>Yes</u> or <u>No</u> to indicate whether the listener thought it was funny. Then listen again and write your *own* response to each joke, using the Vocabulary.

Did the listener think it was funny?			
	Yes	No	Your *own* response to the joke
1	☐	☐	....
2	☐	☐	....
3	☐	☐	....
4	☐	☐	....
5	☐	☐	....
6	☐	☐	....

C **PAIR WORK** Did you both get all the jokes? If there's a joke your partner didn't get (or didn't like), try to explain why it was funny to you. Tell your partner which joke you thought was the funniest, and why.

D **RELATE TO PERSONAL EXPERIENCE** Tell your partner about something funny you saw on TV or in a movie, or a joke or funny story you heard from a friend or family member. Respond to your partner, using the Vocabulary.

DIGITAL INDUCTIVE ACTIVITY
E **GRAMMAR** QUESTIONS IN INDIRECT SPEECH

Indirect questions are a kind of embedded question—a question that is included in a noun clause. Indirect <u>yes</u> / <u>no</u> questions begin with <u>if</u> or <u>whether</u> (or <u>whether or not</u>).

He asked, "Did you find that joke funny?" → He asked **if I had found the joke funny.** OR He asked **whether or not I had found the joke funny.**

My boss asked me, "Were you able to finish the project yesterday?" → My boss asked **if (or whether) I had been able to finish the project the day before.**

Indirect information questions begin with a question word.

She asked, "How did you respond to that offensive joke?" → She asked **how I had responded to that offensive joke.**

People often ask Nora, "How many years have you been studying English?" → People often ask Nora **how many years she has been studying English.**

> **Remember:** Embedded questions always have statement (not inverted) word order. Do not use do, does, or did. My friend asked what movie I wanted to see. NOT My friend asked what movie ~~did I want~~ to see.

 DIGITAL MORE EXERCISES

F GRAMMAR PRACTICE On a separate sheet of paper, rewrite each sentence in indirect speech. Make all necessary backshifts and changes to pronouns and time expressions.

1 The teacher asked her students, "Can you tell me what the joke is about?"
2 Barry sometimes asks himself, "How would I react if someone told an offensive joke?"
3 Lisa asked her boyfriend, "Should you have laughed at that offensive joke?"
4 Dan asked his wife, "Have you finished reading that book of jokes?"
5 Vivian asked me, "Which is the best website for funny animal videos?"

> **PRONUNCIATION BOOSTER** p. 146
> Intonation of sarcasm

NOW YOU CAN   Respond to something funny

A ▶ 3:06 CONVERSATION SPOTLIGHT Read and listen. Notice the spotlighted conversation strategies.

A: Oh, Melanie, **you've got to see this**! I just can't tell you how hilarious it is.
B: What is it?
A: Here. It's this video. Some guy keeps tearing pieces of paper and his baby's laughing hysterically. **Seriously**, come over here and look!
B: Oh, **that's priceless**! Forward me the link, OK?
A: **Totally.**

B ▶ 3:07 RHYTHM AND INTONATION Listen again and repeat. Then practice the conversation with a partner.

 DIGITAL VIDEO — DIGITAL SPEAKING BOOSTER

C CONVERSATION ACTIVATOR Bring a cartoon, photo, or video clip to class. Or use the cartoon below or something from page 50. Use it to create a similar conversation. Start like this: *You've got to see this …* Be sure to change roles and then partners.

DON'T STOP!
• Talk about other cartoons, videos, or video clips you've seen.
• Say why you think they're funny.
• Say as much as you can.

"It could be that it's not plugged in, but that would be too easy."

A **READING WARM-UP**   Who are your favorite comedians and comic actors? Why do they make you laugh?

DIGITAL STRATEGIES   **B** ▶ 3:08 **READING**   Read the article about why people laugh. Provide your own examples to illustrate each theory.

THEORIES OF HUMOR

People of all ages and from all cultures laugh. Although there are many factors that make something funny, three theories are often cited.

THE SUPERIORITY THEORY

The Superiority Theory holds that we tend to find people's small misfortunes and verbal or behavioral mistakes funny. Two examples of the kind of misfortunes often depicted in funny movies and comedy routines are people falling down or bumping into things. Similarly, hearing someone mispronounce a word or use the wrong word makes us laugh, as do the ridiculous mistakes that result from automatic spell check programs. According to this theory, the reason why we laugh at the misfortunes or mistakes of others is that they make us feel superior (and happy that the mistakes and misfortunes are theirs, not ours!).

THE INCONGRUITY THEORY

The Incongruity Theory suggests that humor arises from unexpected, inappropriate, or illogical situations— such as the one about the man who says his brother thinks he's a chicken:

A man goes to a psychiatrist and says, "Doctor, I'm worried about my brother. He thinks he's a chicken." "That IS serious," says the doctor. "Why don't you put him in a mental hospital?" So the man says, "I would, but I need the eggs."

According to the Incongruity Theory, a joke becomes funny when we anticipate that one thing will happen or be said, but something else does instead. When the joke goes in the unexpected direction, we experience two sets of incompatible thoughts and emotions—the ones we had as we were listening and the ones revealed at the end. This incongruity makes us laugh.

THE RELIEF THEORY

According to the Relief Theory, humor is the feeling of relief that comes from the removal of tension. When tension is high, we need a release, and laughter is a way to cleanse our system of the built-up tension. This theory holds that there are certain things we feel tense about, such as bodily functions, physical attractions, and shame about how we look. It is believed that the large number of jokes about those subjects come from our need to laugh about them and thus relieve or reduce our tension about them.

Regardless of the theory, in order to be able to appreciate a situation or joke as funny, some detachment is always necessary; that is, we have to feel uninvolved with the situation. For example, we can often laugh at our own past mistakes because, with the passage of time, we have become detached. Conversely, if the joke or situation is too familiar or realistic, it may "hit too close to home" and evoke sadness instead of laughter. To understand a joke—to "get it"—we might also need some knowledge of cultural, economic, political, and social issues, without which some jokes are impossible to understand. Although humor is universal, there is no universal joke.

C **CLASSIFY**   Complete the chart, checking the theory you think best explains why people laugh. (You may choose more than one.) Explain your choices.

PEOPLE OFTEN LAUGH WHEN THEY ...	THE SUPERIORITY THEORY	THE INCONGRUITY THEORY	THE RELIEF THEORY
discover the strange noise they heard downstairs was only the cat.	☐	☐	☐
see someone slip and fall down.	☐	☐	☐
see someone wearing inappropriate clothes to an event.	☐	☐	☐
arrive at a party where someone is wearing the same outfit.	☐	☐	☐
see a little girl wearing her mother's high heels.	☐	☐	☐
see someone make an embarrassing social mistake.	☐	☐	☐

LISTEN TO APPLY IDEAS Listen to three jokes. Write the theory you think each joke exemplifies. Then discuss with a partner to see if you agreed or disagreed. Provide reasons for your opinion and listen again if necessary to settle differences of opinion.

Joke 1

Joke 2

Joke 3

DIGITAL
EXTRA
CHALLENGE

NOW YOU CAN   Analyze what makes us laugh

DIGITAL
SPEAKING
BOOSTER

DISCUSSION Read the list of common types of jokes to the right and try to explain why people find each kind funny. Use the theories, other reasons, and your own ideas for support.

OPTIONAL WRITING On a separate sheet of paper, write a joke you like. Then write at least two paragraphs analyzing why you and other people find it funny.

DIGITAL
STRATEGIES

▶ 3:10 **Common types of jokes**

a dirty joke	a joke about sex or with sexual content
an ethnic joke	a joke about people of a particular ethnic background
a sexist joke	a joke about men or women
a political joke	a joke about a political candidate, party, opinion, or government official
a verbal joke	a joke that uses language in such a way that the language itself becomes funny

A ▶3:11 **LISTENING WARM-UP** **VOCABULARY** **PRACTICAL JOKES**
Read and listen. Then listen again and repeat.

a practical joke

Don't take it personally!

be the butt of a joke be the person on whom a trick, or "practical joke," is played; be the object of ridicule

can take a joke / be a good sport be able to laugh at a practical joke, even when one is the butt of it, without getting insulted or taking it too personally

be in bad (or **poor**) **taste** be offensive or extremely cruel

cross the line go beyond funny into something mean, hurtful, offensive, or cruel

B ▶3:12 **LISTEN TO ACTIVATE VOCABULARY** Listen to a description of a practical joke a doctor played on another doctor. Complete each statement about the practical joke you heard described.

1 Dr. Adams ....
  a played a practical joke on another doctor
  b was the butt of another doctor's joke

2 The woman thinks her father's joke ....
  a was in pretty good taste
  b may have crossed the line

3 In the end, the younger doctor proved that ....
  a he could take being the butt of a practical joke
  b the joke was in pretty poor taste

4 We can conclude that the man thinks that ....
  a the joke crossed the line
  b the younger doctor was a pretty good sport

C ▶3:13 **LISTEN TO SUMMARIZE** Listen again and write a summary of the story, using indirect speech. Then compare summaries with a partner. Use the example as a way to start:

❝ The woman described a practical joke her father had once played on someone. One day ... ❞

D ▶3:14 **LISTEN TO TAKE NOTES** Listen to people who were the butt of practical jokes. Then listen again to complete the chart. Use the Vocabulary. Listen again if necessary.

Speaker	What was the joke?	How did the person react?
1		
2		
3		

E **DISCUSSION** Which, if any, of the jokes in Exercise D crossed the line? Explain your opinion. Then compare how you would have reacted with the way each speaker reacted.

A FRAME YOUR IDEAS   Read the practical jokes and rate each one, using the scorecard.

SCORECARD

X = I don't get it.
1 = It crosses the line.
2 = It's silly.
3 = It's kind of funny.
4 = It's hilarious!

A   RATING: ☐

Someone in your family leaves a very real-looking toy snake in a drawer with your clothes. You open the drawer and are about to put your hand in when you suddenly see the snake.

B   RATING: ☐

You start getting lots of calls from people who want to buy your house, even though you have no intention of selling. It turns out a friend had secretly created an online real estate ad offering your house at a very cheap price.

C   RATING: ☐

A colleague tells you that another colleague is going to get married. When you see her, you congratulate her happily. She has no idea what you're talking about.

D   RATING: ☐

Someone in your family offers you a cup of coffee or tea. When you take the first sip, it tastes so bad you can hardly swallow it. You realize it has salt in it instead of sugar.

E   RATING: ☐

You're invited to a friend's costume party. When you arrive at the party, everyone is nicely dressed in regular clothes, and you are dressed in a chicken costume.

B PAIR WORK   Compare your ratings on the practical jokes. Do you agree? Then, for each joke, compare how you would have responded if <u>you</u> had been the butt of the joke. Would you have been a good sport? Or would you have been offended?

C DISCUSSION

1 When do you think a practical joke crosses the line?

2 Have you ever played a practical joke on someone else? What was the joke and what happened? Use the Vocabulary from page 58.

3 What is your opinion of practical jokes in the workplace? Are they ever acceptable? Explain.

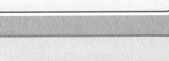

RECYCLE THIS LANGUAGE

· It was so [hysterical / hilarious]!
· It was [too much / too funny]!
· I didn't get it.
· What was so funny about it?
· It went over my head.
· Seriously.
· That just isn't done.
· It was kind of [ridiculous / offensive / silly].

A WRITING SKILL Study the rules.

Paragraphing a story with dialogue

With direct speech, begin a new paragraph each time you introduce a new speaker. Remember that paragraphs should be indented or should have a space above them so the reader can see where new paragraphs begin. See one paragraphing style in the Writing Model.

Punctuation of direct speech

- When the reporting verb comes before a quotation, put a comma after the reporting verb. Put the end punctuation inside the quotation marks.

  Mr. Mann said, "That's not at all funny."

- When the reporting verb comes after a quotation, put a comma, question mark, or an exclamation point at the end of the quoted sentence, inside the quotation marks. Put the speaker's name before or after the reporting verb.

  "Please don't do anything cruel," Ms. Kane said.
  "Didn't anyone object to that mean practical joke?" asked Carlson.

- A reporting verb can also come between two parts of a quotation. Put quotation marks around each part of the quotation. Don't begin the second part of the quotation with a capital letter unless it begins a new sentence.

  "Melanie and Elaine," Mr. Sargent said, "please apologize for hurting Morgan."

- If the reporting verb comes between complete sentences, put a period after the reporting verb. Begin the new sentence with a capital letter.

  "Peter, please apologize to Morgan," continued Mr. Sargent. "You participated in that mean practical joke too."

WRITING MODEL

About a year ago, my grandmoth was walking down the street, stoppir from time to time to look in shop windows. At one store, she stopped to admire a dress in the window. Just as she turned to enter the store, a businessman walking very fast and, not looking where he was going, bumped into her, knocking her down.

"Oh, I'm so sorry!" said the man. "Are you OK?"

My grandmother was too stunned to reply. But then after a moment she said she was fine.

"Look!" she heard someone say from across the street. "An old woman just fell down!"

She quickly sat up and looked around with great concern and said, "Where?"

When she told us this story, we all laughed. But, it really wasn't that funny, and it could have been serious.

B PRACTICE On a separate sheet of paper, rewrite the sentences, correcting the errors in punctuation and capitalization.

1 Norman Cousins said, "That he had cured himself with laughter."

2 "The Superiority Theory" our professor explained. "Is exemplified by finding people's errors funny."

3 "The joke was really cruel," said Claire. "they shouldn't have played it."

4 "Does that example illustrate the Incongruity Theory" asked John?

5 "I learned about all kinds of humor in my psychology class", said my sister.

C PRACTICE On a separate sheet of paper, write the following indirect speech statements in direct speech, using correct punctuation for dialogue.

1 Dr. Summers stated that positive emotions can have a direct effect on emotional and physical health.

2 A psychologist told me many people believed that Norman Cousins's book popularized the idea that laughter therapy could be helpful in treating illness.

3 She said that practical jokes come from our need to feel superior to others.

4 Ms. Barton insisted that traditional medicine is more effective than laughter therapy.

5 Our professor asked whether there is any scientific evidence that laughter can treat illness.

 D APPLY THE WRITING SKILL Write a true or imaginary story telling what happened and what people said, using dialogue. Use the Writing Model for support.

SELF-CHECK

☐ Did I use direct speech in my story?

☐ Did I punctuate direct speech correctly?

☐ Did I correctly paragraph the dialogue?

A ▶3:15 Listen to three examples of jokes. After each one, complete the statement about it. Listen again if necessary.

1 The butt of the joke is ....
   a John   b the manager   c Mark

2 The joke is funny because ....
   a we feel superior to the man   b we are surprised at his response   c we feel relief from tension

3 This joke is an example of ....
   a a verbal joke   b an ethnic joke   c a dirty joke

B Write the response you would give in each situation, using vocabulary from Unit 5 or your own response.

1 Someone tells you a joke you don't understand.

   You: ....
   ....

2 Someone tells an insulting ethnic joke and you want to say something about it.

   You: ....
   ....

3 You hear a joke that you find very funny.

   You: ∧ ....
   ....

4 You have a friend who wants to play a practical joke on someone, but you think it's cruel.

   You: ....
   ....

C On a separate sheet of paper, rewrite the following, changing the direct speech into indirect speech.

1 Mary asked me, "Did you get that joke?"

2 The students insisted, "We didn't play any practical jokes in the gym."

3 My father admitted, "Twenty-five years of practicing medicine have taught me that laughter can be the best medicine."

4 Jess told her friends, "I'll tell you about a joke I told during my job interview yesterday if you promise not to tell anyone."

5 "I can't understand British humor," said Anne.

6 She said, "I may not have enough familiarity with British culture to understand all the pop culture references."

7 The people at the party asked, "Who's going to tell the first joke?"

D Complete each statement about kinds of jokes.

1 A(n) .... joke is a joke that's about sex.

2 A joke that's insulting to all men or to all women is a(n) .... joke.

3 A joke that's insulting to all people of a certain nationality is a(n) .... joke.

4 A joke that makes fun of a candidate for election is a(n) .... joke.

5 A joke that plays a trick on someone to make him or her the butt of the joke is a(n) .... joke.

TEST-TAKING SKILLS BOOSTER p. 155

Web Project: Laughter Therapy
www.english.com/summit3e

61

Troubles While Traveling

COMMUNICATION GOALS

1 Describe some causes of travel hassles
2 Express gratitude for a favor while traveling
3 Discuss staying safe on the Internet
4 Talk about lost, stolen, or damaged property

A FRAME YOUR IDEAS Read about the online contest. On a separate sheet of paper, write your own tips for the common travel hassles.

THE PRACTICAL TRAVELER

HATE TRAVEL HASSLES? ENTER THE TRAVEL TIPS CONTEST!

CONTEST DIRECTIONS: Click on a pull-down menu to enter your own tip for dealing with a specific travel hassle. When you have finished entering all your tips, click on the link to our secure server to submit your tips. Contest winner will be announced on July 15. All decisions final.

CONTEST DEADLINE: July 1

Click here for a full list of prizes for the finalists.

No limit on number of submissions. Enter as many times as you want!

AIR TRAVEL	CAR TRAVEL	OTHER TRAVEL HASSLES
Inedible or no food on flights ▼		Poor air-conditioning or heating ▼
Unexpected checked baggage fees ▼		No phone service or Wi-Fi access ▼
Carry-on luggage fees ▼	Mechanical breakdowns ▼	
Insufficient room in overhead bins ▼	Flat tire ▼	Delays ▼
Overbooked flights ▼	Parking tickets ▼	Unexpected bus or train delays ▼
Missed connections ▼	Getting towed for parking illegally ▼	Uncomfortable seats ▼
Lost luggage ▼	Children arguing in the backseat ▼	Dirty bathrooms ▼
Long lines at check-in and security screening ▼	Finding a bathroom ▼	Loud or rude passengers ▼
	Getting lost ▼	
Items confiscated by security ▼	Traffic jams ▼	CONTINUE ❯ SUBMIT ❯

B ▶ 3:16 VOCABULARY TRAVEL NOUNS Find and circle these words and phrases in the contest. Listen and repeat. Then, with a partner, explain the meaning of each one.

checked baggage fees   security screening
carry-on luggage   a breakdown
an overhead bin   a flat tire
a missed connection   a parking ticket

C DISCUSSION Share your tips. Decide which tips you think are good enough to win the contest.

D ▶3:17 **SPOTLIGHT**   Read and listen to two friends talking about a travel hassle on a business trip. Notice the spotlighted language.

Edison: Oh, no. My folder's missing! It had my passport and my boarding pass in it.

Yuji: Uh-oh! Try to think. When did you see it last? Was it at the hotel?

Edison: Let's see … **I'm drawing a blank**. Oh! I remember now. I'd just finished printing out the boarding pass when the front desk called to say the airport limo was waiting downstairs. So I got my stuff together and split.

Yuji: Do you think you could have left the folder in the room or at the front desk when you checked out? Or what about in the limo?

Edison: Well, I distinctly remember looking back at the seat of the limo before I slammed the door, just to check that I hadn't left anything, and I hadn't. It's got to be in the hotel.

Yuji: Well, don't freak out. **It's a safe bet** they'll find it in the hotel.

Edison: You know, if I hadn't been rushing for the limo, this wouldn't have happened. **The way I see it**, I have no choice but to go back to the hotel. I'll grab a cab outside. You go on. You need to catch that plane.

Yuji: OK.

Edison: But if that folder isn't at the hotel, **I'm toast**. If it weren't for my stupid mistake, I wouldn't be going through this hassle. What'll happen if I miss the dinner?

Yuji: Well, **you'll cross that bridge when you come to it**. But hey, **no sweat**. If the folder's there, you can be back in time to make the four o'clock. We can meet up later. The dinner's not till seven.

Edison: OK. **I'm off**. Keep your fingers crossed!

E **UNDERSTAND IDIOMS AND EXPRESSIONS**   Match the expressions from Spotlight with the statement or phrase that has a similar meaning.

1 I'm drawing a blank.
2 It's a safe bet.
3 the way I see it
4 I'm toast.
5 You'll cross that bridge when you come to it.
6 No sweat.
7 I'm off.

a Don't worry about it.
b It's very probable.
c I'm in big trouble.
d You can worry about that later.
e I can't remember.
f I'm leaving right now.
g in my opinion

F **THINK AND EXPLAIN**   What do you think the outcome of the situation will be? What are Edison's options if the folder isn't found in his room or at the front desk? Explain.

SPEAKING   Check hassles you've experienced and write details about when and where they happened. Then discuss with a partner.

My Experiences	Details
☐ I lost my passport.	
☐ I missed a plane / bus / train.	
☐ I missed a connecting flight.	
☐ My luggage was delayed or lost.	
☐ My car got towed.	
☐ I was in a vehicle that broke down.	
☐ I got a parking ticket.	
☐ My cosmetics were confiscated at security.	
☐ Other	

63

▶ 3:18 **GRAMMAR SPOTLIGHT** Read the interviews about travel hassles. Notice the spotlighted grammar.

ZELLERS: This is Oscar Zellers with another installment of *Nightmares in a Nutshell*. Three callers are on the line from different airports around the world. First up is Isabela Wilson in New York, just arrived from a vacation trip to the south of France.

ZELLERS: Ms. Wilson, I understand you had your perfume taken from you when you went through security.

❶ WILSON: Unfortunately, yes. I got to the airport late and had to take my bag through security. But I'd forgotten the *expensive* French perfume I'd packed in that bag. It's not as if I don't know you can't take liquids through security. If I**'d been thinking** clearly, I **would have arrived** early enough to check my bag. Can you believe it was confiscated?!

ZELLERS: Next up is James Robillard in Montreal. He arrived in Brazil yesterday with an expired business visa and was put on a return flight back to Montreal. How unfortunate, Mr. Robillard!

❷ ROBILLARD: You can say that again! But frankly I'm pretty annoyed that the agent here in Montreal who checked me in didn't notice the expired visa. If she**'d been paying** better attention—instead of worrying about how much my baggage weighed!—she **would have noticed** it. She simply **couldn't have been looking for** the expiration date on the visa. She took a quick glance and saw that my passport was valid, but that was it.

ZELLERS: And last but not least, let's talk to Alice Yang. Ms. Yang started out in Shanghai and flew to Los Angeles, where she connected with her flight to San Salvador. But Ms. Yang's checked luggage wasn't transferred to the San Salvador flight. What bad luck, Ms. Yang!

❸ YANG: It sure was. And I've only got one day here in El Salvador. Tomorrow I'm departing for Bolivia, then the next day, Ecuador, then Peru! My bags may never catch up with me. You know, if I **were traveling** on a weekday, or if I had another day here, it **wouldn't be** such a problem since I could go shopping, but today is Sunday and most stores are closed. Take it from me. If you **have to change** planes, don't even think of checking your bag. Better safe than sorry!

B DISCUSSION Whose situation would be the most frustrating for you? Explain.

C GRAMMAR UNREAL CONDITIONAL SENTENCES: CONTINUOUS FORMS

Use continuous verb forms in unreal conditional sentences to express actions in progress.

Present unreal conditional sentences

You can use <u>were</u> (or <u>weren't</u>) + a present participle in the <u>if</u> clause. You can use <u>would be</u> (or <u>wouldn't be</u>) + a present participle in the result clause. Note: The verb forms should reflect what you want to express. You don't have to use continuous forms in both clauses.

If I **were walking** in traffic, I **wouldn't be talking** on my cell phone.
[continuous forms in both clauses]

If he walked there, he **would be going** through the most dangerous section of town.
[continuous form only in the result clause]

Past unreal conditional sentences

You can use <u>had been</u> (or <u>hadn't been</u>) + a present participle in the <u>if</u> clause. You can use <u>would have been</u> (or <u>wouldn't have been</u>) + a present participle in the result clause. You don't have to use continuous forms in both clauses.

If he**'d been using** his webcam during the conference call, he **would have been wearing** a tie.
[continuous forms in both clauses]

If I **hadn't been checking** my messages, I wouldn't have known the flight was delayed. [continuous form only in the <u>if</u> clause]

Sequence of tenses

The traditional sequence of tenses in all past unreal conditional sentences (past .perfect in the <u>if</u> clause and <u>would have</u> + a past participle in the result clause) can change to express time. Compare the following sentences.

past unreal condition	present or past result
If I **'d gone** to India last year,	I **wouldn't be flying** there right now.
If I **'d gone** to India last year,	I **would have seen** the Taj Mahal.

> **Remember:**
> Conditional sentences usually have two clauses: an if (or "condition") clause and a result clause. The clauses in conditional sentences can be reversed.
>
> Real (or "factual") conditionals describe the results of real conditions. Unreal conditionals describe the results of unreal conditions.

> **Be careful!** Don't use <u>would</u> in the <u>if</u> clause in any unreal conditional sentence.
> If I were watching TV, I would be watching the news.
> NOT If I ~~would be watching~~ TV, …

> **GRAMMAR BOOSTER** p. 137
> The conditional: summary and extension

D UNDERSTAND THE GRAMMAR Choose the sentence that best explains the meaning of each quotation. Then, with a partner, make a statement with <u>should have</u> to indicate what could have prevented the problem.

> **"** I should have made the reservation for the right date. **"**

1 "If the reservation had been made for the right date, I wouldn't be waiting for a standby seat now."
   a The reservation was made for the right date, so I won't have to wait for a standby seat.
   b The reservation was made for the wrong date, so I'm waiting for a standby seat now.
   c The reservation wasn't made for the right date, so I don't have to wait for a standby seat.

2 "If my sister had been watching her bags, they wouldn't have gotten stolen."
   a My sister wasn't watching her bags, so they got stolen.
   b My sister isn't watching, so they might get stolen.
   c My sister was watching her bags, so they didn't get stolen.

3 "I wouldn't have missed the announcement if I hadn't been streaming a movie."
   a I was streaming a movie, and it caused me to miss the announcement.
   b I wasn't streaming a movie, so I didn't miss the announcement.
   c I wasn't streaming a movie, but I missed the announcement anyway.

E GRAMMAR PRACTICE Circle the correct verb phrase to complete each statement.

1 If you (would be / were) at the hotel now, you (would be / would have been) sleeping.

2 If we (had / would have) packed more carefully, we (wouldn't be / wouldn't have been) paying these exorbitant overweight baggage fees!

3 They could (take / have taken) the three o'clock flight if they (would have been / had been) watching the departure board.

4 Karina (would be / would have been) wearing her most comfortable shoes on the tour today if they (wouldn't have been / weren't) sitting in her lost luggage right now.

5 If they (hadn't / wouldn't have) been speeding, they wouldn't (get / have gotten) that ticket.

F PAIR WORK With a partner, take turns completing the unreal conditional sentences, using continuous verb forms.

1 If it were Monday, I ...would be walking to work right now.... .

2 I would have been late to class if ....

3 We would be watching the game now if ....

4 If I were at home, I ....

5 There's no way I would have missed the train if ....

NOW YOU CAN | Describe some causes of travel hassles

A NOTEPADDING Write two travel hassles you or someone you know has faced. Write a statement with <u>should have</u> about how you could have avoided the hassle. Use the chart on page 63 for ideas.

What happened?	How could it have been avoided?
My brother's car got towed last May in New York.	He should have been paying attention to the signs.

What happened?	How could it have been avoided?

B DISCUSSION ACTIVATOR Discuss the travel hassles you experienced. Make at least one statement in the unreal conditional about how you could have avoided the hassle. Say as much as you can.

> **"** If I hadn't been listening to a podcast, I wouldn't have missed the flight announcement. **"**

GOAL Express gratitude for a favor while traveling

A GRAMMAR UNREAL CONDITIONAL STATEMENTS WITH <u>IF IT WEREN'T FOR ...</u> / <u>IF IT HADN'T BEEN FOR ...</u>

Make a present or past unreal conditional statement with <u>if it weren't for</u> / <u>if it hadn't been for</u> + an object to state an outcome that would occur or would have occurred under other circumstances. It's common to use this structure to express regret or relief.

Regret

"If it weren't for the traffic, we **would be** at the airport by now."
(= Under other circumstances, we would be at the airport by now, but unfortunately the traffic caused us not to be. We regret this.)

"If it hadn't been for my bad grades in science, I **would have studied** medicine."
(= Under other circumstances, I would have studied medicine. Unfortunately, my bad grades in science prevented that. I regret this.)

Relief

"If it weren't for this five-hour nonstop flight, the entire trip **would take** ten hours."
(= Under other circumstances, the trip would take ten hours. Fortunately, this nonstop flight caused the trip to be shortened by five hours. I'm relieved about this.)

"If it hadn't been for your help this morning, we **would have missed** the train."
(= Under other circumstances, we would have missed the train. Fortunately, your help prevented our missing the train. We're relieved about this.)

> **Remember:** You can also express strong regret with <u>If only</u>. If only can be followed by <u>were</u> or the past perfect.
> **If only there weren't** so much traffic, we would be at the airport by now.
> **If only I had had** better grades in science, I would have studied medicine.

If it hadn't been for my GPS, I would have gotten hopelessly lost!

B FIND THE GRAMMAR Find and underline a statement using <u>If it weren't for</u> or <u>If it hadn't been for</u> and the unreal conditional in Spotlight on page 63. Is it expressing regret or relief?

C ▶ 3:19 UNDERSTAND THE GRAMMAR Listen to the conversations and infer whether the speakers are expressing regret or relief in each conditional statement.

1 .... 3 .... 5 ....

2 .... 4 .... 6 ....

D ▶ 3:20 LISTEN TO ACTIVATE GRAMMAR Listen again. Complete the paraphrase of what happened, according to what you hear. Use <u>if it weren't for</u> or <u>if it hadn't been for</u>.

1 He might still be waiting for the bus .... Ben.

2 .... the fact that they saw the other car, they might have had an accident.

3 Millie would love to go on the tour .... her cold.

4 They might still be in line .... the fact that she speaks Spanish.

5 They wouldn't be late for the play .... the flat tire.

6 .... her thoughtlessness, she thinks they wouldn't have divorced.

E GRAMMAR PRACTICE On a separate sheet of paper, rewrite each statement, using <u>if it weren't for</u> or <u>if it hadn't been for</u>.

1 Without this cold, I would go to the museum with you tomorrow.

2 I would have totally missed our appointment without the hotel wake-up call.

3 Without that announcement, we would have gone to the wrong departure gate.

4 We would have arrived two hours early without the airline's text message.

5 Without the flight attendant's help with this heavy bag, I would have gotten a backache trying to put it in the overhead bin.

F GRAMMAR PRACTICE First complete the statements with true information, using <u>if it weren't for</u> or <u>if it hadn't been for</u>. Then take turns reading your information with a partner.

1 I wouldn't speak English this well ....

2 I would [or wouldn't] have traveled outside of my country ....

3 I would [or wouldn't] be a great athlete ....

4 I would [or wouldn't] have gone out last night ....

NOW YOU CAN Express gratitude for a favor while traveling

TO GATE 2A

A ▶ 3:21 **CONVERSATION SPOTLIGHT**
Read and listen. Notice the spotlighted conversation strategies.

A: Excuse me. **I wonder if you could do me a favor.**

B: No problem. **How can I help**?

A: I think I left my phone at the counter. Would you mind keeping my place in line?

B: Not at all. **I'd be happy to.**

A: Thanks. I'll be right back.

...

B: Well, that was fast! **It's a good thing** your phone was still there.

A: And if it hadn't been for you, I would have lost my place in line. Thanks!

B ▶ 3:22 **RHYTHM AND INTONATION**
Listen again and repeat. Then practice the conversation with a partner.

DIGITAL VIDEO
DIGITAL SPEAKING BOOSTER

C CONVERSATION ACTIVATOR
Create a similar conversation, using one of the pictures or another idea. Start like this:
Excuse me. I wonder if you could do me a favor... Be sure to change roles and then partners.

... giving me a hand with this bag?

... keeping an eye on my things?

DON'T STOP!

• Explain why you need help.
• Explain the possible consequences of not getting help.
• Continue the conversation with small talk.
• Say as much as you can.

RECYCLE THIS LANGUAGE	
· No sweat.	· Don't freak out.
· I'm off.	· Anytime.
· Wish me luck!	

... grabbing that bag off the carousel?

... pointing me in the right direction?

A **READING WARM-UP**   Do you use public Wi-Fi away from home? Why or why not?

B ▶ 3:23 **READING**   Read about problems with public Wi-Fi. What surprised you the most?

USING PUBLIC
WI-FI
NETWORKS

So it's your first trip away from home, and you've got your smartphone, your tablet, or laptop with you, and you plan to keep up with everything and stay in touch while you're away. You're thinking, "No sweat. There are Wi-Fi hotspots everywhere, and it's free. Well, before you lull yourself into a false sense of security, consider the downside of all that free Wi-Fi.

If you connect to a public Wi-Fi network and send information through websites or mobile apps, it might be accessed by someone else who can, for example, use your credit information to make online purchases. OK. That's not the end of the world, you say, because an unusual buying pattern usually trips a "fraud alert" at the credit card company. They'll contact you, and you'll confirm you didn't make the purchase. The card will be canceled, limiting or preventing any damage, so no harm done.

But here's a downside: An imposter could use your e-mail account to impersonate you and scam people in your contact lists. In addition, a hacker could test your username and password to try to gain access to other websites—including sites that store your financial information.

Worst case scenario? Someone could actually steal your financial identity and pose as you to clean out your bank accounts, removing all your hard-earned money. Repairing a stolen identity can take a long time and cause a lot of hassle. Identity theft is no joke. Prevent it at all costs.

So beware: If you send e-mail, share digital photos and videos, use social networks, or bank online, you're sending personal information over the Internet. How to protect yourself? Think encryption. Encryption scrambles the information you send over the Internet into a code so it's unintelligible and therefore not accessible to others. If you're on a public wireless hotspot, send personal information only to sites that are fully encrypted, and avoid using any mobile apps that require personal or financial information.

And don't just assume a Wi-Fi hotspot is secure either. Most *don't* encrypt the information you send over the Internet and aren't secure. In fact, if a network doesn't require a WPA or WPA2 password, it's probably not secure, and your personal information, private documents, contacts, family photos, and even your log-in credentials (your username and password) for any site you enter could be up for grabs.

HOW TO TELL IF A WEBSITE IS ENCRYPTED

To determine if a website is encrypted, look for "https" at the start of the web address (the "s" is for "secure"). Some websites use encryption only on the sign-in page, but if any part of your session isn't encrypted, your entire account could be vulnerable. Look for "https" on every page you visit, not just when you sign in.

TIPS FOR USING WI-FI SECURELY

▶ Log in or send personal information only to websites you know are fully encrypted. If you find yourself on an unencrypted page, log out right away.

▶ Don't stay permanently signed in to an account. When you've finished using an account, log out.

▶ Do not use the same password on different websites. It could give someone who gains access to one of your accounts access to many of your accounts.

▶ For more control over when and how your device uses public Wi-Fi, consider changing your settings so your device doesn't connect automatically.

C **UNDERSTAND MEANING FROM CONTEXT**   Match each definition with a word or phrase from the article.

...... **1** a person who fraudulently claims to be someone else

...... **2** the location on a website where you identify yourself in order to enter

...... **3** a general term for the username and password you use to identify yourself

...... **4** the disadvantage of something

...... **5** a warning that someone else might be using your credit card

...... **6** pretend to be someone else

...... **7** a place where one can access the Internet, usually for free

...... **8** the use of someone's financial information in order to steal

a a fraud alert

b identity theft

c impersonate

d an imposter

e log-in credentials

f a sign-in page

g downside

h a wireless hotspot

D **PARAPHRASE** On a separate sheet of paper, paraphrase each of the following statements from the article.

1 "An imposter could use your e-mail account to impersonate you and scam people in your contact lists."

> *A person could pretend to be you and trick people in your contact lists.*

2 "Before you lull yourself into a false sense of security, consider the downside of all that free Wi-Fi."

3 "Encryption scrambles the information you send over the Internet into a code so it's unintelligible and therefore not accessible to others."

4 "If a network doesn't require a WPA or WPA2 password, it's probably not secure, and your personal information, private documents, contacts, family photos, and even your login credentials … could be up for grabs."

5 "To determine if a website is encrypted, look for "https" at the start of the web address (the 's' is for 'secure')."

E **FIND SUPPORTING DETAILS** With a partner, discuss and answer the questions. Support your answers with information from the article.

1 What should you look for when sending information to a website when you're using a public Wi-Fi network?

2 How can you know whether a Wi-Fi network is secure?

3 What should you do after concluding your online banking when on a public Wi-Fi network?

4 What could happen if a hacker gained access to your contact list?

DIGITAL EXTRA CHALLENGE
5 What might happen if a credit card company discerns purchases on your card that are not ones you typically make?

NOW YOU CAN Discuss staying safe on the Internet

A **FRAME YOUR IDEAS** Complete the chart with what you do to stay secure on the Internet— at home or away.

	Always	Sometimes	Never
I use public Wi-Fi hotspots.	☐	☐	☐
I check to see if a website is encrypted.	☐	☐	☐
I use different passwords on different sites.	☐	☐	☐
I set my mobile device to automatically connect to nearby Wi-Fi.	☐	☐	☐
I protect myself against credit card fraud.	☐	☐	☐
I actively prevent my identity from being stolen.	☐	☐	☐

B **GROUP WORK** Compare your answers in a small group. Discuss which practices you were familiar with and which were new to you. Then add at least one other thing you do to keep yourself secure on the Internet.

> 66 I change all my passwords once a week. I have a system for scrambling them that makes it easy for me to remember them. 99

GOAL Talk about lost, stolen, or damaged property

DIGITAL
STRATEGIES **A** ▶3:24 **LISTENING WARM-UP** **WORD STUDY** **PAST PARTICIPLES AS NOUN MODIFIERS**
The past participles of transitive verbs can function as noun modifiers. They can precede or
follow the noun they modify. Read and listen. Then listen again and repeat.

"My tire was **damaged**.
I took my **damaged** tire
to the garage."

"My purse was **stolen**
at a store. I found the
stolen purse (without
my wallet!) at the back
of the store."

"My passport was
lost. Luckily, the
police found the
lost passport."

B **WORD STUDY PRACTICE 1** Choose five more past participles of transitive verbs from the chart
on page 122. Write a sentence with each one, using the examples in Exercise A as a model.

C **WORD STUDY PRACTICE 2** On a separate sheet of paper, rewrite each sentence that contains
an underlined object pronoun, using a participial adjective as a noun modifier.

1 When Julie took her skirt out of the closet, she saw that it
was stained. She took <u>it</u> to the cleaners.

> *She took the stained skirt to the cleaners.*

2 While we were at the train station, I found a pair of sunglasses
that were lost. I gave <u>them</u> to the Lost and Found.

3 After walking up the steps to the pyramid, I noticed that the
heel of my shoe was broken. The guy in the shoe repair stand
fixed <u>it</u> in less than ten minutes.

**PRONUNCIATION
BOOSTER** p. 147

· Regular past participle endings
· Reduction in perfect modals

4 We reported that our hotel room had been burglarized.
The front desk sent someone to look at <u>it</u>.

5 The repair shop sells bargain suitcases that are damaged. It's a
good deal because you can pay to have <u>them</u> repaired cheaply.

DIGITAL
STRATEGIES **D** ▶3:25 **LISTEN FOR MAIN IDEAS** Listen to Part 1 of a radio report.
Write a checkmark next to the statement that best expresses its main idea.

☐ Put your name on your luggage to avoid loss or delay.

☐ Know what to do to avoid luggage loss or delay.

☐ Don't check bags that can be carried onto the plane.

Keep your copy
of the luggage
check in case
your bag is lost
or delayed.

E ▶3:26 **LISTEN TO CONFIRM CONTENT** Listen again. Write a checkmark next to the tips Tina
Traveler gave listeners. Write an X next to any tips on the list she didn't give.

☐ **1** Put your address on your luggage inside and out.

☐ **2** Request reimbursement for toiletries if your baggage is delayed.

☐ **3** File a claim with your airline if your bags are lost.

☐ **4** Provide sales receipts to prove what you paid for the
clothes in your lost luggage.

☐ **5** Don't put your prescription medicines in your checked bag.

☐ **6** Keep luggage checks for checked baggage in case you have
to make a claim.

F ▶ 3:27 **LISTEN TO UNDERSTAND MEANING FROM CONTEXT**
Listen again and complete each statement with one of these words
or phrases from Tina Traveler's advice.

a claim	luggage checks
a connecting flight	receipts
depreciated	reimburse
an itinerary	toiletries

1 Cosmetics are an example of ....

2 The list of places and dates of your travel is ....

3 A value lower than the price you paid because the item isn't new is its .... value.

4 If you take two flights to get somewhere, the second one is called ....

5 Slips of paper showing the destination of your checked luggage are ....

6 Slips of paper showing what you paid for something you bought are ....

7 A form that records loss, delay, or damage to property is ....

8 If the airline pays you money to compensate you for a damaged bag, they .... you.

G ▶ 3:28 **LISTEN FOR DETAILS** Listen to Part 2 of Tina Traveler's report. Then answer the
questions. Listen again if necessary.

1 What is the Unclaimed Baggage Center?

2 What's the difference between the Unclaimed Baggage Center and
a Lost and Found office?

3 How many stores does the Center have?

4 Where does the Unclaimed Baggage Center get its merchandise?

5 How does it decide what to buy and what not to buy?

6 What does the center do before selling merchandise?

7 What does it do with merchandise it can't sell?

H **DISCUSSION** Would you shop at the Unclaimed Baggage Center?
Explain why or why not.

NOW YOU CAN   Talk about lost, stolen, or damaged property

A **NOTEPADDING** Write notes about a time your property was lost, stolen, or damaged when you
were traveling. Use words and phrases from Exercise F in your description if possible.

when / where / what?: 2016 / Orlando USA / guitar
brief summary and outcome: *The airline made me check my guitar. It wasn't transferred to my connecting flight in Panama. It was found and delivered to our hotel the next day.*

when / where / what?:
brief summary and outcome:

B **DISCUSSION** Discuss the events you
wrote about on your notepad. Discuss what
happened to your property and what the
final outcome was. Respond to your partner.

> ❝ I freaked out when I didn't see the guitar case on
> the carousel. If it hadn't been for the baggage
> check, I would have been toast! ❞

> ❝ It's a good thing you saved that check! ❞

OPTIONAL WRITING Write about the event you
discussed. Include as many details as possible. Use the words
and phrases from Exercise F and other vocabulary from this unit.

A **WRITING SKILL** Study the rules.

Choose one of these formats for organizing your supporting paragraphs when you want to compare and contrast places, objects, people, ideas, etc., in an essay. (Be sure to include expressions of comparison and contrast.)

WRITING MODEL

Introductory paragraph
Begin with an introductory paragraph that says what you are going to compare and contrast.

(Introductory paragraph)

Public and private transportation have both advantages and disadvantages, so it is fortunate to have options. To make a choice, you can take into account convenience, cost, destination, and the needs and tastes of the people you are traveling with. Other factors to consider are the length of the trip and (if it is important to you) the environmental impact of the means of transportation you choose.

Supporting paragraphs
Choose Format A or B to present and support your ideas.

Format A: Discuss the similarities in one paragraph and the differences in another.

(Format A)

Public and private transportation provide clear advantages for most people. They are similar in certain ways: Both are convenient and cut travel time, allowing people to travel farther to work or school. And with the exception of a bicycle, all vehicles used in public and private transportation are capable of providing a level of comfort available with modern technology, such as air-conditioning and heating.

On the other hand, public and private transportation are different in more ways than they are similar. Cars and bicycles offer a level of privacy and convenience not available in public transportation. You can make your own schedule, take a detour, and not have to pay fares or deal with people you don't want to be with. However, it is only with public transportation that you can move around, relax, and not have to pay attention to traffic or weather conditions.

OR

Format B: Alternatively, you can focus on one specific aspect of the topic in each paragraph, and discuss the similarities and differences within each paragraph.

(Format B)

Regarding scheduling, private and public transportation are very different. When you travel by car, you can make your own schedule and stop when and where you want. Nevertheless, when you travel by bus or train you know exactly when you'll arrive, making planning easy.

In terms of comfort, private transportation has the clear advantage. Public transportation may be crowded and …

Concluding paragraph
Summarize your main ideas in a concluding paragraph.

(Concluding paragraph)

Most people choose to use a mix of private and public transportation, depending on circumstances. However, if I could choose only one means of transportation, I'd go with the car. It has its disadvantages, but I like to travel alone or only with my family and to be able to make my own schedule. All in all, I'd say I'm a car person.

B **APPLY THE WRITING SKILL** On a separate sheet of paper, write an essay comparing and contrasting two means of transportation. Include the paragraph types and formats shown in Exercise A. Use expressions of comparison and contrast.

Expressions to introduce comparisons and contrasts:

Comparisons	Contrasts
Similarly,	While / Whereas …
Likewise,	Unlike …
By the same token,	Nonetheless,
In similar fashion,	Nevertheless,
… as well	In contrast,
… don't either	On the other hand,
	However,

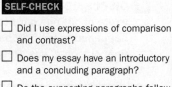

SELF-CHECK

☐ Did I use expressions of comparison and contrast?

☐ Does my essay have an introductory and a concluding paragraph?

☐ Do the supporting paragraphs follow one of the formats illustrated above?

A ▶3:29 Listen to three conversations. On the notepad, summarize what happened in each conversation.

	Conversation Summary
1	
2	
3	

B Choose the correct verb phrase to complete each statement.

1 If it weren't for this long security line, I (will / would) get a cup of coffee.

2 If it hadn't been for the delay in my first flight, my checked bags (wouldn't miss / wouldn't have missed) the connection.

3 We wouldn't have had a flat tire if it (weren't / hadn't been) for all the broken glass on the road.

4 Martin would be here if it (weren't / wouldn't be) for this storm.

5 If it (weren't / wouldn't be) for my broken leg, I would be skiing right now.

C Replace the words or phrases that are crossed out in each statement with ones that make sense.

1 The compartment over your airline seat where you can place your suitcase is the ~~carousel~~.

2 Before you can board an airplane, you have to go through ~~a missed connection~~.

3 If you park in an illegal space, you might get a ~~flat tire~~ or, even worse, your car might get ~~a breakdown~~.

4 A ~~checked~~ bag is one that you take on board with you when you get on a flight.

D Choose the correct idiom or expression.

1 If you can't remember something you're sure you should be able to, you can say, "......"

   a I'm toast.   **b** I'm drawing a blank.

2 When you want to indicate you're about to leave, you can say, "......"

   a I'm off.   **b** I'll cross that bridge when I come to it.

3 If you want to reassure someone that a task won't be hard at all, you can say, "......"

   a No sweat.   **b** It's a good thing.

4 When you think something terrible is definitely going to happen, you can say, "......"

   a I'm off.   **b** I'm toast.

5 When you're sure you've concluded something correctly, you can say, "......"

   a I'm drawing a blank.   **b** It's a safe bet.

TEST-TAKING SKILLS BOOSTER p. 156

Web Project: Travel Nightmares
www.english.com/summit3e

73

GOAL Suggest that someone is being gullible

A **GRAMMAR** NOUNS: INDEFINITE, DEFINITE, UNIQUE, AND GENERIC MEANING (REVIEW AND EXPANSION)

A noun (or noun phrase) is *indefinite* when it doesn't refer to a specific person, place, thing, or idea. Use the indefinite articles (<u>a</u> / <u>an</u>) with indefinite singular count nouns. Indefinite non-count nouns (for example, <u>music</u>, <u>love</u>) have no article.

> You can buy **a smart watch** if you like having everything at a glance. [indefinite, not a specific smart watch]

A noun (or noun phrase) is *definite* when it refers to a specific person, place, thing, or idea. An indefinite noun already mentioned becomes definite when mentioned a second time. Use the definite article (<u>the</u>) with definite singular and plural count nouns and with definite non-count nouns.

> **The wool** they used to make **the sweaters** in this store comes from Canada.
> [definite, specific wool and sweaters]
> I saw a movie last night. **The movie** was a documentary. [definite, second mention]

A count or non-count noun can represent a person, place, or thing that is *unique*; in other words, there's only one. Use <u>the</u>.

> **The president** has named two new foreign ministers.
> Some people claim climate change has no effect on **the environment**.

Count nouns can be used in a *generic* sense to represent all members of a class or group of people, places, or things. When using nouns in a generic sense, use a singular count noun with <u>a</u> / <u>an</u> or <u>the</u>, or use a plural count noun without an article. There is no difference in meaning.

> **A cat** is ⎫
> **The cat** is ⎬ a popular domestic pet in many countries of the world.
> **Cats** are ⎭

> **Remember:** Non-count nouns name things you cannot count. They are neither singular nor plural, but they always use a singular verb. Common categories of non-count nouns are abstract ideas, sports and activities, illnesses, academic subjects, and foods.

> **GRAMMAR BOOSTER** p. 138
> · Article usage: summary
> · Definite article: additional uses
> · More non-count nouns with both a countable and an uncountable sense

B **UNDERSTAND THE GRAMMAR** Read each statement and choose the phrase that describes the underlined word or phrase.

1 <u>Morning snow</u> makes highways dangerous.
  a refers to morning snow in general
  b refers to the snow that fell this morning

2 I think <u>animated movies</u> are boring.
  a refers to all animated movies
  b refers to some animated movies

3 <u>The present</u> they sent me was very expensive.
  a refers to a present as a member of a class
  b refers to a specific present I was sent

4 Some cultures regard <u>the shark</u> as a sign of luck.
  a refers to a specific shark we know about
  b refers to sharks as a class or group

5 <u>The queen</u> will address Parliament this week.
  a refers to a specific queen
  b refers to queens generically

6 <u>A queen</u> can address Parliament.
  a refers to a specific queen
  b refers to queens generically

C **GRAMMAR PRACTICE** Complete the statements about product claims. Insert <u>a</u>, <u>an</u>, or <u>the</u> before a noun or noun phrase where necessary. Write <u>X</u> if the noun shouldn't have an article.

1 .... British company claims to have invented .... machine that allows .... people to talk with their pets. .... company says .... machine, called the PetCom, will be available later in .... year.

2 It's well known that .... carrots are a good source of .... vitamins. In fact, ... research has determined that drinking .... glass of carrot juice every day can add .... years to your life.

3 .... WeightAway diet plan promises to help you lose .... weight fast. .... company guarantees that people following .... plan can lose up to 10 kilograms per week.

4 Last week, the news reported that thousands of people had sent .... money to .... organization advertising a shampoo that .... organization claimed would grow .... hair overnight.

D **DRAW CONCLUSIONS** Complete each statement, based on the information in the article.

1 The factor that doesn't contribute to the placebo effect is ....
  a the appearance of the medication
  b scientific research
  c trust in the doctor
  d the expectation that it will work

2 The knee surgery experiment demonstrates ....
  a the power of suggestion that surgery was performed
  b the value of washing the interior of the knee
  c the need for procedures in surgery
  d the harmful effects of fake procedures

3 The drunkenness experiment is an example of ....
  a the placebo effect
  b the nocebo effect
  c an ethical dilemma
  d the harmful effects of beer

4 ...... is one beneficial use of placebos.
  a The scientific evaluation of the effectiveness of new medications
  b The improvement of the doctor-patient relationship
  c Causing harmful adverse reactions
  d Reducing the cost of antibiotics

5 Under normal circumstances, adverse reactions to medications occur in ....
  a most patients
  b only a few patients
  c the sickest patients
  d the common cold

E **CRITICAL THINKING** Discuss the following questions.

1 What are the pros and cons of telling a patient about potential adverse reactions to a medication?

2 In what way are the placebo effect and the nocebo effect "two sides of the same coin"?

3 In your opinion, are only gullible people susceptible to the placebo and nocebo effect? Explain.

DIGITAL
EXTRA
CHALLENGE

NOW YOU CAN Talk about the power of suggestion

A **NOTEPADDING** Make a list of ways people are susceptible to the power of suggestion. Write what creates the suggestion and how it makes people behave or think.

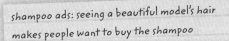
shampoo ads: seeing a beautiful model's hair makes people want to buy the shampoo

Some ideas
· advertisements
· celebrity behavior
· expert opinions
· superstitions
· sexism
· racism

DIGITAL
SPEAKING
BOOSTER

B **DISCUSSION** With a partner, discuss the information on your notepads, providing specific examples to support your opinions.

❝ I think sometimes we just believe what others believe. We think if everyone believes something, it must be right. ❞

RECYCLE THIS LANGUAGE	
· illusion	· What gives you that impression?
· scam	· I wouldn't jump to that conclusion.
· wishful thinking	· Not necessarily.
· claims	· Don't get me wrong.

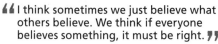

OPTIONAL WRITING Write an essay of at least two paragraphs, describing two or three ways in which people are susceptible to the power of suggestion. Try to explain why it's hard to avoid being influenced by messages in the environment and by wishful thinking.

A ▶ 4:08 **LISTENING WARM-UP** **VOCABULARY** **EXPRESSIONS WITH MIND**
Read and listen. Then listen again and repeat.

make up one's mind

He's afraid of bees and spiders, but he can't make up his mind which are scarier.

change one's mind

She was planning to see the dentist, but it was too scary, so she changed her mind.

put (something) out of one's mind

She's terrified of flying, but she's trying to put any thought of accidents out of her mind.

be all in one's mind

He's afraid there's a monster under the bed. His mom says it's all in his mind.

be out of one's mind

Getting in the elevator would give him palpitations. But they think he's out of his mind to walk down thirty flights of stairs.

B **ACTIVATE VOCABULARY** Complete each definition with the correct form of an expression from the Vocabulary.

1 When you .... , you try not to let it worry or bother you.

2 When you .... to do something, you decide to do it no matter what happens.

3 When something is not real and a person is imagining it, you can tell the person, "................................. "

4 When you .... , you change your opinion or decision about something.

5 If people believe you .... , they think you're behaving in a way that is crazy or foolish.

C ▶ 4:09 **LISTEN FOR DETAILS** Listen to an interview. Then complete each statement, based on the interview.

1 Many people think phobias are ...... because phobias are irrational.

   a scary   **b** funny   **c** enormous

2 People who don't suffer from phobias find them difficult to ....

   a treat   **b** overcome   **c** understand

3 Phobias create both mental and ...... symptoms.

   a economic   **b** physical   **c** irrational

4 People with phobias can't ...... them.

   a control   **b** cure   **c** confront

5 The fight-or-flight response is a set of uncomfortable physical ....

   a fears   **b** anxieties   **c** symptoms

6 Exposure therapy and counter-conditioning are two effective ....

   a treatments   **b** symptoms   **c** responses

D ▶ 4:10 **LISTEN TO CONFIRM CONTENT** Listen to the interview again. Write a checkmark next to the topics that were discussed in the interview and an X next to the ones that weren't. Then with a partner, summarize what was said about each topic that you checked.

☐ The number of people worldwide who suffer from phobias

☐ The way to avoid developing a phobia

☐ Some kinds of phobias that exist

☐ The danger of a rapid heartbeat

☐ The reason why people make jokes about phobias

☐ The physical responses to extreme fear

☐ Two popular treatments for phobias

E ▶ 4:11 **WORD STUDY** **NOUN AND ADJECTIVE FORMS** Read the noun and adjective forms that name and describe a person who suffers from acrophobia. Use the same spelling pattern to complete the chart for the other phobias. Then listen and repeat.

Phobia	Noun	Adjective
acrophobia [heights]	acrophobe	acrophobic
agoraphobia [open spaces]		
arachnophobia [spiders]		
aerophobia [flying]		
claustrophobia [enclosed spaces]		
ophidiophobia [snakes]		
xenophobia [foreigners]		

NOW YOU CAN   Discuss phobias

A **NOTEPADDING** On the notepad, write some things you are afraid of. Look at the list of phobias in Word Study for ideas. Do you think your fears are just run-of-the-mill fears, or could you have real phobias?

Fear	Just afraid, or phobic?	What happens?
bees	I'm really phobic!	I get sweaty palms and palpitations.
		I go inside immediately!

Fear	Just afraid, or phobic?	What happens?

B **PAIR WORK** Compare notes with a partner. Ask your partner questions about his or her fears, their effects on him or her, and why he or she is frightened of the thing. Listen and offer advice.

❝ How come you're so afraid of snakes? Have you ever seen one? ❞

❝ Actually, no, I haven't. But snakes really freak me out. I think I'm just afraid, not phobic. ❞

❝ Well, maybe it would help to read about snakes to find out which are dangerous. Most are actually harmless. ❞

C **DISCUSSION** Discuss the most common fears in your class and how the fears affect your classmates in their everyday and professional lives. Provide examples.

RECYCLE THIS LANGUAGE
• ___ gives me physical symptoms. • I get butterflies in my stomach. • My hands shake. • Don't freak out. • I get palpitations. • Chill. • I lose my voice. • Hang in there. • I get sweaty palms. • I know what you mean.

A WRITING SKILL Study the rules.

When the subject and verb are separated by other words, the subject and verb must still agree.
> **Beliefs** in a supernatural event **are** common in many cultures.
> **The smart thing to do** when someone tells you something is unlucky **is** to just listen.

When two subjects are connected with <u>and</u> in a sentence, the verb must be plural.
> **A black cat** and **a broken mirror are** symbols of bad luck in several cultures.

When verbs occur in a sequence, all the verbs must agree with the subject.
> My sister **believes** in ghosts, **avoids** the number 13, and **wears** a lucky charm on a chain around her neck.

When the subject is an indefinite pronoun like <u>each</u>, <u>everyone</u>, <u>anyone</u>, <u>somebody</u>, or <u>no one</u>, use a singular verb.
> **Nobody** I know **worries** about the evil eye.

When the subject is <u>all</u>, <u>some</u>, or <u>none</u> and refers to a singular count noun or a non-count noun, use a singular verb. Otherwise use a plural verb.
> If salt is spilled by accident, **some is** immediately thrown over the shoulder.
> Some superstitions are old-fashioned, but **some are** not.

> **Remember:** Subjects and verbs must always agree in number.
> **A superstition is** a belief many people think is irrational.
> **Many people believe** certain things can bring good luck.

B PRACTICE Read the paragraph and rewrite it on a separate sheet of paper, correcting the errors in subject-verb agreement.

DIGITAL WRITING PROCESS

C APPLY THE WRITING SKILL On a separate sheet of paper, write a four-paragraph essay. In your first paragraph, introduce the topic of superstitions in general, explaining what they are and why people might believe them. Then write one paragraph each about two superstitions. Include a concluding paragraph and be sure each paragraph has a topic sentence. Be sure all your verbs and subjects agree in number.

ERROR CORRECTION

One common superstition in Western countries concern the number 13. Because they are considered unlucky, many situations involving the number 13 is frequently avoided. For example, in the past, the thirteenth floor of tall apartment buildings were often labeled "fourteen." While that is rare today, there are still many people who are uncomfortable renting an apartment on the thirteenth floor. In addition, there is a general belief that Friday the thirteenth brings bad luck, increases the chance of mishaps, and make it more difficult to get things done effectively.

SELF-CHECK

☐ Did I introduce the topic of superstitions in general in my first paragraph?

☐ Did my second and third paragraphs each describe a superstition?

☐ Did all my paragraphs include topic sentences?

☐ Did all my subjects and verbs agree?

In some cultures, black cats are considered to be unlucky.

A ▶ 4:12 **Listen to the conversations. After each conversation, summarize the claim that the people are talking about. Then listen again. After each conversation, decide whether the people find the claim believable, unlikely, or ridiculous.**

	What is the claim?	believable	unlikely	ridiculous
1		○	○	○
2		○	○	○
3		○	○	○

B Correct the errors in article usage.

A lucky charm is the object that some people carry because they think it will bring the good luck. My lucky charm is a rabbit's foot that I received as gift on my birthday. I don't really know if it has ever brought me a good luck, but I always carry it in my pocket. Since medieval times, the rabbits' feet have been said to bring a good fortune because people believed that witches were capable of turning themselves into rabbits or hares when they were being chased. Both rabbits and hares are very fast animals, so witches stood a good chance of escaping if they turned into rabbits or hares. Since then, the people have carried a rabbits' feet as a good luck charm. They believe the rabbit's foot will protect them.

C Rewrite each sentence, using a present or past passive form of the reporting verb, depending on the information in the sentence.

1 (estimate) Ten percent of people worldwide suffer from some sort of phobia.

....

2 (believe) The mind and body were completely separate, but now we know otherwise.

....

3 (say) If a bee enters your home, you will soon have a visitor.

....

4 (claim) If you say good-bye to a friend on a bridge, you'll never see that friend again.

....

5 (think) The house was damaged by lightning before the fire, but that turned out not to be true.

....

D Choose the correct expression to complete each sentence.

1 If you have a fear of spiders, you should ...... that spiders are very easy to kill.

   a make up your mind   **b** keep in mind

2 Though he was hesitant at first, in the end he ...... to seek help for his problem.

   a was out of his mind   **b** made up his mind

3 She made the decision to get married, but a month before the wedding, she ....

   a changed her mind   **b** kept it in mind

4 People who have a phobia find it very difficult to ....

   a make up their mind   **b** put it out of their mind

TEST-TAKING SKILLS BOOSTER   p. 157

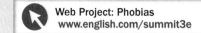
Web Project: Phobias
www.english.com/summit3e

Performing at Your Best

COMMUNICATION GOALS

1 Discuss your talents and strengths
2 Suggest ways to boost intelligence
3 Explain how you produce your best work
4 Describe what makes someone a "genius"

PREVIEW

A **FRAME YOUR IDEAS** Take the EQ quiz.

HOW EMOTIONALLY INTELLIGENT ARE YOU?

The concept of emotional intelligence, developed by psychologist Daniel Goleman, is described as the ability to understand one's own emotions and those of others and use them to motivate actions and achieve goals. According to Goleman, one's emotional intelligence quotient (EQ) can be high even if one's standard intelligence test score (IQ) is low. Take the quiz to calculate your EQ. Check each statement that is true for you. Be as honest as you can!

○ When I feel down, I try to focus on positive things.

○ I like learning about new things.

○ I'm not the kind of person who overreacts to things.

○ I find it easy to admit when I've made a mistake.

○ I see mistakes as opportunities to learn.

○ Most people agree that I have a good sense of humor.

○ When I'm upset about something, I usually know exactly what's bothering me.

○ Understanding the way other people feel or think is important to me.

○ When people criticize me, I use it as an opportunity to improve myself.

○ I don't mind talking with others about uncomfortable topics.

○ I find it fairly easy to get along with people I don't like.

○ I have a good awareness of how my own behavior affects others.

○ I don't mind conflicts or disagreements.

○ I'm good at helping people who disagree with each oth to reach a solution.

○ It's easy to motivate myself to do things I don't really want to do.

○ Before making an important decision, I usually ask othe people for advice.

○ I always think about the ethical consequences of the decisions I make.

○ I have a clear idea of what my strengths and weaknesses are.

○ I feel satisfied with my accomplishments, even if I have received any praise.

○ I generally feel good about who I am, even though ther may be things I'd like to change.

SCORE How many statements did you check?	
17–20 = you have a very high EQ	**5–8** = you have a below-average E
13–16 = you have an above-average EQ	**1–4** = you have a very low EQ
9–12 = you have an average EQ	

B **PAIR WORK** Compare scores with a partner. Do you each feel that your score accurately measures your emotional intelligence? Explain.

C **DISCUSSION** According to Goleman, emotional intelligence is more important for an employee's success than either technical skills or IQ. Based on the quiz, in what ways does EQ seem to measure intelligence differently from IQ? Why might an EQ score be useful for an employer to know?

D ▶ 4:13 **SPOTLIGHT**   Read and listen to a conversation in which someone expresses concern about a family member. Notice the spotlighted language.

Faye: Tony, how's your youngest daughter doing?
Tony: Claire? Here's the thing … She's just a year away from finishing her engineering degree. And, **out of the blue**, she decides to take a part-time job at an animal shelter, taking care of cats!
Faye: Well, that's not surprising. Claire's very responsible. And she's always had a way with animals. I assume she's doing it to help pay for college?
Tony: That's what she said. But in my view she really needs to **put her nose to the grindstone** and focus on her studies right now. Engineering is a tough subject.
Faye: So you're worried it'll affect her grades?
Tony: Exactly. This is her final year. **It's now or never**.
Faye: Have you tried talking with her? Maybe she'll see your point and reconsider.
Tony: Are you kidding? With Claire, everything I say **goes in one ear and out the other**.
Faye: Well, if you don't mind, I'll tell you what I think. Can I be frank?
Tony: Please.

Faye: As I see it, Claire's a pretty sharp young woman. So my **gut feeling** is she'll be just fine. I'll bet she's thinking that working with animals will lessen the stress of her school work. And in any case, if she *does* find herself struggling a bit in her studies, she could always quit the job and concentrate on catching up. I think you should stop worrying about her.
Tony: **I can't help it** … She's my baby girl. But you're probably right. Of my three kids, she's the one I least need to worry about. She's always been very focused on achieving her goals.

E **UNDERSTAND IDIOMS AND EXPRESSIONS**   Match the statement parts to define the idioms and expressions from Spotlight.

1 When you do something "out of the blue," …… .
2 When you "put your nose to the grindstone," …… .
3 When you say "It's now or never," …… .
4 When something "goes in one ear and out the other," …… .
5 When you have a "gut feeling," …… .
6 When you say "I can't help it," …… .

a it's the last opportunity to do something
b you're unable to stop doing something
c someone isn't listening
d you do it suddenly without warning
e you have a strong sense about something
f you're working hard

F **PERSONALIZE IDIOMS AND EXPRESSIONS**
Use two or more idioms from Ex. E to tell a partner about a time when you were concerned about someone or gave someone advice.

❝ My sister wasn't sure what to study, but I had a gut feeling she would like mathematics. So I recommended that she take a course. Unfortunately, my advice went in one ear and out the other … ❞

SPEAKING   Use the EQ quiz to analyze the emotional intelligence of the three characters in Spotlight: Tony, Claire, and Faye. Explain your thinking.

❝ Claire doesn't seem to want to listen to her father's advice. However, according to the quiz, a part of being emotionally intelligent is asking for other people's advice before making important decisions. ❞

❝ I think Faye's a good listener. She seems pretty good at helping people who disagree with each other to reach a solution. ❞

GOAL Discuss your talents and strengths

A ▶ 4:14 **VOCABULARY** EXPRESSIONS TO DESCRIBE TALENTS AND STRENGTHS

Read and listen. Then listen again and repeat.

be good with one's hands	have the ability to use one's hands to make or do things
be mechanically inclined	be able to understand how machines work
have a head for figures	be good at mathematical calculations
have an ear for music	be good at recognizing, remembering, and imitating musical sounds
have an eye for detail	be good at seeing or paying attention to things that others don't usually notice
have a good intuitive sense	be able to draw conclusions based on feelings rather than facts
have a way with words	be able to express one's ideas and opinions well
have a way with [people]	have a special ability to work well with someone or something, for example, plants, children, or animals
have a knack for [learning languages]	have a natural skill or ability to do something well

B **ACTIVATE VOCABULARY** With a partner, use the expressions in the Vocabulary to describe each person's talents and strengths. There may be more than one way to do so. Explain your reasons.

> 66 Clearly Adela has a knack for learning languages! 99

Adela Petran can speak nine languages, including her native Romanian. "It's really not difficult at all," she says.

Miguel Asturias began writing poetry when he was 12. Even though he is still a teen, his teachers have encouraged him to enter his poems in competitions.

Kim Jin-ho was able to solve university math problems at the age of ten. He now teaches math. He argues, "Math's only hard if you think it's going to be hard."

Aiko Kato began playing the violin at the age of three. Today she plays with the Nagoya Philharmonic Orchestra.

Leilah Zaman has been successful at making and selling her own line of women's clothing for five years now. She does all the sewing herself.

As a kid, Felipe Morais liked to take electronic devices apart to figure out how they worked. By the age of 16, he knew he wanted to study engineering.

Blair O'Connor works as an editor. Her job is to check manuscripts for errors and correct them before they get published.

Salesman Bob Pryor is a good listener. He pays attention to his customers' needs and can anticipate what they want before they even know it.

C **PERSONALIZE** Use the Vocabulary to describe five or six people you know.

> 66 My brother Gene, who is a family doctor, has a really good intuitive sense. He can tell what's bothering his patients even when they can't. 99

D **GRAMMAR** USING AUXILIARY <u>DO</u> FOR EMPHATIC STRESS

To add emphatic stress to an affirmative statement in the simple present or past tense, use <u>do</u> or <u>did</u> before the base form of the verb.

> Even if I don't have a head for figures, I **do** have a way with words.
> He **did** like most of his colleagues, but he didn't like his boss.

Be careful!
Use a base form after a form of the auxiliary <u>do</u>.

> She has an eye for detail. → She **does have** an eye for detail. NOT She ~~does has~~ ...
> He liked his job. → He **did like** his job. NOT He ~~did liked~~ ...

▶ 4:15 Listen to emphatic stress on the auxiliary <u>do</u>. Then listen and repeat.
I do have an ear for music.
She does have an ear for music.
He did like his colleagues.

GRAMMAR BOOSTER p. 140
Emphatic stress

E GRAMMAR PRACTICE On a separate sheet of paper, rewrite each item, using <u>do</u> or <u>did</u> for emphatic stress.

1 Sam isn't a great cook. However, he <u>makes</u> great desserts.

2 You're absolutely right! I <u>put things off</u> way too often.

3 She may not sing very well, but she <u>knows</u> how to dance.

4 We made total fools of ourselves, but we <u>got</u> everyone to laugh.

5 He's never lived abroad, but he <u>has</u> a knack for languages.

6 Her decision to quit her job really <u>happened</u> out of the blue.

> *Sam isn't a great cook. However, he does make great desserts.*

> **PRONUNCIATION BOOSTER** p. 148
> Emphatic stress with auxiliary verbs

F PAIR WORK On a separate sheet of paper, write five statements comparing your talents and strengths with your weaknesses, using the auxiliary <u>do</u> for emphatic stress. With a partner, take turns reading your statements aloud.

> ❝ I don't have an eye for detail, but I *do* have a strong intuitive sense. ❞

NOW YOU CAN Discuss your talents and strengths

A ▶4:16 **CONVERSATION SPOTLIGHT** Read and listen. Notice the spotlighted conversation strategies.

A: **Guess what?** I've decided to sign up for an online course.

B: Fantastic! What are you going to be studying?

A: I'm not sure yet. **I can't make up my mind between** engineering and psychology.

B: Which subject do you think you have the most talent for?

A: Well, **I wouldn't say** I'm mechanically inclined, but I do have lots of ability in math.

B: Then maybe engineering would be a good fit.

A: Maybe. But **I've also been told that** I have a good intuitive sense.

B: **I don't think you can go wrong.** Either choice sounds great. Besides, you could always switch subjects down the road if you want.

B ▶4:17 **RHYTHM AND INTONATION** Listen again and repeat. Then practice the conversation with a partner.

C CONVERSATION ACTIVATOR Role-play a similar conversation in which you discuss your talents and strengths. Use the Vocabulary and emphatic stress with the auxiliary <u>do</u>. Start like this: *Guess what?* Be sure to change roles and then partners. OPTION: Tell your classmates about your partner's talents and strengths.

DON'T STOP!

- Provide more details about your talents and strengths.
- Provide more details about what you would like to be able to do.
- Talk about the talents and strengths of people you know.
- Say as much as you can.

RECYCLE THIS LANGUAGE
• I'm [good at / not so good at] ___ .
• I wish I [were / weren't] ___ .
• I wish I [had / hadn't] ___ .
• If only I [could / would] ___ .
• My gut feeling is ___ .
• It's now or never.

GOAL Describe what makes someone a "genius"

A **LISTENING WARM-UP** **DISCUSSION** In your opinion, is there a difference between describing someone as intelligent and calling him or her a genius? Explain.

B ▶ 4:20 **LISTEN FOR MAIN IDEAS** Listen to Part 1 of a lecture on human intelligence. Choose the speaker's main point.

1 Everyone with a high IQ is a genius.

2 Not everyone agrees about how to define genius.

3 A genius is someone with an IQ score over 145.

C ▶ 4:21 **LISTEN TO INFER** Listen to Part 1 again and pay attention to the opposing arguments. Check the one statement that best supports the argument that a high IQ score doesn't determine whether one is a genius.

☐ Albert Einstein had an IQ of 160 and had many impressive achievements.

☐ Most average people have an IQ score that can range from about 85 to 115.

☐ Most people agree that the composer Beethoven was probably a genius.

☐ The 1,500 gifted children in Terman's study had IQs of 140 or more.

☐ None of the people with high IQs in Terman's research had any notable achievements.

Albert Einstein, physicist and Nobel Prize winner

D ▶ 4:22 **LISTEN FOR SUPPORTING DETAILS** Now listen to Part 2 of the lecture. Write at least two arguments the lecturer mentions to support each theory.

in favor of a genetic theory	in favor of an environmental theory
1	1
2	2

E ▶ 4:23 **VOCABULARY** **ADJECTIVES THAT DESCRIBE ASPECTS OF INTELLIGENCE** Read and listen. Then listen again and repeat.

Srinivasa Ramanujan, mathematician

talented	having a natural ability to do something very well
perceptive / observant	good at noticing what people are thinking or feeling
inventive / imaginative	good at thinking of new and interesting ideas; creative
witty	able to use humor intelligently; good at using words for others' enjoyment
curious / inquisitive	having the desire to learn about new things
open-minded	willing to consider new ideas; not close-minded
persistent	willing to continue trying something in spite of difficulty

F **VOCABULARY PRACTICE** Choose the best adjective to complete each description.

1 Comedian Helen Hong's success can be attributed to her (persistent / perceptive) and very funny observations of everyday life.

2 Colombian novelist Gabriel García Márquez was one of the world's most (inventive / inquisitive) writers. He was famous for creating fantastic stories and images.

3 Mark Twain, whose real name was Samuel Clemens, was a (persistent / witty) writer and storyteller. His accounts of his world travels still make people laugh.

4 Jane Goodall is known for her ground-breaking work studying chimpanzees. Her (inquisitive / inventive) mind helped her consider questions about chimp behavior that had never been explained before.

5 Korean film director Bong Joon-ho has been praised as one of the most (talented / persistent) artists in recent years for his excellent imaginative movies.

G **PERSONALIZE THE VOCABULARY**   With a partner, use each adjective to describe a person you know or have heard or read about.

❝I'd call my nephew Sam very imaginative. He's only eight years old, but he entertains us with fantastic stories all the time. ❞

❝I think the Chinese pianist Yuja Wang is really talented. Her interpretations of pieces by classical composers are very perceptive. I always feel like I'm hearing something new when she plays. ❞

NOW YOU CAN   **Describe what makes someone a "genius"**

A **NOTEPADDING**   Identify someone—famous or not—who you would consider to be extremely intelligent or even a genius. In what ways would you describe aspects of this person's intelligence? Write notes about the person on your notepad. Use the Vocabulary from this lesson and from page 88.

Who is it? *my uncle Morris*

List his or her abilities and traits of intelligence:

- *really sharp, has an incredible head for figures and a way with words*

- *a little eccentric, extremely perceptive*

Who is it?

List his or her abilities and traits of intelligence:

Do you think this person's intelligence came from the environment or his or her genes? Why?

Would you call this person a genius? Why or why not?

B **DISCUSSION**   With a partner, discuss the person you wrote about on your notepad. Explain where, in your opinion, the person got his or her intelligence from, providing examples from the person's background and environment.

RECYCLE THIS LANGUAGE		
· difficult	· energetic	· outgoing
· easygoing	· gifted	· passionate
· eccentric	· hardworking	· serious
· egotistical	· moody	· sharp

OPTIONAL WRITING   Write about the person you discussed. Support your view that this person has above-average intelligence with examples.

A WRITING SKILL   Study the rules.

In formal writing, connecting words and phrases are commonly used to clarify relationships between ideas. Use the following to focus on causes or results.

Causes

Use one of these phrases to focus on a cause.

Due to ___ ,	Because of ___ ,
As a result of ___ ,	As a consequence of ___ ,

┌────── cause ──────┐
As a result of a high workload, our work area may get messy.

                                    ┌────────── cause ──────────┐
It may be difficult to stay on task **due to constant interruptions by colleagues.**

Results

Begin a sentence with one of these words or phrases to focus on a result.

As a result,	Consequently,
As a consequence,	Therefore,

                                        ┌────────── result ──────────┐
Colleagues may constantly interrupt your work. **Consequently,** it may be difficult to stay focused.

B PRACTICE   In the Writing Model, underline five sentences with connecting words or phrases that clarify causes and results. Then, on a separate sheet of paper, rewrite each sentence twice, using a different connecting word or phrase.

C APPLY THE WRITING SKILL   Write a three-paragraph essay about the challenges of staying focused while trying to complete a task. Use the "outline" below as a guide. Be sure to include connecting words and phrases to signal causes and results.

Paragraph 1
Describe the things that make staying focused difficult. Summarize the causes.

Paragraph 2
Describe the results of not being able to stay focused.

Paragraph 3
Suggest some ways one might overcome the challenges and become more focused on completing a task.

SELF-CHECK

☐ Did my paragraphs follow the content and sequence suggested in Exercise C?

☐ Did I use connecting phrases to focus on causes?

☐ Did I introduce sentences with connecting words or phrases to focus on results?

WRITING MODEL

When trying to focus on a task, you may discover there are numerous distractions that can keep you from completing your work. You may find it difficult to stay focused due to your staying up late the night before. As a consequence of frequent interruptions by colleagues, you may feel like you are always starting the task all over again. Anything can distract you from a task, and the results can be harmful.

Not being able to stay focused can affect your work in negative ways. You may not be able to produce a report for your manager by the time he or she expects it. Consequently, your manager may wonder whether or not he or she can count on you to deliver what you have promised. Your colleagues may depend on you to finish a task, but you are unable to do it. As a result, you risk your reputation at work.

If you are having difficulty completing a task, it is important that you take actions that help you stay on target. Because of frequent interruptions, you may have to close your office door or ask your colleagues not to disturb you. If you are suffering from a lack of sleep, you may have to take a break and grab a cup of coffee before you start. As long as you make an effort, you should be able to get back on target.

A ▶ 4:24 **Listen to a teacher talking to parents about their children. After each conversation, check the statement that best describes each child's talents and abilities. Listen again if necessary.**

1 Liza
- ☐ has a head for figures.
- ☐ has a way with words.
- ☐ has a knack for languages.

2 Ben
- ☐ is mechanically inclined.
- ☐ has a good intuitive sense.
- ☐ is good with his hands.

3 Stella
- ☐ has a knack for languages.
- ☐ has an ear for music.
- ☐ has a way with words.

4 Steven
- ☐ has a good intuitive sense.
- ☐ has a way with people.
- ☐ has a head for figures.

5 Sophie
- ☐ has an ear for music.
- ☐ has a way with words.
- ☐ has a knack for languages.

6 Dan
- ☐ has an eye for detail.
- ☐ has a good intuitive sense.
- ☐ is mechanically inclined.

7 Karen
- ☐ has a way with words.
- ☐ has an eye for detail.
- ☐ is good with her hands.

8 Sam
- ☐ has a head for figures.
- ☐ has a good intuitive sense.
- ☐ has a way with people.

B **Find and correct the six errors in using the subjunctive.**

Dr. Howard Gardner believes that genius is determined by the environment. Therefore, he recommends that children are provided with greater educational opportunities in order to develop their talents. Other psychologists, however, think that genius is inherited. According to them, if a child is born with talent, it is crucial that he or she receives special attention.

According to Dr. Gardner, people have different kinds of intelligence, and there are different ways of learning suitable for each intelligence type. Consequently, he proposes that a teacher uses learning strategies that are best suited to a particular student's type of intelligence. For example, Gardner suggests that a student studies alone if he or she has intrapersonal intelligence. If, on the other hand, the learner has interpersonal intelligence, it is important that the student works in a team.

Because characteristics such as motivation and emotional control are considered important in the workplace, more and more employers insist that a job applicant takes an EQ test to help the manager make hiring decisions.

C **Write the correct letter to complete each definition.**

1 A person who is witty ....

2 A person who is inquisitive ....

3 A person who is inventive ....

4 A person who is very perceptive ....

5 A person who is really sharp ....

6 A person who is open-minded ....

7 A person who is persistent ....

a keeps trying, even when things are tough

b is probably comfortable with people who disagree with his or her opinions

c is comfortable relying on gut feelings to make decisions

d enjoys learning about new things

e entertains friends with funny and intelligent stories

f has a talent for creating new ideas

g is smart and quick at figuring things out

TEST-TAKING SKILLS BOOSTER p. 158

Web Project: Emotional Intelligence
www.english.com/summit3e

What Lies Ahead?

COMMUNICATION GOALS
1 Discuss the feasibility of future technologies
2 Evaluate applications of innovative technologie
3 Discuss how to protect our future environmen
4 Examine future social and demographic trend

A **FRAME YOUR IDEAS** Complete the survey.

WILL IT COME TRUE?

Which of the following predictions do you think will come true by the end of the 21st century? Which are just too wild to come true? Check your responses on a scale of probability from unlikely to definitely. Add your own predictions if you have any.

MEDICINE AND HEALTH

1 The majority of surgeries will be performed by robots.

UNLIKELY   POSSIBLY   LIKELY   DEFINITELY

2 Scientists will have discovered effective cures for cancer and heart disease.

UNLIKELY   POSSIBLY   LIKELY   DEFINITELY

3 Eyeglasses will have become obsolete.

UNLIKELY   POSSIBLY   LIKELY   DEFINITELY

4 Most people will live to be over 100 years old.

UNLIKELY   POSSIBLY   LIKELY   DEFINITELY

5 Your prediction:

_____

_____

TRANSPORTATION

1 Petroleum will no longer be used as an energy source.

UNLIKELY   POSSIBLY   LIKELY   DEFINITELY

2 Most vehicles will not require a driver.

UNLIKELY   POSSIBLY   LIKELY   DEFINITELY

3 Commercial space travel will be available to anyone who can afford it.

UNLIKELY   POSSIBLY   LIKELY   DEFINITELY

4 Digital technology will have replaced the traditional paper passport.

UNLIKELY   POSSIBLY   LIKELY   DEFINITELY

5 Your prediction:

_____

_____

HOME AND WORK

1 People will be living on another planet.

UNLIKELY   POSSIBLY   LIKELY   DEFINITELY

2 Agricultural work will no longer require human workers.

UNLIKELY   POSSIBLY   LIKELY   DEFINITELY

3 The majority of homes will have a robot to do household chores.

UNLIKELY   POSSIBLY   LIKELY   DEFINITELY

4 Most people will work and make a living from their own homes.

UNLIKELY   POSSIBLY   LIKELY   DEFINITELY

5 Your prediction:

_____

_____

B **PAIR WORK** Compare your responses and explain the reasons for your answers. What made you decide whether a prediction in the survey was just too wild or whether it might actually come true?

C ▶ 5:02 **SPOTLIGHT**   Read and listen to a conversation about the uses for a new technology. Notice the spotlighted language.

Lena: I just read that packages are going to be delivered to people's homes using drones. Is that cool or what?

Nate: Well, it's shocking how much they seem to **be catching on**. You never know where you're going to see them next.

Lena: That's true.

Nate: Unfortunately, no matter how you look at it, it's just going to **open a can of worms**.

Lena: Really? In what way?

Nate: I just think the more drones, the more unintended consequences.

Lena: Sorry. I don't get it. Drones seem pretty harmless to me.

Nate: Well, think about it. Imagine thousands of drones flying all over the place. Who's going to make sure they don't crash into each other? **Before you know it**, somebody's going to get hurt.

Lena: **Come to think of it**, I read last week that some have already crashed into cars … and even people!

Nate: And from what I understand, that's **just scratching the surface**. It gets worse. Pilots have been reporting sightings of drones during takeoffs and landings.

Lena: Wow! That's no joke!

Nate: Exactly. At some point there's going to be a collision—**it isn't a question of if but when**.

Lena: Well, this is definitely a case in which **the bad outweighs the good**.

D **UNDERSTAND IDIOMS AND EXPRESSIONS**   Find these idioms and expressions in Spotlight. Complete each explanation by writing the correct letter.

.... **1** Say something "is catching on" to …

.... **2** Say "It'll open a can of worms" to …

.... **3** Say "Before you know it" to …

.... **4** Say "Come to think of it" to …

.... **5** Say "It's just scratching the surface" to …

.... **6** Say "It isn't a question of if but when" to …

.... **7** Say "The bad outweighs the good" to …

a indicate you suddenly realize or remember something.

b suggest that it provides only a small piece of the total picture.

c suggest that something is going to happen soon.

d suggest that there are more disadvantages than advantages.

e indicate that something is becoming popular.

f state that something is certain to happen.

g express concern about possible problems in the future.

E **DISCUSSION**

1 What are some current uses for drones you're familiar with? What are some possible uses in the future? Use your own ideas.

2 Summarize Nate's concerns about the consequences of an increased use of drone technology. Do you agree with his concerns, or do you think drones are harmless? Explain your views.

SPEAKING   Which of the predictions from page 98 do you think would open a can of worms? Use expressions from Spotlight. Explain your reasons.

❝ I'd worry that digital passports might open a can of worms. Before you know it, criminals or terrorists would be stealing people's identities. ❞

❝ If robots do household chores, people will get lazy! Let's face it … the bad outweighs the good. ❞

GOAL Discuss the feasibility of future technologies

A ▶ 5:03 **GRAMMAR SPOTLIGHT** Read the article and notice the spotlighted grammar.

ENVISIONING THE **FUTURE**

In the 1960s, only large institutions, such as banks, corporations, and the military, had computers. They were expensive, slow, and very large—requiring a special air-conditioned room—and access to them was limited to only a few people. In the 1970s, computer prices came down and then small businesses began to use them. Nevertheless, in 1977, the CEO and founder of Digital Equipment, Kenneth Olsen, predicted that computers would never be used in the home.

> Computers are never going to be used in the home.

Kenneth Olsen

In the early 1980s, Steve Jobs and Bill Gates introduced the personal computer—the Macintosh and the IBM PC, respectively—which made computing at home possible. In 1983, Jobs gave a speech about the future, in which he predicted that, for most people, a great deal of time would be spent interacting with personal computers. He also predicted that, within ten years, computers in the office and at home would be connected so people would be able to use them to communicate.

> In the future, a great amount of our time is going to be spent interacting with our personal computers. And in ten years, home and office computers will have been connected to each other so people can use them to communicate and keep in touch.

Steve Jobs

In 1999, Gates predicted that small devices would be carried around by everyone so that they could get instant information and stay in touch with others. He also claimed that, by the early 21st century, Internet communities would have been formed, based on one's interests or to connect with friends and family.

> Small devices will be carried around by everyone to get information and stay in touch. And in the early 21st century, Internet communities will have been formed.

Bill Gates

B **DISCUSSION** Which of the twentieth century predictions about computers have come true? In what ways?

> PRONUNCIATION BOOSTER p. 149
> Reading aloud

C **GRAMMAR** THE PASSIVE VOICE: THE FUTURE, THE FUTURE AS SEEN FROM THE PAST, AND THE FUTURE PERFECT

Passive voice statements about the future: <u>will be</u> (or <u>be going to be</u>) + a past participle

   In the future, appliances **will be linked** to each other and to the Internet as well.
   In coming years, our lives **are going to be made** easier by new home technologies.

Passive voice statements about the future as seen from the past: <u>would be</u> (or <u>was / were going to be</u>) + a past participle

   Jobs and Gates predicted that computers **would be used** by millions of people at home.
   Olsen thought that computers **were** never **going to be purchased** for use at home.

Passive voice statements in the future perfect: <u>will have been</u> (or <u>be going to have been</u>) + a past participle

   By 2050, commercial airplanes **will have been redesigned** to be much quieter.
   In a few decades, the TV set **is going to have been made** obsolete.

> **Note:** The passive voice is often used when discussing science and technology.
>
> Use a <u>by</u> phrase when it's important to name the agent (the performer of the action).
>
>   Our lives will be improved **by technology**.

> GRAMMAR BOOSTER p. 141
> When to use the passive voice

DIGITAL MORE EXERCISES

D **GRAMMAR PRACTICE** Look at the predictions for a possible moon habitat. On a separate sheet of paper, change the statements from active to passive voice.

A Moon Habitat of the Future
- Rockets will transport lightweight building materials from Earth.
- The construction materials will protect inhabitants from radiation and solar winds.
- The Sun will supply power for electricity.
- Technicians will use robots to mine the Moon's natural resources.
- More than one country will share the costs.

E **GRAMMAR PRACTICE** Read the predictions and complete the statements, putting each prediction into the future perfect in the passive voice. Then, with a partner, discuss the possible downsides to each prediction—or whether you think the good outweighs the bad. Explain your views.

Prediction 1: High-speed maglev trains will replace air travel as the preferred means of transportation.
Maglev trains, which use magnets and can travel at up to 580 kilometers per hour, are already preferred over air travel for many key European routes such as London-Paris. Will they replace even more routes? Some say it's not a question of if, but when.

By the end of the 21st century, ...
....
....
....

Prediction 2: Alternative methods of identification will replace passports for international travel.
Customs agencies will require cards with electronic chips that can be easily swiped, or perhaps they will rely on fingerprints to identify travelers. No matter how you look at it, stamping a passport is a thing of the past.

By the second half of the 21st century, ...
....
....
....

Prediction 3: Drone technology will make airplane pilots obsolete. Would you fly on a pilotless plane? You may not have a choice. Once drones have become widely accepted, who needs pilots?

By 2075, ...
....
....
....

Prediction 4: A private company will construct a space hotel with a spectacular view of the Earth.
Got money to burn? How about a vacation in outer space? After decades of experience maintaining the International Space Station, a space hotel is the next logical step. Only the wealthy will be able to afford it. But what a view!

By the year 2100, ...
....
....
....

NOW YOU CAN Discuss the feasibility of future technologies

A **NOTEPADDING** On your notepad, write at least three wild predictions about the future, using the passive voice of <u>will</u> or <u>be going to</u> or the future perfect.

In the future	By 2050	By the end of the century

 DIGITAL VIDEO

B **DISCUSSION ACTIVATOR** What future technologies do you think will catch on? Are you optimistic or pessimistic about the use of science and technology in the future? Why? Use the predictions on your notepad. Say as much as you can.

101

GOAL Evaluate applications of innovative technologies

DIGITAL STRATEGIES

A ▶ 5:04 **VOCABULARY** **INNOVATIVE TECHNOLOGIES**
Read and listen. Then listen again and repeat.

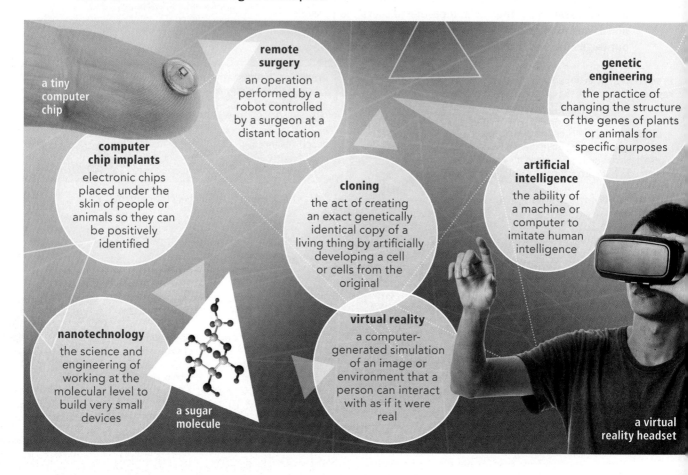

a tiny computer chip

remote surgery
an operation performed by a robot controlled by a surgeon at a distant location

genetic engineering
the practice of changing the structure of the genes of plants or animals for specific purposes

computer chip implants
electronic chips placed under the skin of people or animals so they can be positively identified

cloning
the act of creating an exact genetically identical copy of a living thing by artificially developing a cell or cells from the original

artificial intelligence
the ability of a machine or computer to imitate human intelligence

nanotechnology
the science and engineering of working at the molecular level to build very small devices

a sugar molecule

virtual reality
a computer-generated simulation of an image or environment that a person can interact with as if it were real

a virtual reality headset

B ▶ 5:05 **LISTEN TO ACTIVATE VOCABULARY** Listen to conversations about applications of innovative technologies. After each, write the technology they're discussing, using the Vocabulary. Listen again and describe how the technology is being used.

	Innovative technology	How it's being used
1		
2		
3		
4		
5		
6		
7		

C ▶ 5:06 **LISTEN TO IDENTIFY POINT OF VIEW** Listen again. Circle whether the speaker is for or against each technology. Then, with a partner, explain each answer.

1 He's (for / against) it.

2 She's (for / against) it.

3 She's (for / against) it.

4 She's (for / against) it.

5 She's (for / against) it.

6 He's (for / against) it.

7 They're (for / against) it.

D GRAMMAR   THE PASSIVE VOICE IN UNREAL CONDITIONAL SENTENCES

The present unreal conditional

If effective cancer-fighting drugs **were developed** through genetic engineering, that technology **might be** more widely **accepted**.

> **Note:** The passive voice can be used in one or both clauses in an unreal conditional sentence.

The past unreal conditional

If antibiotics **had been discovered** earlier, the death toll from pneumonia might have been lower.
If the computer chip **hadn't been developed**, smartphones and tablets **would** never **have been invented**.

E GRAMMAR PRACTICE   Read the true statements. Then, on a separate sheet of paper, write unreal conditional statements with your own opinions, using the passive voice in if clauses.

Example: Operations aren't always performed by robots.

1 Chips aren't implanted in our bodies at birth.

2 Genetic engineering isn't prohibited.

> *If operations were always performed by robots, there would never be any surgical errors.*

3 Human cloning isn't permitted.

4 The airplane was invented in the early 1900s.

5 The dinosaur was made extinct.

6 Written language was developed thousands of years ago.

7 Electricity was discovered in the seventeenth century.

F PAIR WORK   Compare the seven opinions you wrote for Exercise E with a partner. Explain your opinions, providing examples.

NOW YOU CAN   Evaluate applications of innovative technologies

A ▶ 5:07 CONVERSATION SPOTLIGHT   Read and listen. Notice the spotlighted conversation strategies.

A: I've been thinking about it and this human cloning sounds like a good thing to me. **For one thing**, couples who weren't able to have kids would finally be able to.

B: **Well, if you ask me**, I think it's pretty scary.

A: Really? What makes you say that?

B: It's a slippery slope. **I mean**, before you know it, someone's going to use it for something bad, like making designer babies.

A: **I see your point**. But people have always worried about new things.

> ▶ 5:09 **Ways to express a concern about consequences**
> It's a slippery slope.
> It's like opening a can of worms.
> It's like playing with fire.
> It's like opening Pandora's box.

B ▶ 5:08 RHYTHM AND INTONATION   Listen again and repeat. Then practice the conversation with a partner.

C NOTEPADDING   On your notepad, write an innovative technology that exists in the present and one you'd like to see in the future. Write one important application or use of each technology.

Present technology	Application
genetic engineering	create disease-resistant seeds

Present technology	Application

Future technology	Application

D CONVERSATION ACTIVATOR   Create a conversation similar to the one in Exercise A, using one of the innovative technologies on your notepad. Start like this: *I've been thinking about it and ___ sounds ___ to me.* Be sure to change roles and then partners.

DON'T STOP!

- Provide more reasons you are for or against a particular technology.
- Evaluate applications of other technologies.
- Say as much as you can.

GOAL Discuss how to protect our future environment

A READING WARM-UP   What threats today will affect the environment of the future?

DIGITAL STRATEGIES **B** ▶ 5:10 **READING**   Read the article. What environmental threats does it address?

ORDINARY PEOPLE WITH BIG IDEAS— PRACTICAL STRATEGIES TO PROTECT THE EARTH

All around the globe, there are quiet hard-working people doing what it takes to protect our environment. They are changing minds and attitudes and demonstrating that ordinary people can make a difference.

HERE ARE TWO INSPIRING STORIES.

▲ California's huge redwoods

REVERSING GLOBAL WARMING ONE TREE AT A TIME

Old-growth forests play a key role in keeping the earth's atmosphere clean. In these forests, most trees are over 100 years old—many even 1,000 years or more. Unfortunately, after centuries of logging, development, pollution, and disease, about 98% of these forests have been destroyed, contributing to global warming. However, David Milarch and Leslie Lee, co-founders of a U.S. environmental group called Archangel Ancient Tree Archive, are doing something to turn things around.

Tree experts told him it couldn't be done, but Milarch and his sons, Jared and Jake, have been cloning trees from among more than sixty of the world's best-known, oldest, and largest species, creating exact copies of these ancient trees. These include California's huge redwoods and sequoias (some are 2,000 to 3,000 years old!), Ireland's imposing ancient oaks, and Lebanon's historic cedars.

Milarch and Lee want people to buy their cloned trees and plant them—millions of them. The trees then can produce oxygen, which is good for the environment; absorb carbon, which is bad for the environment; and in some cases even be used in the manufacture of much-needed medications. Eventually Milarch hopes to clone over 200 different species and return some of the old-growth forests we have lost through human activity. "I'm a workaholic. I work 16 hours a day, 365 days a year," says Milarch. When asked how he wants to be remembered, he says, "He caused us to stop and think and take action."

◀ David Milarch

PROTECTING WILDLIFE BY CHANGING MINDS

Cambodia is experiencing a rise in population and unregulated development, which has been destructive for the environment. More and more inexperienced farmers are taking up agriculture near the edges of Cambodia's forests. Unfortunately for Cambodia's wild Asian elephants, this has caused a conflict with humans. As elephants search for food, they have destroyed farms. In turn, poor and uneducated farmers have killed the elephants to protect their livelihoods. By the early years of this century, the population of elephants had fallen dramatically from about 2,000 to 500.

Tuy Sereivathana (known as Vathana) grew up in the countryside, where he learned to respect both nature and the elephants. After choosing to study forestry, he committed himself to conservation of Cambodia's natural resources. Eventually, working for the country's national parks, he focused his attention on understanding the problems the Cambodian farmers were facing.

Vathana realized that the farmers needed to know more about the elephants' migration patterns and how to apply practical solutions for protecting their farms. He helped them build electric fences. He taught them how to use hot chili peppers and other native plants that elephants don't like in order to discourage the animals from eating their crops. He convinced the farmers to organize themselves to guard their farms at night, using fireworks and other loud noises to scare the elephants off. He also helped them improve their farming techniques so they would not have to go farther into the elephants' habitat.

Vathana worked to establish community schools to increase literacy and provide wildlife conservation education. And he helped redevelop the cultural pride Cambodians have long had in their elephants. The farmers are now the elephants' greatest protectors. Vathana is now known as "Uncle Elephant." There has not been a single killing of a wild Asian elephant since 2005.

Tuy Sereivathana ▶

C **UNDERSTAND MEANING FROM CONTEXT**   Find the underlined words and phrases in the article. Then complete each statement. Explain your answers.

1 If you <u>turn things around</u>, it means you are making something ....

   a worse   **b** better   **c** stay the same

2 <u>Redwoods</u>, <u>sequoias</u>, <u>oaks</u>, and <u>cedars</u> are types of ....

   a clones   **b** trees   **c** medications

3 When trees <u>absorb</u> carbon, it is actually ....

   a good for the environment   **b** bad for the environment   **c** causing global warming

4 <u>Unregulated</u> development is ....

   a good for the environment   **b** bad for the environment   **c** good for farmers

5 If something falls <u>dramatically</u>, it means it ....

   a hasn't changed   **b** has changed a little   **c** has changed a lot

6 A <u>native</u> plant is one that has ...... another place.

   a been brought in from   **b** not been brought in from   **c** been cloned at

D **DRAW CONCLUSIONS**   In small groups, discuss the following questions. Find information in the article to support your answers.

1 What do old-growth forests do that's beneficial to this planet?

2 Why does Milarch focus specifically on cloning ancient tree species?

3 What were the benefits of Vathana's decision to work closely with the farmers?

4 What might be a long-term benefit of teaching wildlife conservation in Cambodian schools?

NOW YOU CAN | Discuss how to protect our future environment

A **FRAME YOUR IDEAS**   Complete the questionnaire and compare answers with a partner. Which of you appears to be the more environmentally conscious?

HOW ENVIRONMENTALLY CONSCIOUS ARE YOU?

Check off the things that you do—and add some more.

TO REDUCE POLLUTION

☐ I use energy-efficient appliances.

☐ I use energy-efficient compact fluorescent light bulbs or LED bulbs instead of incandescent bulbs.

☐ I walk as often as I can or take public transportation instead of driving.

☐ And I ...

TO PRESERVE WATER

☐ I place a brick in the toilet's reservoir tank.

☐ I take showers instead of baths whenever I can.

☐ I turn off the water while I brush my teeth or shave.

☐ And I ...

TO AVOID WASTING FOOD

☐ I use leftovers to create new meals.

☐ I compost food to use in the garden.

☐ I only buy as much food as I need.

☐ And I ...

B **PRESENTATION**   In a small group, choose one of the three categories in the questionnaire. Develop an action plan and present it to your class.

GOAL Examine future social and demographic trends

DIGITAL STRATEGIES **A** ▶ 5:11 **LISTENING WARM-UP** **VOCABULARY** **DESCRIBING SOCIAL AND DEMOGRAPHIC TRENDS**
Read and listen. Then listen again and repeat.

dem·o·graph·ic /ˈdɛməˈgræfɪk ◀ / n. **1 demographics** [plural] information about the people who live in a particular area, such as how many people there are or what types of people there are: *the changing demographics of Southern California* **2** [singular] a part of the population that is considered as a group, especially for the purpose of advertising or trying to sell goods: *Cable television is focused on the 18 to 49 demographic (= people who are 18 to 49 years old).*

rate /reɪt/ n. [C] **1** the number of times something happens, or the number of examples of something within a certain period: **[+ of]** *The rate of new HIV infections has risen again.* | **at a rate of sth** *Refugees were crossing the border at a rate of 1,000 a day.* | *The unemployment rate rose to 6.5% in February.* | *The city still has a high crime rate.*

sta·tis·tic / stəˈtɪstɪk / n. **1 statistics** [plural] a collection of numbers which represents facts or measurements: *official crime statistics* **2** [singular] a single number which represents a fact or measurement: *a depressing statistic.* / **a statistic that** *I read a statistic that over 10,000 Americans a day turn 50.*

trend / trɛnd / n. [C] a general tendency in the way a situation is changing or developing: *Social and economic trends affect everyone.* | **[+ in]** *The researchers studied trends in drug use among teenagers.* | **[+ toward]** *There is a worldwide trend toward smaller families.* | *Davis is hoping to* **reverse the trend** *of rising taxes (= make a trend go in the opposite direction).* | **a current / recent / present trend** *If current trends continue, tourism will increase by 10%.* | *There is a growing trend in the country toward buying organic foods.*

Excerpted from *Longman Advanced American Dictionary*

B **APPLY THE VOCABULARY** Write whether each example is <u>a demographic</u>, <u>a statistic</u>, <u>a rate</u>, or <u>a trend</u>. Explain your choices.

1 An increasing number of customers are choosing to stream movies at home rather than go to a theater to see them. ....

2 The social media site *Pinterest* is used by more women than men. ....

3 The number of births per family is lower in wealthier developed countries. ....

4 Fifteen percent of seniors in the U.S. are living in poverty. ....

DIGITAL STRATEGIES **C** ▶ 5:12 **LISTEN TO ACTIVATE VOCABULARY** Listen to people discussing demographic trends. Write the number of the conversation next to the rate (or rates) they are discussing. (One rate is not discussed at all.) Then circle whether the rate is rising or falling. Listen again to check your work.

▶ 5:13 **Listen and repeat.**
literacy = ability to read and write
fertility = ability to reproduce
mortality = death

☐ **crime rate**	(rising / falling)	☐ **literacy rate**	(rising / falling)
☐ **birthrate**	(rising / falling)	☐ **fertility rate**	(rising / falling)
☐ **mortality rate**	(rising / falling)	☐ **divorce rate**	(rising / falling)

D ▶ 5:14 **LISTEN TO CONFIRM CONTENT**
Now listen to a lecture predicting world population trends. Read the list of subjects. Then listen again and check the subjects that were mentioned.

☐ a decrease in world population
☐ unemployment rates
☐ life expectancy
☐ marriage trends
☐ divorce rates
☐ fertility rates
☐ mortality rates
☐ literacy rates

1 According to the U.N. report, if the world's fertility and infant mortality rates don't decrease, the world's population will increase by (less than / more than / approximately) 30% by 2040.

2 By 2050, the country with the second highest population in the world will be (China / India / the U.S.).

3 By 2050, populations in Japan, Russia, and Germany will be (higher / lower / the same).

4 Worldwide, the number of older people will be (the same as / lower than / higher than) the number of younger people.

5 In 2050, the total number of children in the continent of Africa will be (lower than / higher than / the same as) the total number in the rest of the world.

F **SUPPORT AN OPINION**   Which of the statistics about future world demographics concern you the most? Explain your reasons.

NOW YOU CAN   Examine future social and demographic trends

A **NOTEPADDING**   With a partner, examine some social and demographic trends in your country that concern you. Write them on your notepad. Decide which of the trends present the greatest challenges.

Marriage and divorce: *Fewer and fewer people are getting married.*

Marriage and divorce:
Government and politics:
The news media:
Education:
Family life:
Seniors:
Other:

B **DISCUSSION**   Discuss with your partner some possible solutions to meet the challenges you identified in Exercise A. Then present your ideas to your class and invite your classmates to share their own ideas.

DIGITAL
SPEAKING
BOOSTER

OPTIONAL WRITING   On a separate sheet of paper, write three paragraphs about one of the trends you discussed. In the first paragraph, explain the problem and give examples. In the second paragraph, explain the challenges. In the third, suggest some solutions.

A **WRITING SKILL** Study the rules.

A formal essay should include a thesis statement somewhere in the introductory paragraph. The thesis statement presents an argument or point of view. The supporting paragraphs should be organized to provide reasons, facts, or examples to support your thesis. The outline on the left indicates an effective way to organize a formal essay to support a thesis.

To write a thesis statement ...
• Narrow the topic to one or two main ideas.
• Make sure it expresses your point of view.

I. Introductory paragraph (with a thesis statement)

Your introduction should include a thesis statement—a sentence that presents your argument. The remaining sentences should suggest what specific topics the essay will include.

II. Supporting paragraphs (with supporting examples)

Each supporting paragraph should include a topic sentence that supports your thesis statement, followed by supporting examples.

III. Concluding paragraph (with a summary)

Your conclusion should summarize the main points of the entire essay and restate your thesis.

WRITING MODEL

In twenty years, cars will probably all be powe by alternative energy sources, and they will be equipped with new technologies that take over many of the responsibilities of driving. There are good reasons to be optimistic about these prediction since car manufacturers are already moving in this direction. Undoubtedly, new technological advances will make these developments almost certain to become reality.

Many experts predict that most cars of the future will be powered by electricity. Unlike today's electric cars, which have limitations that keep them from being as popular as gas-powered vehicles, electric cars in the future will be much easier to maintain. For example, ..

Advances in computing will also make human drivers obsolete. Cars of the future will have advanced technological features, some of which are being applied today, that do the thinking for the driver. First of all, car will all be able to park themselves. In addition, ...

Based on the direction the car industry is heading today, we can confidently predict some of the key advances we will see in the cars of the future. The industry is already offering both electric and hybrid vehicles, and it has introduced some "driverless" features, so we can expect much more development in those two areas.

B **PRACTICE** Essay tests often suggest topics in the form of a question. On a separate sheet of paper, write a thesis statement for each topic. Be sure to apply the guidelines above.

1 How can we end poverty?

> *Poverty can only be ended if the government makes that one of its highest priorities.*

2 Are hospitals and medical care getting too expensive?

3 How are fast-food restaurants changing the way people eat?

4 What are the best ways to avoid becoming a crime victim?

5 Do video games affect young people in negative ways?

6 What are the best places to go on vacation?

C **APPLY THE WRITING SKILL**

Write a four- or five-paragraph essay on one of the suggested topics. State your argument in the introduction with a thesis statement. Support your argument with two or three supporting paragraphs. In your conclusion, restate your argument and summarize the main points.

Suggested topics
• Transportation in the future
• Communication in the future
• Health care in the future
• Education in the future
• The future of the earth
• Your own idea: ....

SELF-CHECK

☐ Does my thesis statement clearly state my argument?

☐ Does each of my supporting paragraphs have a topic sentence that supports my point of view?

☐ Does my conclusion summarize my main points and restate my thesis?

A ▶ 5:16 **Listen to the conversations. Complete each statement with the technology the people are referring to and circle the word or phrase that reflects each person's opinion.**

1 He's (skeptical / excited) about ....

2 She (doesn't think / thinks) .... is a great idea.

3 He's (skeptical / excited) about ....

4 He's (bothered / not bothered) by ....

B **Write statements, using the underlined idioms in your statements.**

> I'm certain that home delivery of restaurant meals using drones will catch on someday.

1 something you think is going to <u>catch on</u> in the future

....

2 something that would be like <u>opening a can of worms</u>

....

3 a situation in which someone <u>turned things around</u>

....

C **Complete the paragraph with words and phrases from the list. Make any necessary changes.**

trend	statistics	mortality rate	birthrate	population growth	demographic

.... indicate that there are over 6 billion people in the world, with an increase of a
(1)
million people each year. This .... is not a result of an increased .... In fact, the
(2)   (3)
worldwide .... is for women to have fewer children. This increase in population is mainly the
(4)
result of a decrease in the child .... with more children living to adulthood. People are living
(5)
much longer lives. When the first humans walked the earth, the average person lived only to the age of

twenty. Today, the senior .... is rapidly increasing in size, especially in developing countries.
(6)

D **Rewrite each of the following sentences in the passive voice. Do not include a <u>by</u> phrase.**

1 In two years, engineers will have designed a new factory.

....

2 Engineers are going to equip the factory with air filters.

....

3 Workers will recycle paper, metal, and plastic.

....

4 They're going to treat waste before they release it into rivers.

....

5 New technologies are going to reduce energy demands by 50 percent.

....

6 Pipes will collect rainwater, and they will transport it to tanks.

....

7 Pipes will also carry excess heat from one building to another.

....

TEST-TAKING SKILLS BOOSTER p. 159

Web Project: Animal Conservation
www.english.com/summit3e

COMMUNICATION GOALS
1 React to news about global issues
2 Describe the impact of foreign imports
3 Discuss the pros and cons of globalization
4 Suggest ways to avoid culture shock

PREVIEW

A FRAME YOUR IDEAS Complete the quiz.

GET THE FACTS!

Test your knowledge about English in today's world.

1 English is NOT an official language in ....
- ☐ Canada
- ☐ South Africa
- ☐ the U.S. or the U.K.
- ☐ Nigeria

2 There are approximately ...... people in the world who can speak English.
- ☐ 1.5 million
- ☐ 1 billion
- ☐ 10 million
- ☐ 1.5 billion

3 Approximately ...... of the world's population are native speakers of English.
- ☐ 5%
- ☐ 20%
- ☐ 10%
- ☐ 30%

4 There are about ...... million people who speak English as a foreign language.
- ☐ 6
- ☐ 70
- ☐ 10
- ☐ 700

5 ...... is the country with the most English speakers.
- ☐ China
- ☐ the U.K.
- ☐ the U.S.
- ☐ India

6 Approximately ...... million children are studying English in China.
- ☐ 1
- ☐ 100
- ☐ 10
- ☐ 500

7 In France, there are approximately ...... post-secondary degree programs offered in English.
- ☐ 20
- ☐ 300
- ☐ 100
- ☐ 700

8 Approximately ...... of the information stored in the world's computers is in English.
- ☐ 10%
- ☐ 50%
- ☐ 30%
- ☐ 80%

9 Approximately ...... new words are added to the English language each year.
- ☐ 10
- ☐ 400
- ☐ 100
- ☐ 4,000

ANSWERS 1. Neither the U.S. nor the U.K. has an official language. English is the main language in those countries by history and tradition. Both English and French are official languages in Canada. South Africa has 11 official languages, including English. Nigeria has only one—English. **2.** According to some estimates, 1.5 billion people in the world speak English—that's one out of every six people, and the number is growing. **3.** There are about 380 million native speakers of English, a little over 5% of the world's population. **4.** There are anywhere from 700 million to one billion people who have learned—or are currently learning—English—English in addition to their own language. **5.** The U.S. has the most English speakers, native and non-native, at 298 million. Ranking highest after that are India (125 million), Pakistan (92 million), Nigeria (82 million), and the U.K. (64 million). But there are more English speakers in Asia than in the U.S., U.K., and Canada combined. **6.** 100 million children are learning English in China. That's more than the population of the U.K. **7.** French universities offer 700 degree programs in English. France attracts more foreign university students than any other non-English-speaking country. **8.** Eighty percent of the world's digitally stored information is in English, but the proportion of information stored in other languages is growing. **9.** Four thousand new words are added yearly, making English the language with the largest vocabulary in the world.

B PAIR WORK Did any of the answers surprise you? Explain why or why not.

C ▶ 5:17 **SPOTLIGHT** Read and listen to a conversation about someone's plans. Notice the spotlighted language.

Paul: Are you still thinking about going overseas for a master's program?

Hyo: Actually, I've been checking out engineering programs in both Los Angeles and London. But I guess I'm still **on the fence**—I haven't made up my mind which I prefer.

Paul: Well, why don't you check out ECE Paris? They have a top-notch engineering program.

Hyo: Are you serious? **It's bad enough that** I wouldn't be able to handle the coursework in French. But between the culture shock and not being able to use my English there, I'd feel like **a fish out of water**.

Paul: Well, believe it or not, they're offering their engineering program in English.

Hyo: In Paris? You**'re pulling my leg**, right?

Paul: No way! I kid you not.

Hyo: No offense, Paul, but isn't France like the *last* place you'd expect anyone to be offering classes in English? I heard the French government actually tried to keep all university instruction in French.

Paul: That was probably true some years ago, but I guess they decided it was **a losing battle**. Apparently universities *had* to offer classes in English in order to continue attracting students from abroad—like you!

Hyo: **How do you like that!** I guess **money talks** ...

Paul: At any rate, I'm sure you'd fall in love with my hometown. And besides, you could pick up some French while you're there.

D **UNDERSTAND IDIOMS AND EXPRESSIONS 1** Circle the correct word or phrase to complete each explanation.

1 If you're "on the fence," you haven't (made a decision / changed your plans).
2 If you feel like "a fish out of water," everything seems (exciting / unfamiliar) to you.
3 If someone "pulls your leg," he or she is (being serious / only kidding).
4 If something is "a losing battle," it's probably best to (give up / keep trying).

E **UNDERSTAND IDIOMS AND EXPRESSIONS 2** Complete each statement with the correct lettered explanation.

1 When Hyo says "It's bad enough that ... ," he's ......
2 When Hyo says "How do you like that!" he's ......
3 When Hyo says "Money talks," he's ......

a emphasizing a problem.
b offering an explanation.
c expressing surprise.

F **THINK AND EXPLAIN** With a partner, discuss the questions and explain your answers.

1 Why does Paul suggest that Hyo study in Paris? What would be the benefits?
2 What explanation is Hyo offering when he says, "I guess money talks ... "?

SPEAKING Read the opinions. Explain why you agree or disagree. Discuss how you think you will use English in your own lives.

If you want to be considered proficient in English, you should never make mistakes, and you should sound like a native speaker.

These days, speaking English is like knowing how to use a computer—you need both skills for a better job.

The most important goal in learning English is to be able to function socially and communicate successfully.

I think the only real reason to learn English is to travel or work overseas. If those aren't your plans, it's not particularly useful.

GOAL React to news about global issues

DIGITAL STRATEGIES

A ▶ 5:18 **VOCABULARY** PHRASAL VERBS* TO DISCUSS ISSUES AND PROBLEMS
Read and listen. Then listen again and repeat.

bring about make something happen; to cause to occur or exist

We need to agree about what the problems are if we expect to bring about changes.

carry out achieve or accomplish a plan or project

It's time the president carried out her promise to vaccinate all school-age children.

come down with become sick with a particular illness

More than a million people have come down with the mosquito-borne virus.

come up with think of something such as an idea or a plan

Municipal governments need to come up with a new approach to reduce homelessness.

go without live without something you need or usually have

No one should have to go without clean drinking water.

lay off end the employment of workers due to economic conditions

The company recently announced they were laying off two hundred employees.

put up with accept a bad situation or person without complaining

For many years, people in small villages have put up with inadequate roads.

run out of use up all of something and not have any more of it

If we're not careful, we'll run out of oil before alternative energy sources have been found.

wipe out end or destroy something completely so it no longer exists

Ten years ago, few people could read or write in this country, but now illiteracy has been nearly wiped out.

*****Remember:** Phrasal verbs contain a verb and one or more particles that together have their own meaning. Particles are most commonly prepositions and adverbs.

B ▶ 5:19 **LISTEN TO ACTIVATE VOCABULARY**
Listen to the conversations about global issues. After each conversation, complete the statement.

Conversation 1 The refugees will ....
   a go without food soon   **b** come down with something   **c** carry out a plan

Conversation 2 Lots of people have been ....
   a putting up with vaccinations   **b** coming down with the disease   **c** coming up with a plan

Conversation 3 The government hasn't ....
   a carried out the president's plan yet   **b** run out of supplies   **c** laid off anyone

C **VOCABULARY PRACTICE 1**   Circle the correct phrasal verb to complete each sentence.

1 Because of increased availability of the flu vaccine this year, very few people have (come up with / come down with) the disease.

2 Many believe that it is essential to (carry out / wipe out) terrorist organizations.

3 A decrease in donations to humanitarian organizations will force thousands to (go without / put up with) the food they need to survive.

4 The oil company claims it will have to (bring about / lay off) one-third of its workforce on three continents.

5 Attempts to help the earthquake survivors were successful until the United Nations relief agencies (ran out of / laid off) supplies.

6 Change was (brought about / run out of) through the work of volunteers.

7 City residents will have to (put up with / lay off) the presence of foreign military troops.

8 Hopefully someone will (put up with / come up with) a plan to reverse global warming.

9 The actress's volunteer work is helping human rights groups (wipe out / carry out) their mission to help war refugees settle into their new lives overseas.

UN HUNGER RELIEF

The UN World Food Program (WFP) is the world's largest humanitarian organization dealing with the issue of hunger and how to **(1)** _____ malnutrition, especially among children. Its goal is to **(2)** _____ improvements in food production and to **(3)** _____ its plans to provide food assistance to millions of people in seventy-five countries around the world. Whenever people are forced to **(4)** _____ food because of droughts or war, the WFP tries to help. Under these famine conditions, people are unable to feed their families and they are forced to **(5)** _____ being hungry on a daily basis. Making the situation worse, many of its malnourished victims are more vulnerable due to weakened immune systems and may **(6)** _____ contagious diseases. It is the WFP's responsibility to make sure that relief groups do not **(7)** _____ essential emergency supplies. In the 1990s, the WFP **(8)** _____ a successful money-saving idea for responding more quickly to emergencies using small teams of experts to assess the situation before committing full-scale resources.

NOW YOU CAN React to news about global issues

A ▶5:20 **CONVERSATION SPOTLIGHT** Read and listen. Notice the spotlighted conversation strategies.

A: **Can you believe** what's been happening in Northern Africa?
B: You mean the drought? It's just horrendous.
A: Awful. **But on the bright side**, people have been donating tons of money for relief. I find that really inspiring.
B: Totally. **It just goes to show you** how powerful social media can be.
A: But on the other hand, it's appalling how much corruption there is.
B: **Well, that's another story** … It makes you feel hopeless, doesn't it?
A: Yeah. **You'd think** someone could do something to stop it.

B ▶5:21 **RHYTHM AND INTONATION** Listen again and repeat. Then practice the conversation with a partner.

C **CONVERSATION ACTIVATOR** Create a similar conversation, using one of these news stories. Start like this: *Can you believe …?* Be sure to change roles and then partners.

IGITAL VIDEO
IGITAL PEAKING BOOSTER

DON'T STOP!

- Describe the news in more detail.
- Say more about your response to the news.
- Say as much as you can.

RECYCLE THIS LANGUAGE
· It's a slippery slope. / It's like opening a can of worms.
· The good outweighs the bad.
· Before you know it, …
· Don't get me wrong.
· What [bothers / concerns] me is …

PRONUNCIATION BOOSTER p. 150
Intonation of tag questions

Celebrities Raise Millions for Famine Victims

The North African drought has forced four million people to go without adequate food and water. Some of the world's best-known celebrities have come up with a plan to use social media to raise money for humanitarian efforts.

TERRORIST ATTACK ATTRACTS INTERNATIONAL ACTIVISM

After hearing about the bombing in Beirut that left forty dead, Colombian businesswoman Leticia Gómez decided to use her connections to carry out a campaign to help the families of the victims. Gómez lost her husband to a bombing in Bogotá in the eighties and knows firsthand how devastating terrorism can be.

STEPS TAKEN TO AVOID EPIDEMIC IN THE PHILIPPINES

Hundreds have come down with an unknown illness in Mindanao, causing authorities to restrict both domestic and international travel. Doctors Without Borders has agreed to send a team to investigate.

China Carries Out Conference Recommendations

The government has come up with a long-term plan for reducing factory emissions in China, where urban residents have had to put up with high levels of pollution with its resulting health consequences.

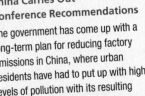

GOAL Describe the impact of foreign imports

A ▶ 5:22 **GRAMMAR SPOTLIGHT** Read the people's opinions and notice the spotlighted grammar.

Gina Falcone, U.S.

"I do a lot of business travel, and it's amazing how you **run into** so many foreign things—for example, a Starbucks coffee shop from the U.S. in Bogotá, Colombia. Hello! Colombia already *has* great coffee! Recently I **came across** the Japanese clothing chain UNIQLO in New York. Almost everywhere you go now, you can **count on** being able to find a restaurant that serves Indian, Thai, Japanese, or Mexican food. In any city, people can **take up** tai chi from China, yoga from India, or capoeira from Brazil. Seems like every place is becoming the same."

Mehmet Demirkahn, Turkey

"Every time my kids **turn** their tablets or smartphones **on**, I worry. I'm concerned about the influence foreign games and websites will have on them. I don't particularly **care for** some of the values they teach. But my kids are crazy about their gadgets. If I were to ask my kids to **give** them **up**, I'd never hear the end of it! They can't imagine **going without** them. I've been trying to **talk** them **into** doing other things, but it's a bit of a losing battle, I'm afraid. I guess I just have to learn to **put up with** their devices."

"Nowadays you see foreign brands everywhere you look. Before you **throw** the packaging from a food item **away**, read the label—it might say it comes from the U.S. or Mexico. **Try** a blouse **on** at the store—nine times out of ten, it'll have come from China, Vietnam, or Bangladesh. Or **try** some new product **out** at the electronics store and there's a good chance it's imported from Korea. Some people worry that imports will **wipe out** our own local products. But the way I see it, we can enjoy foreign things and still value and appreciate our own."

Sophia Freitas, Brazil

B **ACTIVATE PRIOR KNOWLEDGE** Would people in your country express opinions similar to the ones in the Grammar Spotlight? Explain.

GRAMMAR BOOSTER	p. 142
Phrasal verbs: expansion	

DIGITAL INDUCTIVE ACTIVITY

C **GRAMMAR** **SEPARABILITY OF TRANSITIVE PHRASAL VERBS**

Remember: Transitive verbs are verbs that can have direct objects. Transitive *phrasal verbs* can be separable or inseparable.

Separable

A direct object noun can generally come after or before the particle of a separable phrasal verb.

Check out their website. OR **Check** their website **out**.

However, a direct object pronoun must come before the particle.

Check it **out**. NOT ~~Check out it~~.

Inseparable

A direct object noun or pronoun always comes after the particle of an inseparable phrasal verb.

They **cater to** younger customers. NOT ~~They cater younger customers to~~.

I **ran into** her at the park. NOT ~~I ran her into the park~~.

Be careful! Some phrasal verbs are always separated. The particle never comes directly after the verb.

I **talked** them **into** contributing money. NOT ~~I talked into them~~ contributing money.

Separable

bring about	give up	wipe out	turn on / off
carry out	lay off	try on	throw away
figure out	pick up	try out	
find out	take up		

Inseparable

care for	come down with	put up with
cater to	count on	run into
come across	go after	run out of
come up with	go without	

Always separated

do (sth.) over   start (sth.) over   talk (s.o.) into (sth.)

For a complete list with definitions, see pp. 124–126.

D UNDERSTAND THE GRAMMAR Which phrasal verbs in the Grammar Spotlight are separable? Rewrite each of those sentences, with the direct object in a different position.

E GRAMMAR PRACTICE Complete the sentences, using a form of the phrasal verb with the pronoun it or them. Pay attention to whether or not the phrasal verb is separable.

1 Yoga is really popular. Even my great-grandmother has (take up) ....
2 Although only a small minority of the population can understand English, English words are visible everywhere. You often (come across) .... on signs, product ads, and even clothing.
3 The workers who have been laid off have highly developed skills. It may not be so easy to (talk into) .... learning all new skills.
4 Because young adults are tech-savvy and have tremendous economic power, many Internet companies have developed marketing campaigns that (go after) .... exclusively.
5 At the International Trade Fair, foreign companies offer samples of their products. People can (try out) .... before deciding whether to buy them.
6 Once a foreign brand has become popular, it's hard to for people to (give up) ....

NOW YOU CAN Describe the impact of foreign imports

A NOTEPADDING On your notepad, list examples of imports from foreign countries or cultures that you come across regularly.

Foods:	Entertainment:
Music:	Vehicles:
Products for your home:	Sports and games:
Clothing / personal accessories:	Other:

B DISCUSSION ACTIVATOR Have the imports you listed on your notepad had a positive or negative impact? Explain, providing examples. Say as much as you can.

DIGITAL VIDEO

C PAIR WORK Read the statements about foreign imports. Discuss whether you agree or disagree with them, providing examples. Use phrasal verbs when you can.

There's a growing trend towards **giving up** local traditions and replacing them with imported things. But I question the wisdom of just **throwing away** our long-held traditions like that.

Young people **are picking up** values from foreign media, so culturally we're becoming more and more alike. I wonder what would happen if we lose the things that make us different.

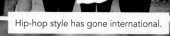
Hip-hop style has gone international.

Chinese restaurants are popular in Peru.

People dance salsa in Japan.

115

A **READING WARM-UP** Do people in your country generally view increased international trade positively or negatively? Explain.

DIGITAL STRATEGIES **B** ▶ 5:23 **READING** Read the article on the effects of globalization. Do you share its concerns? Why or why not?

GLOBALIZATION

DOES IT LIVE UP TO EXPECTATIONS?

Globalization and increased free trade in this century have brought the world's cultures and economies together. We depend more than ever on each other to thrive. Along with advances in technology and communication, we have become more interconnected as people, corporations, and brands travel across borders more easily than ever before. Nevertheless, most people agree that the social, economic, environmental, and political changes caused by globalization have brought both positive and negative results.

THE PROMISE

Advocates of globalization believed it would make the world smaller and bring diverse people and cultures closer. They were right. People in cities on opposite sides of the world can easily get in touch by phone, e-mail, instant messaging, or teleconference. Ease of communication and freer global trade have resulted in improved efficiency and competition. Companies are able to respond quickly to economic changes and market demands. As cooperation—and competition—have increased, new technologies are shared and developed.

Many countries have experienced improvements in their standard of living. For many people, an economic benefit of increased imports and exports has been an increase in income. Consumers enjoy a wider variety of choices when they shop. And as a result of increased prosperity, it has been possible to increase investment in new infrastructure—roads, bridges, and buildings.

THE OTHER SIDE OF THE STORY

While globalization promised to benefit everyone with an increase in worldwide wealth and prosperity, critics cite evidence of a widening gap between rich and poor. In developed countries, such as the U.S., corporations outsource both manufacturing and customer service jobs to developing countries in Asia and Latin America, where labor costs are lower. For example, India's economy benefits from the establishment of call centers, where English-speaking staff provide 24/7 technical support by phone and Internet to customers all over the world. Their technicians can do so at about one-fifth the cost of what companies would have to pay workers in developed economies for the same service. So while Indian workers benefit, workers in other countries complain that their jobs have been taken away.

Critics of globalization argue that free trade has made the world so competitive that criminal activities have flourished. For example, child labor, which is illegal in many countries, has increased to fill manufacturing demands for gold and textiles. Recent news reports have exposed the use of slavery on merchant ships, where workers are mistreated and forced to work without receiving any wages. Economic opportunities made possible by globalization have also encouraged corruption, in which government officials agree to ignore unethical business practices. Some argue that a global economy has helped drug cartels and terrorists move people and materials across borders more easily.

As internationally recognized fast-food chains have expanded throughout the world, critics complain that the fried foods and sugary drinks they serve have been replacing healthier local eating traditions and increasing the consumption of unhealthy junk food among young people. Some argue that globalization has led to a homogenization of culture in general—that local traditions are quickly being replaced by imported ones.

Even worse, without international regulation, developing countries such as Nigeria are becoming dumping grounds for hazardous industrial waste. In other countries such as China, increased development has brought with it uncontrolled pollution, reaching sky-high levels that threaten public health and contribute to global warming. And globalization has also been a strain on the environment as more and more natural resources are tapped for manufacturing.

Obviously, we can't turn back the clock on globalization. And we know that those countries that have embraced it have experienced increased economic growth. However, it is also clear that there are challenges to overcome despite globalization's many benefits.

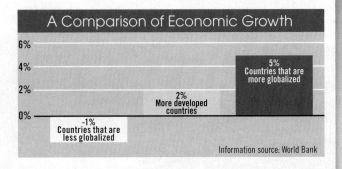

A Comparison of Economic Growth

- 6%
- 4%
- 2%
- 0%
- -1% Countries that are less globalized
- 2% More developed countries
- 5% Countries that are more globalized

Information source: World Bank

C **UNDERSTAND MEANING FROM CONTEXT** Match each word from the article with its definition.

...... **1** globalization   **a** money put into a company or business to encourage growth and make a profit
...... **2** exports   **b** the act of making it easier to produce products and trade them internationally
...... **3** investment   **c** products sold to other countries
...... **4** infrastructure   **d** use other countries' services rather than one's own
...... **5** prosperity   **e** financial success
...... **6** outsource   **f** things that make transport of products efficient
...... **7** homogenization   **g** causing things to become more similar

D **IDENTIFY SUPPORTING IDEAS** Answer the questions, supporting your answers with information in the article.

1 What are some specific examples of both improved and decreased standard of living, caused by globalization?

2 What are some areas where businesses or governments could make investments that might address some of the challenges of globalization?

3 What are two examples given that describe workers who lose or are denied income?

4 What examples are given to illustrate the pros and cons of availability of foreign imports?

E **INTERPRET INFORMATION IN A GRAPH** According to the graph, who benefits the most from globalization? Who benefits the least? Explain.

Increased imports and exports have led to economic growth in many countries.

NOW YOU CAN Discuss the pros and cons of globalization

A **NOTEPADDING** On your notepad, write the names of international companies that have had an economic, social, environmental, or political impact in your country.

B **DISCUSSION** What benefits or problems have these companies brought to your country? Overall, do you think globalization is good or bad for your country? Explain.

have had an economic impact	have had a social impact
have had an environmental impact	**have had a political impact**

> 66 Toyota's investment in local factories has been good for the country. It provides employment and pays good wages, raising the standard of living for a lot of people. 99

Some well-known international companies

Apple	Nestle
British Petroleum (BP)	Samsung
IKEA	The Gap

GOAL Suggest ways to avoid culture shock

A **LISTENING WARM-UP** **DISCUSSION** Read the definition of culture shock. What feelings of anxiety or confusion might someone experiencing culture shock have? Give some examples of situations that might cause culture shock.

> **culture shock** *n.* the feelings of anxiety and confusion that people have when they visit a foreign country and experience a new culture for the first time

DIGITAL STRATEGIES

B ▶ 5:24 **LISTEN TO SUMMARIZE** Listen to the radio program. In your own words, summarize the characteristics of each of the four stages of culture shock.

Susan Cahill

Stage one:

Stage two:

Berat Yildiz

Stage three:

Stage four:

C ▶ 5:25 **LISTEN TO CONFIRM INFORMATION** Listen again. Check the correct answers, according to the program.

1 Which of the following disorienting experiences did not cause negative feelings for Berat in London?
☐ the traffic   ☐ the money   ☐ the weather   ☐ the food   ☐ people's behavior

2 Which symptoms of culture shock did Berat experience?
☐ headaches   ☐ disappointment   ☐ sadness   ☐ lack of sleep   ☐ loneliness

3 Which of the following were mentioned as signs that Berat was in the final stage of culture shock?
☐ dressing right for cold weather   ☐ making friends   ☐ calling home
☐ appreciating cultural differences   ☐ finding Turkish restaurants

▶ 5:26 **LISTEN TO UNDERSTAND MEANING FROM CONTEXT** Listen to the excerpts from the radio program. Use the context to help you complete each statement.

1 When Susan Cahill says that Berat Yildiz knows about culture shock "firsthand," she means he knows it from ....

   a experience   **b** his studies   **c** his culture

2 When Berat says he felt like he was "in heaven," he means he felt ....

   a worried   **b** shocked   **c** great

3 When Berat says he found some things "disorienting," he means he felt ....

   a comfortable   **b** confused   **c** angry

4 When Susan says there is "a light at the end of the tunnel," she means that things will ....

   a get better   **b** get worse   **c** stay the same

5 When Berat says he got his "feet back on the ground," he means he stopped ....

   a feeling confused   **b** feeling happy   **c** thinking about Turkish food

---

NOW YOU CAN Suggest ways to avoid culture shock

A **NOTEPADDING** Check the aspects of your culture you think might cause culture shock to a visitor to your country. Add others. Then choose the three from the list you think are the most difficult to deal with. Write notes suggesting ways to avoid the negative effects of each one.

1 ....

- [ ] local dishes
- [ ] eating and drinking customs
- [ ] the way people act at work
- [ ] greeting customs
- [ ] the way people socialize
- [ ] local holidays
- [ ] sense of humor
- [ ] formality and informality
- [ ] traditional leisure activities
- [ ] apologizing
- [ ] the do's and don'ts for clothing
- [ ] treatment of children
- [ ] customs for keeping pets
- [ ] how people shop
- [ ] public transportation
- [ ] driving or walking in traffic
- [ ] other ....
....

2 ....

3 ....

Try it. It's delicious!

B **PAIR WORK** Tell your partner why you chose the three topics. Describe your ideas for helping a visitor avoid the worst symptoms of culture shock.

OPTIONAL WRITING Write an article for visitors to this country, suggesting ways to be prepared for culture shock and avoid the most negative symptoms.

A **WRITING SKILL** Study the rules.

When writing a rebuttal to an opposing argument or point of view, support your ideas by presenting them one by one. Following is an outline to organize your essay effectively.

I. Introductory paragraph

Explain the issue and summarize the opposing point of view. Include a thesis statement stating your own point of view.

II. Supporting paragraphs

In each paragraph, state one aspect of the point of view you are rebutting. Use details and examples to support your own point of view.

III. Concluding paragraph

Summarize your point of view.

Expressions for introducing others' arguments:

According to [Bill Gates], …
[Some people] say / think / feel that …
[Many experts] argue / believe that …
It may be true that …
It has been argued / said / pointed out that …

Transitions and subordinating conjunctions for your rebuttal:

However, …   All the same, …
Nevertheless, …   In spite of this, …
Even so, …

WRITING MODEL

I There are many people who feel that globalization is causing more problems than it is solving. **Nevertheless, it is my opinion that, overall, globalization has contributed to a better world.** We need to accept it as a reality of today's world and do what we can to make it work for everyone.

II **Critics argue that** many countries have not benefited as much as others. **All the same**, we shouldn't assume that all countries will benefit at the same speed or time. It is a fact that free trade has been a tremendous benefit to nations in East and Southeast Asia. Their economies have grown substantially in this century and their standard of living has greatly improved. There's no reason to believe this won't happen elsewhere, for example in West Africa.

It has been argued that globalization has increased the spread of disease, worsened pollution, and made it easier for criminals to cross borders. **In spite of this**, I believe that free trade and increased international cooperation have also made it easier for nations to fight these problems more effectively. With attention, these are problems that can be solved.

III Clearly, globalization has areas for improvement. **Even so, I believe the advantages of globalization far outweigh the problems.**

B **PRACTICE** On a separate sheet of paper, write five sentences that introduce arguments for or against globalization. Paraphrase—using your own words—arguments from the article on page 116. Use the expressions for introducing others' arguments.

> People who defend globalization argue that the standard of living has improved in many countries.

C **PRACTICE** Now write statements to rebut each of the arguments opposing globalization that you introduced in Exercise B. Use the suggested transitions and subordinating conjunctions.

> Even so, it can be argued that too many countries have not enjoyed the benefits.

D **APPLY THE WRITING SKILL** Write an essay of at least four paragraphs in which you present your point of view about globalization and rebut the opposing point of view.

SELF-CHECK

☐ Did I summarize the point of view I want to rebut in my introduction?

☐ Did I rebut each argument by providing details and examples to support my own?

☐ Did I use the suggested expressions and transitions or subordinating conjunctions to link my ideas clearly?

☐ Did I summarize my point of view in my conclusion?

A ▶ 5:27 Listen to three news reports on globalization-related topics. After each report, complete each statement so that it is true, according to the information presented in the report. Listen again if necessary.

Report 1: WorldWatch is concerned that improving living standards in developing countries …… .

    a will cause natural resources to run out
    b will bring about an increase in prices for luxury goods

Report 2: According to the report, most people think that globalization …… .

    a is causing social and economic problems
    b is not causing social and economic problems

Report 3: The chairman of Starbucks believes that his customers appreciate …… .

    a the convenience of having Starbucks stores in so many locations
    b both the coffee and the experience of being in the store

B Complete each phrasal verb with the correct particle. Use the phrasal verb list on pages 124–126 if necessary.

1 The island voted to carry ………… the governor's plan to find foreign investors to develop the island into a tourist resort.

2 Technological advances such as social media have brought ………… great changes in the way people communicate.

3 The president is determined to figure ………… how to increase trade with other countries without causing a rise in unemployment.

4 Clerks were handing ………… free cups of Colombian coffee at a Tokyo supermarket in the hopes that it would catch ………… with local shoppers.

5 I picked ………… a little French when I visited my uncle in Paris last summer, but I wouldn't say that I'm fluent.

6 A lot of families have been putting ………… large purchases because they're afraid they may soon be out of work if the economy doesn't improve.

7 To be honest, I'm worried that the cultures of wealthier nations will one day wipe ………… the traditional cultures of poorer nations.

8 Asian martial arts have become really popular recently. I know so many people who have taken ………… tae kwon do, karate, or judo.

C On a separate sheet of paper, rewrite each sentence, replacing the underlined phrase with the pronoun *it* or *them*.
1 We should check out <u>that new French film</u>. | *We should check it out.*
2 We're trying to go without <u>imported products</u>.
3 They voted to give up <u>protections against imports</u>.
4 Falling profits forced the factory owner to lay off <u>the workers</u>.
5 Just turn on <u>your TV</u> and you'll see news and films from all over the world.
6 I talked <u>my friends</u> into buying tickets for the U2 concert.
7 Manufacturers of luxury products cater to <u>wealthier consumers</u>.
8 If you take up <u>karate</u>, you'll probably be in great shape.

TEST-TAKING SKILLS BOOSTER p. 160

Web Project: Global Warming
www.english.com/summit3e

Reference Charts

IRREGULAR VERBS

base form	simple past	past participle	base form	simple past	past participle
be	was / were	been	mean	meant	meant
beat	beat	beaten	meet	met	met
become	became	become	mistake	mistook	mistaken
begin	began	begun	pay	paid	paid
bend	bent	bent	put	put	put
bet	bet	bet	quit	quit	quit
bite	bit	bitten	read /rid/	read /rɛd/	read /rɛd/
bleed	bled	bled	ride	rode	ridden
blow	blew	blown	ring	rang	rung
break	broke	broken	rise	rose	risen
breed	bred	bred	run	ran	run
bring	brought	brought	say	said	said
build	built	built	see	saw	seen
burn	burned / burnt	burned / burnt	sell	sold	sold
burst	burst	burst	send	sent	sent
buy	bought	bought	set	set	set
catch	caught	caught	shake	shook	shaken
choose	chose	chosen	shed	shed	shed
come	came	come	shine	shone	shone
cost	cost	cost	shoot	shot	shot
creep	crept	crept	show	showed	shown
cut	cut	cut	shrink	shrank	shrunk
deal	dealt	dealt	shut	shut	shut
dig	dug	dug	sing	sang	sung
do	did	done	sink	sank	sunk
draw	drew	drawn	sit	sat	sat
dream	dreamed / dreamt	dreamed / dreamt	sleep	slept	slept
drink	drank	drunk	slide	slid	slid
drive	drove	driven	smell	smelled / smelt	smelled / smelt
eat	ate	eaten	speak	spoke	spoken
fall	fell	fallen	speed	sped / speeded	sped / speeded
feed	fed	fed	spell	spelled / spelt	spelled / spelt
feel	felt	felt	spend	spent	spent
fight	fought	fought	spill	spilled / spilt	spilled / spilt
find	found	found	spin	spun	spun
fit	fit	fit	spit	spit / spat	spit / spat
fly	flew	flown	spoil	spoiled / spoilt	spoiled / spoilt
forbid	forbade	forbidden	spread	spread	spread
forget	forgot	forgotten	spring	sprang / sprung	sprang / sprung
forgive	forgave	forgiven	stand	stood	stood
freeze	froze	frozen	steal	stole	stolen
get	got	gotten	stick	stuck	stuck
give	gave	given	sting	stung	stung
go	went	gone	stink	stank / stunk	stunk
grow	grew	grown	strike	struck	struck / stricken
hang	hung	hung	string	strung	strung
have	had	had	swear	swore	sworn
hear	heard	heard	sweep	swept	swept
hide	hid	hidden	swim	swam	swum
hit	hit	hit	swing	swung	swung
hold	held	held	take	took	taken
hurt	hurt	hurt	teach	taught	taught
keep	kept	kept	tear	tore	torn
know	knew	known	tell	told	told
lay	laid	laid	think	thought	thought
lead	led	led	throw	threw	thrown
leap	leaped / leapt	leaped / leapt	understand	understood	understood
learn	learned / learnt	learned / learnt	upset	upset	upset
leave	left	left	wake	woke / waked	woken / waked
lend	lent	lent	wear	wore	worn
let	let	let	weave	wove	woven
lie	lay	lain	weep	wept	wept
light	lit	lit	win	won	won
lose	lost	lost	wind	wound	wound
make	made	made	write	wrote	written

VERBS FOLLOWED BY A GERUND

acknowledge	celebrate	discontinue	escape	imagine	postpone	recall	risk
admit	complete	discuss	explain	justify	practice	recommend	suggest
advise	consider	dislike	feel like	keep	prevent	report	support
appreciate	delay	don't mind	finish	mention	prohibit	resent	tolerate
avoid	deny	endure	forgive	mind	propose	resist	undestand
can't help	detest	enjoy	give up	miss	quit		

EXPRESSIONS THAT CAN BE FOLLOWED BY A GERUND

be excited about	be committed to	make an excuse for	look forward to
be worried about	be opposed to	have a reason for	blame [someone or something] for
be responsible for	be used to	believe in	forgive [someone or something] for
be interested in	complain about	participate in	thank [someone or something] for
be accused of	dream about / of	succeed in	keep [someone or something] from
be capable of	talk about / of	take advantage of	prevent [someone or something] from
be tired of	think about / of	take care of	stop [someone or something] from
be accustomed to	apologize for	insist on	

VERBS FOLLOWED DIRECTLY BY AN INFINITIVE

afford	can't wait	demand	hope	need	pretend	swear	want
agree	care	deserve	hurry	neglect	promise	threaten	wish
appear	choose	expect	intend	offer	refuse	volunteer	would like
arrange	claim	fail	learn	pay	request	wait	yearn
ask	consent	grow	manage	plan	seem		
attempt	decide	hesitate	mean	prepare	struggle		

VERBS FOLLOWED BY AN OBJECT BEFORE AN INFINITIVE*

advise	cause	enable	force	need*	persuade	require	want*
allow	challenge	encourage	hire	order	promise*	teach	warn
ask*	choose*	expect*	instruct	pay*	remind	tell	wish*
beg	convince	forbid	invite	permit	request*	urge	would like*

* In the active voice, these verbs can be followed by the infinitive without an object (example: *want to speak* or *want someone to speak*).

VERBS THAT CAN BE FOLLOWED BY A GERUND OR AN INFINITIVE

with a change in meaning		without a change in meaning				
forget	remember	begin	continue	like	prefer	try
regret	stop	can't stand	hate	love	start	

ADJECTIVES FOLLOWED BY AN INFINITIVE*

afraid	ashamed	depressed	eager	fortunate	lucky	relieved	surprised
alarmed	certain	determined	easy	glad	pleased	reluctant	touched
amazed	content	disappointed	embarrased	happy	prepared	sad	upset
angry	curious	distressed	encouraged	hesitant	proud	shocked	willing
anxious	delighted	disturbed	excited	likely	ready	sorry	

*Example: I'm willing **to accept** that.

PARTICIPIAL ADJECTIVES*

alarming	–	alarmed	embarrassing	–	embarrassed	paralyzing	–	paralyzed
amazing	–	amazed	enlightening	–	enlightened	pleasing	–	pleased
amusing	–	amused	entertaining	–	entertained	relaxing	–	relaxed
annoying	–	annoyed	exciting	–	excited	satisfying	–	satisfied
astonishing	–	astonished	exhausting	–	exhausted	shocking	–	shocked
boring	–	bored	fascinating	–	fascinated	soothing	–	soothed
confusing	–	confused	frightening	–	frightened	startling	–	startled
depressing	–	depressed	horrifying	–	horrified	stimulating	–	stimulated
disappointing	–	disappointed	inspiring	–	inspired	surprising	–	surprised
disgusting	–	disgusted	interesting	–	interested	terrifying	–	terrified
distressing	–	distressed	irritating	–	irritated	tiring	–	tired
disturbing	–	disturbed	moving	–	moved	touching	–	touched

STATIVE VERBS

amaze	contain	feel*	look like	please	smell*
appear*	cost	forget	look*	possess	sound
appreciate	desire	hate	love	prefer	suppose
astonish	dislike	have*	matter	realize	surprise
be*	doubt	hear	mean	recognize	taste*
believe	envy	imagine	mind	remember*	think*
belong	equal	include*	need	resemble	understand
care	exist	know	owe	see*	want*
consist of	fear	like	own	seem	weigh*

*These verbs also have action meanings. Example: *I see a tree.* (non-action) *I'm seeing her tomorrow.* (action)

TRANSITIVE PHRASAL VERBS

Some transitive phrasal verbs have more than one meaning. Not all are included here.

Abbreviations
s.o.	=	someone
sth.	=	something
e.g.	=	for example
inf.	=	informal

SEPARABLE

blow sth. **out**   stop a flame by blowing on it
blow sth. **up**   **1** make sth. explode **2** fill sth. with air, e.g., a balloon **3** make sth. larger, e.g., a photo
bring sth. **about**   make sth. happen
bring sth. **back**   **1** return sth. to a store **2** revive or renew sth., e.g., a custom or tradition
bring sth. **out**   **1** introduce a new product **2** make a quality more noticeable
bring s.o. **up**   raise a child
bring sth. **up**   start to talk about an issue
burn sth. **down**   burn a structure completely
call s.o. **back**   return a phone call
call sth. **off**   cancel sth.
call s.o. **up**   call s.o. on the phone
carry sth. **out**   conduct a plan
check s.o./sth. **out**   look at s.o. or sth. more closely
cheer s.o. **up**   make s.o. feel happier
clean s.o./sth. **up**   clean s.o. or sth. completely
clear sth. **up**   clarify sth.
close sth. **down**   force a business or institution to close
cover sth. **up**   **1** cover sth. completely **2** change facts to avoid responsibility
cross sth. **out**   draw a line through sth.
cut sth. **down**   make sth. fall by cutting, e.g., a tree
cut sth. **off**   **1** remove sth. by cutting **2** stop the supply of sth.
cut s.o. **off**   interrupt s.o who is speaking
dream sth. **up**   invent or think of a new idea
drink sth. **up**   drink a beverage completely
drop s.o./sth. **off**   leave s.o. or sth. somewhere
empty sth. **out**   empty sth. completely
figure s.o./sth. **out**   understand s.o. or sth. after some thought
fill s.o. **in**   tell s.o. about recent events
fill sth. **out**   complete a form
fill sth. **up**   fill a container completely
find sth. **out**   learn new information
follow sth. **through**   do everything to complete a task
get sth. **across**   help s.o. understand an idea
give sth. **away**   give sth. you do not need or want
give sth. **back**   return sth. to its owner
give sth. **out**   distribute sth.
give sth. **up**   quit doing sth.
hand sth. **in**   submit work, e.g., to a boss or a teacher
hand sth. **out**   distribute sth.
hang sth. **up**   put sth. on a hanger or hook, e.g., clothes
help s.o. **out**   assist s.o.
keep s.o./sth. **away**   cause s.o. or sth. to stay at a distance
lay s.o. **off**   fire s.o. because of economic conditions
leave sth. **on**   **1** not turn sth. off, e.g., an appliance **2** not remove sth. such as clothing or jewelry

leave sth. **out**   omit sth.
let s.o. **down**   disappoint s.o.
let s.o./sth. **in**   allow s.o. or sth. to enter
let s.o. **off**   allow s.o. to leave a bus, car, taxi, etc.
let s.o./sth. **out**   allow s.o. or sth. to leave
light sth. **up**   illuminate sth.
look s.o./sth. **over**   examine s.o. or sth.
look s.o./sth. **up**   **1** try to find s.o. **2** try to find sth. in a book, the Internet, etc.
make sth. **up**   create a fictional story
pass sth. **out**   distribute sth.
pass sth. **up**   decide not to take an opportunity
pay s.o. **off**   bribe s.o.
pay sth. **off**   pay back money one owes
pick s.o./sth. **out**   identify or choose s.o. or sth.
pick s.o. **up**   stop a vehicle so s.o. can get in
pick s.o./sth. **up**   lift s.o. or sth.
pick sth. **up**   **1** get or buy sth. from somewhere **2** learn sth. new **3** get an infectious disease
point s.o./sth. **out**   show s.o or sth. to another person
put sth. **away**   put sth. in its appropriate place
put sth. **back**   return sth. to its original place
put s.o./sth. **down**   **1** stop holding or lifting s.o. or sth. **2** insult s.o.
put sth. **off**   delay or postpone sth.
put sth. **on**   get dressed or place sth. on one's body
put sth. **together**   **1** put sth. on a wall **2** build sth.
put sth. **up**   build or erect sth.
set sth. **off**   cause sth. to explode
set sth. **up**   **1** establish a new business, organization, etc. **2** prepare equipment for use
show s.o./sth. **off**   display the best qualities of s.o. or sth.
shut sth. **off**   stop a machine or supply
straighten sth. **up**   make sth. neat
switch sth. **on**   start a machine, turn on a light, etc.
take sth. **away**   remove sth.
take sth. **back**   **1** return sth. to a store **2** accept sth. returned by another person
take sth. **down**   remove sth. that is hanging
take sth. **in**   **1** notice and remember sth. **2** make a clothing item smaller
take sth. **off**   remove clothing, jewelry, etc.
take s.o. **on**   hire s.o.
take sth. **on**   agree to do a task
take s.o. **out**   invite s.o. somewhere and pay for his/her meal, show, etc.
take sth. **up**   start doing an activity habitually
talk sth. **over**   discuss sth.
tear sth. **down**   destroy sth.

tear sth. **up**	tear sth. into small pieces	turn sth. **in**	submit a paper, application, etc.
think sth. **over**	consider sth.	turn sth. **off**	stop a machine, light, etc.
think sth. **up**	invent or think of a new idea	turn s.o. **off**	cause s.o. to lose interest (inf.)
throw sth. **away**	put sth. in the garbage	turn sth. **on**	start a machine, light, etc.
throw sth. **out**	put sth. in the garbage	turn sth. **out**	make or manufacture sth.
touch sth. **up**	improve sth. with very small changes	turn sth. **over**	turn sth. so the bottom is at the top
try sth. **on**	try clothing to see if it fits	turn sth. **up**	raise the volume, heat, etc.
try sth. **out**	use sth. to see if one likes it or if it works	use sth. **up**	use sth. completely
turn sth. **around**	**1** turn so the front is at the back **2** cause things to get better	wake s.o. **up**	cause s.o. to stop sleeping
		wipe sth. **out**	remove or destroy sth.
turn s.o./sth. **down**	reject s.o. or sth.	work sth. **out**	**1** resolve a problem **2** calculate a math problem
turn sth. **down**	lower the volume, heat, etc.	write sth. **down**	write sth. to have a record of it

ALWAYS SEPARATED

ask s.o. **over**	invite s.o. to one's home	see sth. **through**	complete a task
bring s.o./sth. **down**	remove a ruler or government from power	start sth. **over**	begin sth. again
do sth. **over**	do sth. again	talk s.o. **into** sth.	persuade s.o. to do sth.
keep sth. **on**	not remove sth. such as clothing or jewelry		

INSEPARABLE

cater to s.o.	provide what s.o. wants or needs	**go over** sth.	examine sth. carefully
carry on sth.	continue sth. another person has started	**go without** sth.	live without sth. one needs or wants
come across s.o./sth.	find s.o. or sth. unexpectedly	**run into** s.o.	meet s.o. unexpectedly
count on s.o./sth.	depend on s.o. or sth.	**run into** sth.	accidentally hit or crash into sth.
do without s.o./sth.	live without s.o. or sth. one needs or wants	**stick with** s.o.	stay close to s.o.
go after s.o./sth.	pursue s.o. or sth.	**stick with** sth.	continue doing sth. as before

INTRANSITIVE PHRASAL VERBS

Some intransitive phrasal verbs have more than one meaning. Not all are included here.

blow up	**1** explode **2** suddenly become very angry	go off	explode; make a sudden noise
break down	stop functioning	go on	continue to talk about or describe sth.
break out	start suddenly, e.g., a war, disease, or fire	go out	**1** leave a building **2** leave one's home to meet people, enjoy entertainment, etc.
burn down	burn completely		
call back	return a phone call	go up	be built
carry on	**1** continue doing sth. **2** behave in a silly or emotional way	grow up	become an adult
catch on	become popular	help out	do sth. helpful
check in	report one's arrival at an airport or hotel	hang up	end a phone call
check out	pay one's bill and leave a hotel	hold on	wait during a phone call
cheer up	become happier	keep away	stay at a distance
clear up	become better, e.g., a rash or the weather	keep on	continue
close down	stop operating, e.g., a factory or a school	keep up	go or think as fast as another person
come along	accompany s.o.	lie down	rest on a bed
come back	return	light up	**1** begin to shine brightly **2** look pleased or happy
come in	enter	make up	end an argument and reestablish a friendly relationship
come off	become unattached		
come out	**1** appear, e.g., the sun **2** be removed, e.g., a stain	pass out	become unconscious
dress up	wear more formal clothes or a costume	pay off	be worthwhile
drop in	visit unexpectedly	pick up	improve, e.g., the economy
drop out	quit a class, school, or program	play around	have fun or not be serious
eat out	eat in a restaurant	run out	no longer in supply
empty out	empty completely	show up	appear
fall off	become unattached	sign up	register
fill out	become bigger	sit down	sit
fill up	become completely full	slip up	make a mistake
find out	learn new information	stand up	rise to one's feet
follow through	continue working on sth. until it is completed	start over	begin again
fool around	have fun or not be serious	stay up	not go to bed
get ahead	make progress or succeed	straighten up	make neat
get along	to not argue	take off	depart by plane
get back	return from a place	turn in	go to bed (inf.)
get together	meet somewhere with a friend or acquaintance	turn out	have a particular result
get up	get out of bed	turn up	appear
give up	quit	wake up	stop sleeping
go along	**1** accompany s.o. **2** agree	watch out	be careful
go back	return	work out	**1** exercise **2** be resolved; end successfully

THREE-WORD PHRASAL VERBS

Some three-word phrasal verbs have more than one meaning. Not all are included here.

catch up on sth.   **1** do sth. one didn't have time to do earlier
                    2 get the most recent information
catch up with s.o.   exchange information about recent activities
check up on s.o.   make sure s.o. is OK
come away with sth.   learn sth. useful from s.o. or sth.
come down to sth.   be the most important point or idea
come down with sth.   get an illness
come up against s.o./sth.   be faced with a difficult person or situation
come up with sth.   think of an idea, plan, or solution
face up to sth.   accept an unpleasant truth
fall back on sth.   use an old idea because new ideas have failed
follow through on sth.   continue doing sth. until it is completed
get around to sth.   finally do sth.
get away with sth.   avoid the consequences of a wrong act
get back at s.o.   harm s.o. because he / she harmed you
give up on s.o.   stop hoping that s.o. will change

give up on sth.   stop trying to make sth. happen
go along with sth.   agree to do sth.
go through with sth.   do sth. difficult or painful
grow out of sth.   stop doing sth. as one becomes an adult
keep up with s.o.   stay in regular contact
look down on s.o.   think one is better than another person
look out for s.o.   protect s.o.
look up to s.o.   admire or respect s.o.
make up for sth.   do sth. to apologize
put up with s.o./sth.   accept s.o. or sth. without complaining
run out of sth.   no longer have enough of sth.
stand up for sth.   support an idea or a principle
stand up to s.o.   refuse to let s.o. treat anyone badly
team up with s.o.   do a task together
think back on s.o./sth.   think about and remember s.o. or sth.
walk out on s.o.   end a relationship with a wife, boyfriend, etc.
watch out for s.o./sth.   protect s.o. or sth.

Verb forms: overview

SUMMARY OF VERB FORMS

	Present time	Past time	Future time
Simple	**Simple present** walk / walks	**Simple past** walked	**Simple future** will walk
Continuous	**Present continuous** am walking / is walking / are walking	**Past continuous** was walking / were walking	**Future continuous** will be walking
Perfect	**Present perfect** have walked / has walked	**Past perfect** had walked	**Future perfect** will have walked
Perfect continuous	**Present perfect continuous** have been walking / has been walking	**Past perfect continuous** had been walking	**Future perfect continuous** will have been walking

SIMPLE VERB FORMS: USAGE

	Present time	Past time	Future time
Simple verb forms describe habitual actions or events that occur at a definite time.	**Simple present[1]** **Habitual action** *The department **meets** once a month to review the status of projects.* **Facts and generalizations** *The Earth **rotates** around the sun every 365 days.*	**Simple past** **Completed action that occurred at a definite time in the past** *Last year researchers **discovered** a new cancer treatment.* **Habitual action in the past[2]** *When I was young we **visited** my grandparents every week.*	**Simple future[3]** **Action that will occur at a definite time in the future** *Next year they **will offer** a course on global trade.* **Habitual action in the future** *Next month I'**ll go** to the gym three times a week.*

[1] The simple present tense can also express a future action: *Her flight arrives this evening at eight.*

[2] Used to and would also express habitual actions in the past: *When I was a child, we used to spend the summer in the mountains. In the mornings we would go hiking and in the afternoons we would swim in a nearby lake.*

[3] Be going to can also express a future action: *Next year they are going to offer a course on global trade.*

CONTINUOUS VERB FORMS: USAGE

	Present time	Past time	Future time
Continuous verb forms describe continuous actions or events that occur at a definite time.	**Present continuous*** **Action in progress now** *The business managers **are discussing** next year's budget right now.*	**Past continuous** **Action in progress at a definite time in the past** *None of the computers **were working** when I came in this morning.*	**Future continuous** **Action that will be in progress during a definite time in the future** *We'll **be listening** to the speech when you arrive.*

*The present continuous can also express a future plan: *They're getting married next month.*

PERFECT VERB FORMS: USAGE

	Present time	Past time	Future time
Perfect verb forms describe actions or events in relation to other time frames.	**Present perfect*** **Completed action that occurred at an indefinite time before the present** *She **has made** many contributions to the field.* **Recently completed action** *He **has** just **published** an article about his findings.* **Uncompleted action (action that began in the past, continues into the present, and may continue into the future)** *They **have studied** ancient cultures for many years.*	**Past perfect** **Action that occurred at some point before a definite time in the past** *By 2016, he **had started** a new business.* **Action that occurred before another past action** *They **had** already **finished** medical school when the war broke out.*	**Future perfect** **Action that will be completed by some point at a definite time in the future** *By this time next year, I **will have completed** my research.*

*Many statements in the present perfect can also be stated correctly using the simple past tense, depending on the speaker's perspective: *She made many contributions to the field.*

PERFECT CONTINUOUS VERB FORMS: USAGE

	Present time	Past time	Future time
Perfect continuous verb forms describe continuous actions or events in relation to other time frames.	**Present perfect continuous** **Uncompleted continuous action (action that began in the past, continues into the present, and may continue into the future)** *She **has been lecturing** about that topic since 2015.* **Very recently completed action** *The workers **have been protesting**. They're finished now.*	**Past perfect continuous** **Continuous action that occurred before another past action or time** *By 2015, researchers **had been seeking** a cure for AIDS for more than thirty years.*	**Future perfect continuous** **Continuous action that occurred before another action or time in the future** *When the new director takes over, I **will have been working** at this company for ten years.*

Grammar Booster

The Grammar Booster is optional. It provides more explanation and practice, as well as additional related grammar concepts and review.

Describing past actions and events: review

The past of <u>be</u> and the simple past tense
Use for completed actions and states that occurred at a specific time in the past.
> He **was** here at 10:00 and **left** this message.

The past continuous
Use for one or more recurring actions or actions in progress at a specific time in the past.
> Steven **was** always **talking** in class.
> The baby **was sleeping** and the older children **were eating** dinner when we arrived.

The present perfect
Use for actions completed at an unspecified time in the past.
> She **has** already **informed** her manager about the problem.
> New York **has been called** the capital of the world.

The past perfect
Use for an action that occurred before another past action.
> They **had** already **made** a decision when we called.

The past perfect continuous
Use for a continuing action that was occurring before another past action.
> We **had been working** for two hours when the storm began.

Used to / would
Use <u>used to</u> for past situations and habits that no longer exist. Use <u>would</u> or <u>used to</u> for actions that were repeated regularly in the past.
> When she was younger, she never **used to be** afraid of anything.
> In those days, we **would** (or **used to**) **take** a long walk every evening.

The future as seen from the past
Use <u>was</u> / <u>were going to</u> + the base form of a verb to express future plans someone had in the past.
> He **was going to start** his own business, but he couldn't get a loan.

<u>Would</u> + the base form of the verb can also express the future as seen from the past, but only after statements of knowledge or belief.
> We always thought that she **would become** an actor, but she decided to study law.

A Correct the errors with past forms.

1 Florence has been walking for several hours before she realized that her wallet was missing.

2 As a child, he was practicing the piano for hours every day. Then he stopped taking lessons.

3 "I have seen that movie last year, and I thought it was great," Frank exclaimed.

4 Before this morning, I never took a yoga class.

5 He was working on the problem all morning when he finally found the solution.

6 My husband believed he will never get married, but then he met me.

Stative verbs

Stative (non-action) verbs express mental states, emotions, perceptions, descriptions, relationships, possession, measurements, and other conditions, rather than actions. They are not usually used in continuous verb forms, even when they describe a situation in progress.
> Many people **believe** the environment should be our top priority. NOT Many people ~~are believing~~ the environment should be our top priority.
> She **has** always **understood** that job satisfaction was important. NOT She ~~has always been understanding~~ that job satisfaction was important.

Some stative verbs have both non-action and action meanings. A stative verb that has an action meaning may be used in the continuous.

Non-action meaning	Action meaning
That's ridiculous! (description)	You're being ridiculous! (act in a ridiculous way)
She has two children. (possession)	She's having another baby soon. (act of giving birth)
We think these laws are unfair. (mental state: opinion)	We're thinking of organizing a protest. (act of planning)
How does the soup taste? (perception)	I'm tasting the soup to see if it needs salt. (act of tasting)
This garden looks neglected. (description)	The child is looking at the flowers. (act of looking)

NOTE: In informal spoken English, certain stative verbs, especially <u>want</u>, <u>need</u>, and <u>have to</u>, are becoming common in the continuous:
> I'm really **wanting** a cup of good coffee. Let's go into that coffee bar.

For a complete list of stative verbs, see the Reference Charts, page 124.

B Decide if each stative verb in parentheses has an action or a non-action meaning. Then complete each sentence with the simple present tense or the present continuous.

	action	non-action	
1	☐	☐	Sara .... (doubt) that she'll get a promotion at her job.
2	☐	☐	Our skills are excellent, and we .... (have) experience in the field.
3	☐	☐	Philip .... (think) about moving abroad to teach for a year.
4	☐	☐	We .... (have) dinner at 6:00 today so we can go to the lecture on climate change.
5	☐	☐	Michael .... (not remember) where the meeting will take place.
6	☐	☐	The book .... (include) some diagrams to support the hypothesis.
7	☐	☐	The doctor .... (see) another patient now.

UNIT 2

Adjective clauses: overview

Purpose	Examples			
To identify or give additional information about a person · relative pronoun can be subject or object of clause	The physicist	{ who that	made that discovery }	teaches at my university.
	The psychologist	{ whom that who	he interviewed }	did a study about lying.
To identify or give additional information about a place or thing · relative pronoun can be subject or object of clause	The building	{ that which	is on your left }	was formerly a bank.
	The article	{ (that)* (which)*	I read yesterday }	is fascinating.
To show possession	The woman **whose house you admired** is a famous author. Paris, **whose museums hold so many treasures**, is a favorite destination for tourists.			
To modify a noun of place	The town	{ where they live in which they live that they live in which they live in	} has many beautiful parks and squares.	
To modify a noun of time	I can't remember the year	{ (when)* (that)* (in which)*	we visited them for the first time. }	

*Note: These relative pronouns may be omitted.

A Underline the best word or words to complete each sentence.

1 Parents (who / which) spend time with their children give them a sense of security.

2 The city (that / in which) my father grew up was destroyed during the war.

3 The Miller family, (whose / who) house is for sale, hopes to find a buyer soon.

4 The star of the film, (whom / which) we had hoped to meet, didn't come to the reception.

5 I will never forget the time (when / who) I told the truth and was punished for it.

6 The woman (who / which) used to teach English at my school is now the director there.

7 The *Sun Times*, (whose / which) is the best newspaper in town, recently published an article about the social uses of lying.

Grammar for Writing: adjective clauses with quantifiers

Some adjective clauses may include a quantifier that refers to a previously mentioned noun or noun phrase.
These clauses are constructed as follows: quantifier + of + relative pronoun (whom, which, or whose).

He consulted three doctors, **all of whom** confirmed the original diagnosis.

I can think of several possible explanations, **none of which** justifies their behavior.

The reporters questioned the president, **one of whose** strengths is his ability
to remain calm under pressure.

Adjective clauses that include quantifiers appear more often in written than spoken English.

Some expressions of quantity used with of		
a few of	half of	none of
all of	little of	one of
a number of	many of	several of
both of	most of	some of
each of	neither of	

B Complete each sentence with a quantifier from the box and the correct relative pronoun.
Use each quantifier only once.

all of	each of	neither of	one of	both of

1 I've bought several of the company's products, only .... works.

2 He's upset with all three of his children, ... makes up a different excuse to avoid sharing chores at home.

3 The teacher sent six of her students to speak with the director, ... were caught cheating on the test.

4 The two articles, ... deal with the issue of honesty in the workplace, should be required reading for everyone in the company.

5 My parents, ... has ever told a lie, are the most honest people I know.

Grammar for Writing: reduced adjective clauses

Adjective clauses can be reduced to adjective phrases.

clause: Hawaii, **which is known for its beautiful topography and climate**, lies in the middle of the Pacific Ocean.

phrase: Hawaii, **known for its beautiful topography and climate**, lies in the middle of the Pacific Ocean.

There are two ways to reduce an adjective clause to an adjective phrase:

1 When the adjective clause contains a form of the verb be, drop the relative pronoun and the verb be.
Herodotus, **who was the first Greek historian**, wrote about the wars between ancient Greece and Persia. →
Herodotus, **the first Greek historian**, wrote about the wars between ancient Greece and Persia.

2 When the adjective clause does not contain a form of the verb be, drop the relative pronoun and use
the present participle of the verb.
The human skeleton, **which contains** 206 separate bones, is a strong and flexible structure. →
The human skeleton, **containing** 206 separate bones, is a strong and flexible structure.

Those **who tamper** with the smoke detector will be prosecuted. →
Those **tampering** with the smoke detector will be prosecuted.

Adjective phrases often begin with an article or one, a type of, or a kind of.
My grandmother, **a very practical and hardworking woman**, made clothes for the entire family.
The largest city in Turkey, Istanbul is at the point where Europe joins Asia.
They're looking for a quiet place to live, preferably **one in the suburbs**.
Chanterelles, **a type of edible mushroom with a rich yellow color**, are very expensive.
The llama and alpaca are camelids, **a kind of mammal native to South America**.

> **Remember**
> A clause is a group of words that has both a subject and a verb.
> A phrase is a group of words that doesn't have both a subject and a verb.

> The use of commas in reduced adjective clauses follows the same rules as those for full adjective clauses. See page 000 for the use of commas in restrictive and non-restrictive adjective clauses.

C Reduce the adjective clause in each sentence to an adjective phrase.

1 Daniel Craig and Rachel Weisz, who are two of the U.K.'s best-known movie actors, do charity work with underprivileged teens.

2 Philanthropy, which is the act of giving time and money to help others, can be very time-consuming.

3 Executives who fail to accept responsibility for their mistakes risk losing the trust of their employees.

4 The United Nations, which hosts a number of humanitarian organizations, invited Angelina Jolie to be a goodwill ambassador to countries in need of assistance.

5 Truthfulness, which is believed to be taught to us by our parents, develops in children from a very young age.

D On a separate sheet of paper, combine each pair of sentences. Use the second sentence as an adjective phrase.

1 Amal Hijazi is also known for her humanitarian work. (Hijazi is a Lebanese pop singer currently living in Beirut.)

> Amal Hijazi, a Lebanese pop singer currently living in Beirut, is also known for her humanitarian work.

2 Telling a white lie can still get us into big trouble. (A white lie is the type of lie we tell to protect others.)

3 My mother taught me a lot about how to be honest. (My mother is the only person I know who is unable to tell a lie.)

4 My brother frequently volunteers in a hospital. (My brother is a man of great compassion.)

5 A lot of money was raised at last night's concert. (Last night's concert was the biggest charity event of the year.)

UNIT 3

Embedded questions: review and common errors

Remember: A question can be embedded in a noun clause.
Use if or whether to begin an embedded yes / no question.
If and whether have the same meaning.

Yes / no questions	Embedded yes / no questions
Does she get fed up when she's frustrated?	Let's ask **whether she gets fed up when she's frustrated**.
Do you know what I mean?	I'd like to know **if you know what I mean**.
Have you ever asked your boss for a raise?	Could you tell me **if you've ever asked your boss for a raise?**

Use a question word to begin embedded information questions.

Information questions	Embedded information questions
What's she afraid of?	I can't remember **what she's afraid of**.
Why have you decided to stay home?	I don't understand **why you've decided to stay home**.
When was it found?	Do you know **when it was found**?

Phrases that are often followed by embedded questions

Ask …	I'd like to know …
Tell me …	Don't tell them …
I wonder …	I can't remember …
Let's ask …	Do you know …?
Don't say …	Can you tell me …?
I don't know …	Can you remember …?
Let me know …	Could you explain …?

Question words and phrases

how	what color	which
how many	what day	who
how much	when	whom
what	where	why

Punctuation of embedded questions
Use a period with an embedded question within a statement.
Use a question mark with an embedded question within a question.

> **I don't know** who is singing.　　　　**Would you mind telling me** who is singing?

Social use of embedded questions
You can use an embedded question to soften a direct question.

> Why isn't this printer working? → Can you tell me **why this printer isn't working**?
> Where's the bathroom? → Do you know **where the bathroom is**?

Embedded questions: common errors
Remember: Use regular statement word order, not inverted (question) word order, in embedded questions.

> Do you know **why your parents won't** fly?　NOT　Do you know why ~~won't they~~ fly?
> Can you tell me **whether this bus runs** express?　NOT　Can you tell me ~~does this bus run~~ express?

A On a separate sheet of paper, combine the two parts of each item to write an embedded question, using if or whether, as indicated. Punctuate each sentence correctly.

1 I can't remember (Is there going to be a late show?) [whether]

2 We're not sure (Was it John or Bill who found the wallet?) [whether]

3 Could you tell me (Is the movie going to start soon?) [if]

4 I wonder (Will the traffic be bad at this hour?) [if]

5 Would she like to know (Is there a possibility of getting a seat on the plane?) [if]

6 Do you know (Does this movie have a good cast?) [whether]

B On a separate sheet of paper, combine the two parts of each item to write an embedded question. Punctuate each sentence correctly.

1 Please let me know (When do you expect to arrive?)

2 I wonder (Where were your parents when the earthquake occurred?)

3 Can you tell me (How do you know that?)

4 We're not sure (Where can we buy flowers to take to the hostess of the dinner party?)

5 They'd like to understand (Why don't you just call the restaurant for reservations?)

6 Please tell us (What time does the performance begin?)

C On a separate sheet of paper, rewrite the sentences, correcting errors, including punctuation errors.

1 Please tell me what do you usually say when you feel frustrated.

2 Can you remind me what day is the party?

3 Could you explain how did you make this omelet?

4 Tell me what is your favorite color?

5 I wonder what should they do.

6 Do you think is something wrong?

Count and non-count nouns

Non-count nouns made countable

A non-count noun is neither singular nor plural. Except in certain circumstances, it is not preceded by an article.
A non-count noun can be preceded by certain quantifiers such as <u>much</u>, <u>a lot of</u>, <u>a little</u>, and <u>some</u>.

   I always like **a little** sugar in my oatmeal. NOT I like a sugar in my oatmeal. OR Sugar are good in oatmeal.

Many non-count nouns can be made countable by using a phrase to limit them or give them a form.

   If you want to serve fruit for dessert, serve each person **two pieces of** fruit instead of one. One piece might not be enough.

   They got scared when they heard **a clap of** thunder.

Some phrases to make non-count nouns countable

The following phrases are used to make non-count nouns countable. The list includes abstract ideas, natural phenomena, foods, drinks and liquids, and household products. Many phrases are used in more than one category.

an article of (clothing)	**a cloud of** (smoke)	**a liter of** (gasoline / oil)
a bar of (chocolate / soap)	**a cup of** (sugar / rice / coffee / tea)	**a loaf of** (bread)
a bottle of (water)	**a drop of** (rain / water)	**a piece of** (fruit / paper / wood / metal / advice)
a bowl of (rice / soup / cereal)	**a game of** (tennis / soccer / chess)	**a teaspoon of** (salt / sugar)
a box of (rice / pasta)	**a glass of** (juice / milk)	**a type (or kind) of** (energy / behavior / music)
a carton of (milk / juice)	**a grain of** (sand / salt / rice)	

Phrases that are used to make a number of non-count nouns countable

Here are four common phrases that are used to make a number of non-count nouns countable.

a piece of	**a sense of**	**an act of**	**a state of**
advice	achievement	anger	confusion
equipment	community	defiance	disrepair
furniture	confidence	generosity	emergency
gossip	control	insanity	mind
information	humor	justice	war
news	heroism	kindness	
paper	identity		

Nouns used in both countable and uncountable sense

Some nouns can be used in both a countable and an uncountable sense.

a chance	=	a possibility		a coffee	=	a cup of coffee
chance	=	luck		coffee	=	a type of beverage
a light	=	a light source, such as a light bulb, lamp, etc.		a hair	=	a single hair
light	=	a type of energy		hair	=	all the hair on the head
a metal	=	a specific substance, such as gold or steel		a shampoo	=	a brand of shampoo
metal	=	a type of substance		shampoo	=	soap for your hair

D On a separate sheet of paper, rewrite the statements, using a phrase to make each underlined non-count noun countable.

1 If you're going to play <u>tennis</u> tomorrow morning, give me a call.

2 When I plant my garden in April, I wait eagerly for the first <u>rain</u> to make sure the plants grow.

3 If you sew or repair <u>clothing</u> yourself instead of taking it to someone else, you will save a lot of money in the long run.

4 They say that turning <u>bread</u> upside down after a slice has been cut from it will keep it fresh.

5 When I make chicken soup, I like to serve <u>rice</u> on the side.

E Choose the best word from the box to complete each sentence.

| act | bar | glass | piece | sense | state |

1 The group's donation was a true .... of generosity.

2 My sister has an amazing .... of humor.

3 The woman slipped on a .... of soap in the shower.

4 Our town has been in a .... of emergency since the hurricane.

5 The park just installed a new .... of equipment in the playground.

6 I asked the waitress for a .... of orange juice.

UNIT 4

Grammar for Writing: more conjunctions and transitions

Purpose	Coordinating conjunctions	Subordinating conjunctions	Transitions
To add information *Marc is working as a photographer, **and** he has experience in graphic design.* ***In addition to** working as a photographer, Marc has experience in graphic design.*	and	in addition to besides	In addition, Furthermore, Moreover, Besides, More importantly,
To clarify information *Smaller cars are more efficient; **in other words,** they use less fuel.*			That is, In other words, In fact,
To illustrate or exemplify information *Many European cities are found along waterways.* ***For example,** London, Paris, Vienna, and Budapest all lie on major rivers.*			For instance, For example, To illustrate,
To show contrast *Meg does not usually perform well under pressure, **but** she gave a brilliant recital.* *Meg does not usually perform well under pressure.* ***Despite this,** she gave a brilliant recital.*	but yet	even though although though while whereas despite the fact that	However, Nevertheless, Nonetheless, In contrast, Even so, Still, Despite [this / that], In spite of [this / that], All the same, On the other hand,
To express cause or result *They have a new baby, **so** they rarely get a good night's sleep!* ***Now that** they have a new baby, they rarely get a good night's sleep!*	so for	because since due to the fact that now that so that	Therefore, Consequently, Accordingly, As a consequence, As a result,

Remember
- A <u>coordinating conjunction</u> links two independent clauses in a sentence. It is preceded by a comma.
- A <u>subordinating conjunction</u> introduces a dependent clause in a sentence. When a dependent clause starts a sentence, the clause is followed by a comma.
- A <u>transition</u> links ideas between sentences or paragraphs. It usually begins a sentence and is followed by a comma. A transition can be preceded by a semicolon.

	or (else)	(only) if	Otherwise,
To express a condition		provided that	
*Pollution can be reduced **provided that** car manufacturers mass-produce cars with greater fuel efficiency.*		as long as	
*Car manufacturers should mass-produce cars with greater fuel efficiency. **Otherwise,** pollution will not be reduced.*		unless	
		even if	
		whether (or not)	
To show similarity			Similarly,
*Water is necessary for life. **Similarly,** oxygen is required by all living things.*			Likewise,

A On a separate sheet of paper, combine each pair of sentences two ways: once with the connecting word(s) in <u>a</u> and once with the connecting words in <u>b</u>. Use a semicolon before a transition. Change the wording as necessary to retain the meaning.

1 John is a bit of a perfectionist. His brothers are pretty easygoing. (**a** while   **b** in contrast)

2 Nicole has always struggled with being disorganized. She has made a lot of progress recently. (**a** although   **b** despite that)

3 My boss tends to be very negative. He gets angry too quickly. (**a** in addition to   **b** furthermore)

4 I need to stop procrastinating. I won't ever finish the class assignment on time. (**a** unless   **b** otherwise)

5 Carla has been trying not to be so controlling at work. She gets along better with her colleagues. (**a** now that   **b** as a result)

Cleft sentences: more on meaning and use

Cleft sentences with <u>What</u>

Cleft sentences with <u>What</u> are often used to clarify what someone said, thought, or meant.

A: Do you think Gail would like to go somewhere for her birthday?
B: Actually, **what she'd really like is** for us to take her out to a nice restaurant.

A: Were you surprised that Rob called you after your argument?
B: Actually, **what surprised me was** that he was even willing to talk to me!

Cleft sentences with <u>It</u>

Cleft sentences with <u>It</u> are used to clarify who, what, when, where, or why.

A: Did you try calling me a few minutes ago? Your number popped up in my missed calls.
B: Actually, **it was my sister** who called you. She was using my phone. (clarifies who)

A: Our neighbor had a great party last night. But I have to say, the noise really got to me.
B: Well, **it was not getting an invitation** that really bugged me. (clarifies what)

A: Don't I see you in the computer lab on Mondays?
B: I doubt it. **It's usually on Tuesdays and Thursdays** that I go to the lab. (clarifies when)

A: Did you hear about the bus accident this morning?
B: Yeah. And **it was just down the street from me** where it happened! (clarifies where)

A: Thanks for helping me with the homework.
B: Well, **it's because you're always so nice** that I did it. (clarifies why)

B Clarify what B said, thought, or meant. Complete each cleft sentence using the underlined information.

1 **A:** <u>Are you excited about</u> going on vacation next week?
  B: Actually, ... getting to see my aunt and uncle again.

2 **A:** <u>Did you think</u> your boss was going to lose her temper?
  B: On the contrary. .... that she was going to give me a promotion.

3 **A:** It's 6:15. I thought <u>you said</u> you'd be here at 6:00.
  B: .... we should plan to meet at 6:00, but that I might be a little late.

4 A: <u>What did Gary mean</u> when he said his tablet cost an arm and a leg?

   B: .... it was a lot more expensive than he thought it would be.

5 A: <u>Should you be eating</u> that cake?

   B: According to my doctor, ... nothing but healthy food. But I don't care!

C Write cleft sentences with <u>It</u> to clarify who, what, when, where, or why. Use the prompts.

1 A: Is feeding a parrot a lot of work?

   B: Are you kidding? .... (clean the cage)

2 A: Did Gina write that song?

   B: No. .... (her sister)

3 A: Will the traffic be really bad at this time?

   B: I don't think so. .... (at 5:00)

4 A: These cookies are so good!

   B: Thanks. .... (because / I add / nuts)

5 A: Aren't we supposed to meet Jason at the coffee shop?

   B: No. .... (at the bus stop)

UNIT 5

Indirect speech: review and expansion

Imperatives in indirect speech

When imperatives are used to report commands, requests, instructions, and invitations, the imperative form changes to the infinitive. The negative infinitive is used for negative commands, requests, and instructions.

Direct speech	Indirect speech
"Could you please **go** to the store?"	She asked me **to go** to the store.
The chef said, "**Add** two eggs and stir the mixture."	The chef said **to add** two eggs and stir the mixture.
"Please **have** dinner with us," he said.	He invited me **to have** dinner with them.
She told the child, "**Don't cross** the street."	She told the child **not to cross** the street.

> **Remember**
> Indirect questions end with a period, not a question mark. Like in embedded questions, verbs in indirect questions follow the same changes as the verbs in indirect statements.

Changes to pronouns and possessives

Remember: In indirect speech, pronouns and possessives change to reflect the point of view of the reporter rather than the original speaker.

My manager said, "**You** have to finish **your** report and give it to **me** as soon as possible."	→	My manager said (that) **I** had to finish **my** report and give it to **her** as soon as possible.
I told her, "**You**'ll have **this** report on **your** desk by noon."	→	I told her (that) **she** would have **that** report on **her** desk by noon.
Peter asked them, "Are **these** coats **yours**?"	→	Peter asked them if **those** coats were **theirs**.

A On a separate sheet of paper, write each sentence in indirect speech.

1 Marian advised Claire, "Turn on the TV at 9:00 because there's a funny movie on."

2 Dr. Baker advised his patient, "Don't let emotional tension make you sick."

3 She told me, "Be a good sport and laugh about it."

4 "Don't laugh at that joke," Fred instructed his son. "It's disgusting."

5 "Laugh first, cry later," an old saying advises us.

6 Lucas told us, "Never touch the green button on the printer."

7 "Take the penguin to the zoo tomorrow," Mr. Franklin's neighbor told him.

8 Nick said, "Please don't ask how the meeting went."

B On a separate sheet of paper, write these conversations in indirect speech, using correct pronouns and possessives.

1 MARIA: Your cartoon is great. Your drawing is so funny.

   JACK: Yours is hilarious, too! It really cracked me up!

> *Maria said Jack's cartoon was great and that...*
> *Jack answered that...*

2 KATHERINE: Allison, I'm not sure if this tablet is yours.

   ALLISON: It's definitely mine. Thanks!

3 RICHARD: My paper on the health benefits of humor has just been published in a medical journal.

   ME: I'm happy for you! I'd appreciate it if you could give me a copy.

4 KIM: I bought a new MP3 player last week.

   BEN: I know. I saw it on your desk. It looks much better than your old one.

5 SAM: I got all these articles about humor on the Internet last weekend.

   PIRI: That's great. Would you let me read them when you've finished them?

Say, tell, and ask

Remember: Use <u>tell</u> when you mention the listener. You can use <u>say</u> in indirect speech when you mention the listener, but you must use the preposition <u>to</u> and introduce the indirect speech with <u>that</u>.

   Marie **told** Dr. Barton she had to change the time of her appointment. (listener mentioned)

   Dr. Barton **said** that wouldn't be a problem. (listener not mentioned)

   Dr. Barton **said to** the nurse that it wouldn't be a problem. (listener mentioned)

Use <u>ask</u> either with or without mentioning the listener. Don't use <u>to</u> after <u>ask</u> when you mention the listener.

   Marie **asked** if she could make an appointment later in the week. OR Marie **asked** Dr. Barton if she could make an appointment later in the week.

> **BE CAREFUL!**
> DON'T SAY: He ~~said the manager~~ that he completely disagreed with her.
> DON'T SAY: He ~~told~~ that he completely disagreed with the manager.
> DON'T SAY: He ~~told to the manager~~ that he completely disagreed with her.
> DON'T SAY: He ~~asked to the manager~~ if she agreed.

C Complete the sentences with a form of <u>say</u>, <u>tell</u>, or <u>ask</u>.

1 She .... the waiter if she could pay with a credit card.

2 We .... that we would come back later when they were less busy.

3 He .... his friends that he would be a few minutes late.

4 She .... to her teacher that she needed a bit more time.

5 They .... the reporter that they were ready to provide information about the case.

6 I .... them if they enjoyed the movie.

Grammar for Writing: other reporting verbs

Writers use a variety of reporting verbs to describe actions more specifically and accurately.

claim

   "Things are definitely getting better," **claims** Charles Wilder, a patient trying out humor therapy for the first time.

   Charles Wilder, a patient trying out humor therapy for the first time, **claims** that things are definitely getting better.

declare

   "The nursing staff has been doing a brilliant job!" **declared** the head doctor on Tuesday.

   On Tuesday, the head doctor **declared** that the nursing staff had been doing a brilliant job.

explain

   "You should always discuss dieting with your doctor," Dr. Fish **explained**.

   Dr. Fish **explained** that people should always discuss dieting with their doctors.

report

   The New York Times **reports**, "Obesity is a growing problem in Asia."

   Last year, the New York Times **reported** that obesity was a growing problem in Asia.

state

   The new CEO **stated**, "Things are going to change around here."

   The new CEO **stated** that things were going to change at the company.

> **More reporting verbs**
> | | |
> |---|---|
> | add | maintain |
> | announce | mention |
> | answer | promise |
> | comment | remark |
> | complain | reply |
> | exclaim | reveal |
> | imply | write |

D On a separate sheet of paper, restate each sentence with a different reporting verb. Use a dictionary if necessary.

1 The Bangkok Post says that the president of Chile will be visiting Thailand next month.
2 The minister of education said yesterday that major improvements had been made in schools across the country.
3 The secretary of the United Nations says that more should be done to alleviate world hunger.
4 The scientists who conducted the study said that more research would have to be conducted.
5 The children who wrote on the walls said that they wouldn't do it again.
6 The BBC said that it would increase its coverage of the news in the Middle East.

UNIT 6

The conditional: summary and extension

Type	Use	If clause (states the condition)	Result clause (states the result)	Examples
Factual conditional	To express a general or scientific fact	simple present Note: In this type of conditional, if can be replaced by <u>when</u> or <u>whenever</u>.	simple present	*If it rains, the gardens close early.* *Water freezes if the temperature falls below zero degrees Celsius.*
	To talk about what will happen in the future under certain conditions	simple present Note: Don't use a future form in the <u>if</u> clause.	<u>will</u> / <u>be going to</u> + base form of the verb Note: Use <u>can</u>, <u>may</u>, <u>might</u>, <u>should</u> if the result is not certain.	*If you plan your trip carefully, things will go smoothly.* *If we arrive late, they're going to start without us.* *If we hurry, we may be able to catch the train.*
Present unreal conditional	To talk about present unreal or untrue conditions	simple past or <u>were</u> Note: Don't use <u>would</u> in the <u>if</u> clause.	<u>would</u> + base form of the verb Note: Use <u>could</u> or <u>might</u> if the result is not certain.	*If I had the time, I would explain the problem to you.* *If he were here, he might make a lot of changes.*
Past unreal conditional	To talk about past unreal or untrue conditions	past perfect Note: Don't use <u>would have</u> in the <u>if</u> clause.	<u>would have</u> + past participle Note: Use <u>could have</u> or <u>might have</u> if the result is not certain.	*If they had known about the storm, they would have taken a different flight.* *If you had told us about the delay, we could have made other arrangements.*
Mixed time frames	To talk about past unreal or untrue conditions in relation to the present	past perfect Note: Don't use <u>would</u> in the <u>if</u> clause.	<u>would</u> + base form of the verb Note: Use <u>could</u> or <u>might</u> if the result is not certain.	*If I had prepared for the interview, I wouldn't be so nervous.* *If we had left earlier, we might be on time now.*
	To talk about present unreal or untrue conditions in relation to the past	simple past or <u>were</u> Note: Don't use <u>would have</u> in the <u>if</u> clause.	<u>would have</u> + past participle Note: Use <u>could have</u> or <u>might have</u> if the result is not certain.	*If she were honest, she would have told us the truth.* *If I spoke Russian, I might have understood the guide.*

Extension: other uses

Use <u>should</u>, <u>happen to</u>, or <u>should happen to</u> in the <u>if</u> clause in factual conditionals when the condition is less likely.

If you ⎰ **should** / **happen to** / **should happen to** ⎱ see Peter, tell him to call me.

To express inferences in conditional sentences, different combinations of tenses can be used.
If Julie **went** to the party last night, she definitely **saw** what happened.
If you **don't know** the answer to this question, you **didn't do** your homework.
If the results **didn't come out** yesterday, they**'ll** definitely **come out** today.
If you still **haven't finished** packing by now, you**'re not going to catch** your flight.

A Circle the correct word or words to complete each sentence.

1 If Sam (does / will do) well this year, he will apply to medical school.

2 Water (boils / is going to boil) when the temperature reaches 100 degrees Celsius.

3 If you (will / should) find my scarf, please hold it for me.

4 If you (happen / happen to) see a good camera at the market, please buy it for me.

5 If it (wouldn't have been / hadn't been) for her savings, Anna wouldn't have been able to attend university.

6 If we (would have known / had known) that car insurance was so expensive, we would not have bought a car.

7 If you didn't get a reply today, you (would definitely hear / will definitely hear) from us tomorrow.

8 If I (had / would have) a garden, I would grow several types of flowers.

9 If I (would have practiced / had practiced) my speech a bit more, I might not be so worried now.

10 If I (should happen to / will) see John, I'll tell him to call you.

UNIT 7

Article usage: summary

Note where indefinite or definite articles are used or omitted.

	Indefinite article	Definite article	No article
General statement	Use with singular count nouns: *A cat* may symbolize good fortune.	Use with singular count nouns: *The cat* may symbolize good fortune. Use with non-count nouns: Freud called attention to *the importance* of dreams.	With plural count nouns: *Cats* may symbolize good fortune. With non-count nouns: *Misfortune* may strike at any time.
First mention	Use with singular count nouns: I found *a lucky charm*.		With plural count nouns: I have (some) lucky *charms*. With non-count nouns: I bought (some) *shampoo*.
Second mention		Use with singular count nouns: *The* lucky *charm* was in a box. Use with plural count nouns: *The* lucky *charms* were in a box. Use with non-count nouns: *The shampoo* is in the closet.	

A On a separate sheet of paper, rewrite the paragraph, correcting eleven errors and making any necessary changes.

The homes are expensive these days, but Peter got lucky and bought small house last week. A house has two bedrooms and one bathroom. It also has large kitchen and the living room. Peter will use a living room as his home office. Bedrooms are in bad condition, and Peter will need a help painting them. Then he wants to have the party so his friends can admire a house. Later Peter will buy a furniture—when he saves some money!

Definite article: additional uses

When a noun represents a unique thing	Use with singular count nouns: *The sun* rises in the east.

With a comparative or superlative adjective to make a noun unique (or with <u>right</u>, <u>wrong</u>, <u>first</u>, <u>only</u>, <u>same</u>)	Use with singular count nouns:
	    Telling the truth is *the best course* of action. It's always *the right thing* to do.
	    The robin is *the first sign* of spring.
	Use with plural count nouns:
	    People in different places often have *the same superstitions*.
	Use with non-count nouns:
	    That's *the only information* I was able to find on the Internet.

When context makes a noun specific	Use with singular count nouns: **The hospital** in this town has an excellent emergency room. Use with plural count nouns: **The buildings** in this town are no higher than ten stories. Use with non-count nouns: **The air** in this city is polluted.
When an adjective clause makes a noun specific	Use with singular count nouns: **The mirror that you broke** will bring you bad luck. Use with plural count nouns: **The mirrors that you broke** will bring you bad luck. Use with non-count nouns: **The progress that she made** was due not to good luck but to hard work.
When an adjective represents a certain group of people	Use with a noun derived from an adjective, such as the blind, the deaf, the dead, the living, the young, the old, the poor, the rich, the unemployed, the privileged, the underprivileged: **The unemployed** must often learn new job skills.

B Complete the paragraphs with words from the box. Use a definite article when appropriate.

tourists	gasoline	view	world	wealthy	sky	ballooning	first men

On March 20, 1999, Bertrand Piccard of Switzerland and Brian Jones of Britain were ....
1

to travel around .... in a balloon. The numerous balloonists who had been attempting this
2

journey for decades beforehand ran into various problems with weather and equipment.

In the past several years, ... has become a popular adventure sport. Due to the high cost of balloons
3

and .... , however, it is a sport reserved for .... can get a taste of ballooning during
4   5   6

their travels. .... of a city or landscape from .... is always breathtaking.
7   8

More non-count nouns with both a countable and an uncountable sense

With some non-count nouns, the change in meaning is subtle: The countable meaning refers to something specific and the uncountable meaning refers to something general.

a fear = the anticipation of a specific danger; a phobia He had **a fear** of heights.	fear = a general anticipation of danger Irrational **fear** can lead to anxiety.
a victory = a specific event in which mastery or success is achieved The battle of Waterloo was **a great victory** for the English.	victory = the phenomenon of winning She led her party to **victory**.
a time = a specific moment in the past or future; a specific occasion There was **a time** when food was much cheaper. How **many times** did you read it?	time = the general concept; clock time **Time** passes so quickly! What **time** did you arrange to meet?
a superstition = a specific belief or practice **A** common **superstition** is that a black cat brings bad luck.	superstition = a general attitude The prevalence of **superstition** today is surprising.

C Write a before a noun where necessary. Write X if a noun should not have an article.

1 a Will people ever learn to control their phobias? Only .... time can tell.

b There has never been .... time when people didn't try to interpret their dreams.

2 a If you have .... fear of flying, you shouldn't take a job that requires overseas travel.

b Psychologists agree that .... fear is a universal emotion.

3 a Ignorance and fear may sometimes lead to .... superstition.

   b There is .... widely held superstition that knocking on wood brings good luck.

4 a The coach's tactics helped the team win .... major victory in last night's game.

   b Everyone cannot always experience the joy of .... victory; someone has to lose.

Grammar for Writing: indirect speech with passive reporting verbs

A passive reporting verb can be followed by an infinitive phrase.
  Most superstitions are believed **to be** false.

The infinitive phrase reflects the time of the reporting verb. It can be simple, continuous, perfect, or perfect continuous.
  This book is said **to be** excellent.
  The robber was reported **to be running away** from the scene of the crime.
  The car is believed **never to have been** in an accident before.
  She was thought **to have been preparing** dinner when she got sick.

D On a separate sheet of paper, change each of the following sentences from the active voice to the passive voice.

1 Many people believe that flying isn't as safe as driving.

2 They reported the driver was talking on his phone when he crashed into the back of that van.

3 Everyone says the tour was overpriced, but others think the price was very fair.

4 People have said the article was a lie, but it turned out to be perfectly true.

UNIT 8

Grammar for Writing: emphatic stress

In informal writing, you can underline the verb <u>be</u>, a modal, or an auxiliary verb to indicate emphatic stress.
The addition of <u>do</u> for emphatic stress does not require underlining. In more formal writing, with the exception of
adding the auxiliary <u>do</u>, emphatic stress is avoided.
  She <u>is</u> good at math, isn't she?
  Even though it was getting late, I <u>would</u> have liked to stay longer.
  I suddenly realized that I <u>had</u> been there before.
  BUT She didn't answer her phone, but she did text me.

> In the modal-like expression <u>had better</u>,
> underline <u>better</u>, not <u>had</u>.
>   He'd <u>better</u> pay attention in class!

A Use the prompts to write B's response with emphatic stress. Add the auxiliary <u>do</u> if possible,
and underline stressed verb <u>be</u>, modal, or other auxiliary verb.

1 A: Do you worry much about global warming?

  B: .... (I think about it) from time to time.

2 A: Would you say you have a way with words?

  B: .... (I express myself) clearly.

3 A: I'm thinking of applying to medical school, but I haven't made up my mind yet.

  B: Well, ... (you should apply).

4 A: Do you have to pass any kind of tests to get a job at the Mason Corporation?

  B: .... (you have to take) an EQ test.

5 A: Shouldn't Jamie hurry if she wants to catch the 3:00 bus?

  B: .... (She'd better hurry). That's the last bus.

6 A: Would you like me to introduce you to my brother?

  B: .... (I'd like to meet) him.

7 A: Would you like to grab dinner somewhere together?

  B: .... (I've already had) dinner.

Infinitives and gerunds in place of the subjunctive

Certain statements in the subjunctive can be rephrased less formally by changing <u>that</u> to <u>for</u> and using an infinitive.

It is essential **for** John **to find** the time each day to relax. (= It is essential that John **find** the time each day to relax.)

An infinitive can also be used without a <u>for</u> phrase. It usually refers to "people in general."

It is essential **to find** the time each day to relax.

Certain statements in the subjunctive can be rephrased using a gerund if it refers to "people in general."

Dr. Sharpe recommends **spending** a few moments relaxing. (= Dr. Sharpe recommends that people **spend** a few moments relaxing.)

B Rewrite each sentence less formally, using infinitives and gerunds. Make any necessary changes.

1 It is crucial that you practice feng shui.

2 The article suggests that you carry lucky charms.

3 The manager recommended that they finish the project fast.

4 It is important that we get enough sleep every night.

5 The directions advise that you add salt.

6 It is necessary that she arrive at the theater by 4:00 P.M.

UNIT 9

Grammar for Writing: when to use the passive voice

Passive sentences focus attention on the result of an action rather than on the performer (agent) of the action. Writers prefer the passive voice in the following situations:

1 To emphasize the result of an action, or if the agent is unimportant or unknown. This use is common in academic writing, scientific articles, and news reports.

Some sophisticated treatments **have been developed**. (emphasizes the treatments, not the people who developed them)

Hundreds of people **were made** homeless by yesterday's floods. (emphasizes the result, not the floods themselves)

2 To describe a process. This use is found in technical and scientific writing.

There are four basic steps in the commercial production of orange juice. First the oranges **are unloaded** from trucks and **placed** on a conveyor belt. Then they **are washed** and **sorted**. Next they **are put** into machines that remove the juice and put it into cartons.

3 To use an impersonal or indirect tone, which suggests formality, impartiality, or objectivity. This use is favored in official documents, formal announcements, and signs, or to avoid placing blame.

Walking on the grass **is prohibited**.

An error **has been made** in your account. It **will be corrected** on next month's statement. (The writer avoids mentioning who made the mistake and emphasizes the fact that it will be corrected, rather than who will do the correcting.)

4 To keep the reader's attention focused on a previously mentioned noun, because it is the central topic of the paragraph.

They caught the thief later that evening. He **was placed** in jail and **was allowed** to call a lawyer. (The topic is the thief. By using the passive voice in the second sentence, the writer keeps the reader's attention focused on the thief.)

5 To avoid using a "general subject." General subjects include the impersonal <u>you</u>, <u>we</u>, and <u>they</u>; <u>people</u>; <u>one</u>; <u>someone</u> / <u>somebody</u>; <u>anyone</u> / <u>anybody</u>. This use is common in formal documents, in official signs, and in newspaper editorials and other texts that express an opinion.

People must show their IDs before boarding. PREFERRED: IDs **must be shown** before boarding.

Someone should inform consumers of their rights. PREFERRED: Consumers **should be informed** of their rights.

6 To avoid awkward sentence constructions. This is a common solution when the agent has a long or complex modifier.

The Tigers, whose new strategy of offense and defense seemed to be working, defeated the Lions.

PREFERRED: The Lions **were defeated** by the Tigers, whose new strategy of offense and defense seemed to be working.

A On a separate sheet of paper, write each sentence in the passive voice.

1 Construction workers built the museum in less than six months.

2 People must present their passports at the border.

3 First, engineers perfect the design for the new product. Then, workers build a prototype. Next, engineers test the prototype. After engineers approve the design, the factory begins production.

4 We have credited the sum of eighty-five dollars to your VISTA account.

5 The reporter, whose investigation uncovered many shocking facts and a pattern of corrupt behavior, exposed the official for taking bribes.

Phrasal verbs: expansion

The passive form of phrasal verbs

Transitive phrasal verbs are always inseparable in the passive voice, even when they are separable or always separated in the active voice.

> I couldn't **turn on** the TV (OR **turn** the TV **on**). → The TV couldn't be **turned on**.
>
> They **turned** the empty lot **into** a beautiful → The empty lot was **turned into** garden. a beautiful garden.

> **Remember**
> Intransitive phrasal verbs are always inseparable. They can't be used in the passive voice since they don't have direct objects.

Transitive and intransitive meanings

Some phrasal verbs have both a transitive and an intransitive meaning.

> He went to bed without **taking off** his clothes. (transitive meaning: remove)
>
> What time does your plane **take off**? (intransitive meaning: leave)
>
> She **broke in** the new employees by showing them the procedures. (transitive meaning: train someone)
>
> Thieves **broke in** and stole her jewelry. (intransitive meaning: enter by force)

For a complete list of transitive and intransitive phrasal verbs, see the Reference Charts, pages 124–125.

Three-word phrasal verbs

A three-word phrasal verb consists of a verb, a particle, and a preposition that together have a specific meaning. The verb, the particle, and the preposition in three-word phrasal verbs are inseparable.

> As a result of his controversial ideas, the senator **came up against** members of his own party, who opposed him vigorously.
>
> Does society have an obligation to **look out for** people who are disadvantaged?
>
> Temper tantrums are not uncommon in young children. As they mature, they **grow out of** this behavior.
>
> I'm going to close my door and not take any calls today; I've just got to **catch up on** my work.

For a complete list of three-word phrasal verbs, see the Reference Charts, page 126.

A On a separate sheet of paper, rewrite each sentence in the passive voice. Do not include a <u>by</u> phrase.

1 We have to call the meeting off.

2 He talked the client into a better deal.

3 They covered the mistake up.

4 She dropped the children off in front of the school.

5 One of the applicants filled the form out incorrectly.

6 I paid the balance off last month.

7 Someone threw the document away.

8 The speaker handed pamphlets out at the end of the presentation.

B Underline the phrasal verb in each sentence. Then decide if it has a transitive or an intransitive meaning.

	transitive	intransitive	
1	☐	☐	The photographer blew up the photo 200 percent so we could use it for the poster.
2	☐	☐	The plane blew up shortly before it was supposed to land.
3	☐	☐	The workers won't give up until they're paid fair wages.
4	☐	☐	She has tried to give up smoking several times, without success.
5	☐	☐	Phil has to wake up at 5:00 A.M. every morning to get to work on time.
6	☐	☐	The children played quietly in order not to wake up their parents.
7	☐	☐	He works out three or four times a week in order to stay healthy.
8	☐	☐	World leaders are meeting to work out a plan to eradicate poverty.

Pronunciation table

These are the pronunciation symbols used in *Summit 2*.

	Vowels				Consonants		
Symbol	**Key Word**	**Symbol**	**Key Word**	**Symbol**	**Key Word**	**Symbol**	**Key Word**
i	beat, feed	ə	banana, among	p	pack, happy	z	zip, please, goes
ɪ	bit, did	ɚ	shirt, murder	b	back, rubber	ʃ	ship, machine, station, special, discussion
eɪ	date, paid	aɪ	bite, cry, buy, eye	t	tie	ʒ	measure, vision
ɛ	bet, bed	aʊ	about, how	d	die	h	hot, who
æ	bat, bad	ɔɪ	voice, boy	k	came, key, quick	m	men, some
ɑ	box, odd, father	ɪr	beer	g	game, guest	n	sun, know, pneumonia
ɔ	bought, dog	ɛr	bare	tʃ	church, nature, watch	ŋ	sung, ringing
oʊ	boat, road	ɑr	bar	dʒ	judge, general, major	w	wet, white
ʊ	book, good	ɔr	door	f	fan, photograph	l	light, long
u	boot, food, student	ʊr	tour	v	van	r	right, wrong
ʌ	but, mud, mother			θ	thing, breath	y	yes, use, music
				ð	then, breathe	t̬	butter, bottle
				s	sip, city, psychology	t̚	button

Pronunciation Booster

The Pronunciation Booster is optional. It provides a pronunciation lesson and practice to support speaking in each unit, making students' speech more comprehensible.

UNIT 1

Sentence stress and intonation: review

Sentence stress

Remember: Content words are generally stressed in a sentence.

I've **ALWAYS DREAMED** about **BEING** a **PHOTOGRAPHER**.

You've been **TALKING** about **DOING** that for **YEARS**!

Have you **EVER THOUGHT** about a **CAREER** in **LAW**?

Intonation

Lower pitch after the stressed syllable in the last stressed word in statements, commands, and information questions. Raise pitch after the last stressed syllable in yes/no questions.

I love the outdoors, so I've decided to become a naturalist.   What's stopping you?

Tell me something about your experience.   Have you made plans to get married?

If the last syllable in the sentence is stressed, lengthen the vowel and lower pitch. In yes/no questions, lengthen the vowel and raise pitch.

I just gave notice at the bank.   Have you decided on a career?

Content words

nouns	photographer, Robert, career
verbs	think, study, discuss
adjectives	important, young, successful
adverbs	carefully, ever, recently
possessive pronouns	ours, yours, theirs
demonstrative pronouns	this, that, these
reflexive pronouns	myself, yourself, ourselves
interrogative pronouns	who, what, why

In compound nouns, stress only the first word.

She has just been accepted to a top **BUSINESS** school.

Have you made any progress with your **JOB** search?

A ▶6:02 **Listen and practice.**

1 I've always dreamed about being a photographer.
2 You've been talking about doing that for years!
3 Have you ever thought about a career in law?

B ▶6:03 **Listen and practice.**

1 I love the outdoors, so I've decided to become a naturalist.
2 Tell me something about your experience.
3 What's stopping you?

4 Have you made plans to get married?
5 I just gave notice at the bank.
6 Have you decided on a career?

C **Circle the content words.**

1 It was very difficult for Dan to hide his disappointment.
2 He was rejected by two law schools.
3 What does he plan to do now?

4 He just accepted a position teaching math at the university.
5 MediLabs has an opening for a junior lab specialist.

▶6:04 **Now practice reading each sentence aloud. Listen to compare.***

D **Circle the last stressed content word in each sentence.**

1 He wants to start his own travel agency.
2 I don't really know how to get started.
3 Do I need to have experience in the tourism industry?

4 Why are you looking for a change?
5 Tell me about your plans for the coming year.
6 Do you want to become a flight attendant?
7 Have you applied for that job?

▶6:05 **Now practice reading each sentence aloud, using the intonation patterns you have learned. Listen to compare.***

UNIT 2

Emphatic stress and pitch to express emotion

Use emphatic stress and higher pitch on content words to indicate intensity of emotion.

I'm **SO SORRY**!
I'm **REALLY UPSET**!
What do you **MEAN**?

How could you **DO** that?
What **GREAT NEWS**!
Thank you **SO MUCH**!

A ▶6:06 **Listen and practice.**

1 I'm so sorry!
2 I'm really upset!

3 What do you mean?
4 How could you do that?

5 What great news!
6 Thank you so much!

B ▶6:07 **Practice reading each sentence aloud, using intonation to express emotion. Listen to compare.***

1 **JOHN**, what **HAPPENED**?
2 You look **WORRIED**.
3 I feel **JUST TERRIBLE**!
4 How did **THAT** happen?

5 Why didn't you slow **DOWN**?
6 We could have been **KILLED**!
7 How could you **SAY** that?

*NOTE: Whenever you see a listening activity with an asterisk (*), say each word, phrase, or sentence in the pause *after* the number. Then listen for confirmation.

Vowel reduction *to* /ə/

Remember: The /u/ sound in the function word <u>to</u> is often reduced to /ə/ in spoken English.

We tried **to** cheer him up. /tə/
They were scared **to** death. /tə/
It was starting **to** get me down. /tə/
You just need **to** give it a little more time. /tə/

Do not reduce the /u/ sound when <u>to</u> comes before another /ə/ sound.

        /tə/   /tu/
She was trying **to** e-mail a message **to** a friend.

When <u>to</u> occurs before <u>her</u> or <u>him</u>, you can say it two ways (Note the change in syllable stress, too):

Use /tə/ and pronounce /h/   →   I sent it **to her** yesterday. /təˈhər/
Use /tu/ and drop /h/   →   I sent it **to her** yesterday. /ˈtuər/

In the phrases <u>have to</u>, <u>ought to</u>, and <u>be going to</u>, /u/ generally reduces to /ə/, and there are often other sound changes.

I didn't **have to** walk very far. /hæftə/
You really **ought to** be careful next time. /ɔtə/
We're definitely **going to** take a cell phone on our next trip. /gʌnə/

Function words

prepositions	of, from, at, to
conjunctions	and, but, or
determiners	a, the, some
personal pronouns	he, she, they
possessive adjectives	my, her, their
auxiliary verbs	have [+ past participle]
	be [+ present participle]

Be careful! When an auxiliary verb is negative or used in short answers, it is generally stressed.

I **CAN'T GO**.   He **WON'T LIKE** it.
No, they **DON'T**.   Yes, I **HAVE**.

A ▶6:08 **Listen and practice.**

1 We tried to cheer him up.
2 They were scared to death.
3 It was starting to get me down.
4 You just need to give it a little more time.
5 She was trying to e-mail a message to a friend.

6 I sent it to her yesterday.
7 I sent it to her yesterday.
8 I didn't have to walk very far.
9 You really ought to be careful next time.
10 We're definitely going to take a cell phone on our next trip.

B Circle the words in the following sentences that you think contain sounds that will be reduced, according to what you have learned about vowel reduction.

1 I'm learning to sail my ship.
2 They had sent an SOS text message from a cell phone to a friend in London.
3 They got several messages telling them to be strong.
4 The helicopters had been unable to take off because of the severe weather.
5 You ought to tell your brother that you can't talk to him right now.
6 Don't let it get to you.
7 I'm going to refuse to give up.
8 We have to keep trying, no matter how tired we are.

▶6:09 **Now practice reading each sentence aloud and listen to compare.***

Shifting emphatic stress

You can shift stress within a sentence to change emphasis. Place emphatic stress on key words to get your meaning across.

A: I think I'm too critical of other people.
B: Really? I don't think I'm critical **ENOUGH**.

A: I don't think I'm critical enough.
B: Really? I think I'm **TOO** critical.

A: I think I'm too critical of other people.
B: I don't see you that way at all. **I'M** too critical.

A: I think I'm too critical of other people.
B: Really? Not me ... At least I don't **THINK** I'm too critical.

A ▶6:10 **Listen and practice.**

1 I don't think I'm critical **ENOUGH**.

2 I think I'm **TOO** critical.

3 **I'M** too critical.

4 I don't **THINK** I'm too critical.

B **Study each conversation, paying attention to emphatic stress.**

1 "You know what my problem is? I'm a perfectionist."

RESPONSE: Well, **I'M** just the opposite.

2 "You know what my problem is? I'm a perfectionist."

RESPONSE: Not me. I'm just the **OPPOSITE**.

3 "What set Sam off this morning?"

RESPONSE: I have no idea. But he's **ALWAYS** angry about **SOMETHING**.

4 "Why did Sam tell Paul off in front of everyone?"

RESPONSE: It's just the way he is. He's always **ANGRY** about something.

5 "Why was Judy so angry this morning?"

RESPONSE: I don't know. I've **NEVER** seen her lose her cool like that.

6 "Can you believe how angry Judy was this morning?"

RESPONSE: Not really. I've never seen her lose her cool like **THAT**.

▶6:11 **Now practice reading each response aloud, using emphatic stress as shown. Listen to compare.***

UNIT 5

Intonation of sarcasm

Saying the opposite of what you mean in order to show that you don't think a joke is funny is a type of sarcasm. When someone thinks a joke is funny, the response is usually said with raised pitch. The same response can convey sarcasm if it is said with flattened pitch and at a slower pace.

Pleasure	Sarcasm
How funny! (= It's funny.)	How funny. (= It's not funny.)
That's hysterical! (= It's funny.)	That's hysterical. (= It's not funny.)
That's terrific! (= It's great.)	That's terrific. (= It's not great.)
I love it! (= It's great.)	I love it. (= It's not great.)

A ▶6:12 **Listen and practice.**

1 How funny! / How funny.

2 That's hysterical! / That's hysterical.

3 That's terrific! / That's terrific.

4 I love it! / I love it.

B ▶6:13 **Practice saying each statement two ways, first with intonation showing pleasure and then sarcasm. Listen to compare.* (Note that your choices may differ from what you hear on the audio.)**

1 That's hilarious! / That's hilarious.

2 That's so funny! / That's so funny.

3 What a funny story! / What a funny story.

4 That's great! / That's great.

5 That's too much! / That's too much.

6 That really made me laugh! / That really made me laugh.

Regular past participle endings

There are three pronunciations of the past participle ending -ed,
depending on the final sound of the base form of the verb.

With voiced sounds (except /d/)
When the base form ends with a voiced sound, pronounce the -ed ending as /d/.

moved   canceled   described   stayed   agreed

With voiceless sounds (except /t/)
When the base form ends with a voiceless sound, pronounce the -ed ending as /t/.

helped   asked   crushed   watched

HOWEVER: When the base form ends with the sound /t/ or /d/, pronounce the -ed ending as a new syllable,
/ɪd/ or /əd/. In American English, the final sound before the -ed ending is always /t̬/, no matter whether the base
form ended in the sound /t/ or /d/. Link /t̬/ with the -ed ending.

wai ted	→	/weit̬ɪd/
re por ted	→	/rɪpɔrt̬ɪd/
nee ded	→	/nit̬ɪd/
in clud ed	→	/ɪnklut̬ɪd/

Voiced sounds		Voiceless sounds
/b/	/i/	/p/
/g/	/ɪ/	/k/
/ð/	/eɪ/	/θ/
/v/	/ɛ/	/f/
/z/	/æ/	/s/
/ʒ/	/ɑ/	/ʃ/
/dʒ/	/ɔ/	/tʃ/
/m/	/oʊ/	/t/
/n/	/ʊ/	
/ŋ/	/u/	
/r/	/ʌ/	
/l/	/d/	

Reduction in perfect modals

The auxiliary have in perfect modals is generally reduced. The /h/ is dropped and /æ/ is reduced to /ə/.

/wʊt̬əv/
If I'd looked at the expiration date, I **would have** renewed my passport.

/maɪt̬əv/
If I weren't Japanese, I **might have** needed a visa to enter the country.

/wʊt̬ənəv/
If we'd left on time, we **wouldn't have** missed our flight.

Perfect modals	
would have	
could have	
should have	+ [past participle]
might have	
may have	

A ▶6:14 Listen and practice.

1 moved	5 agreed	9 watched	12 needed
2 canceled	6 helped	10 waited	13 included
3 described	7 asked	11 reported	
4 stayed	8 crushed		

B ▶6:15 Listen and practice.

1 If I'd looked at the expiration date, I would have renewed my passport.

2 If I weren't Japanese, I might have needed a visa to enter the country.

3 If we'd left on time, we wouldn't have missed our flight.

C Circle the correct pronunciation of each -ed ending.

1 avoided	/ɪd/	/t/	/d/	9 promised	/ɪd/	/t/	/d/
2 looked	/ɪd/	/t/	/d/	10 covered	/ɪd/	/t/	/d/
3 summarized	/ɪd/	/t/	/d/	11 added	/ɪd/	/t/	/d/
4 arrived	/ɪd/	/t/	/d/	12 changed	/ɪd/	/t/	/d/
5 owed	/ɪd/	/t/	/d/	13 reported	/ɪd/	/t/	/d/
6 ruined	/ɪd/	/t/	/d/	14 discussed	/ɪd/	/t/	/d/
7 kicked	/ɪd/	/t/	/d/	15 investigated	/ɪd/	/t/	/d/
8 refunded	/ɪd/	/t/	/d/	16 enjoyed	/ɪd/	/t/	/d/

▶6:16 **Now practice saying each word aloud and listen to compare.***

D ▶6:17 **Practice saying each sentence aloud, paying attention to reductions. Listen to compare.***

1 If I'd put my passport in my briefcase, it wouldn't have gotten lost.

2 If you'd checked the luggage limits, you might have avoided extra charges.

3 If my friend's luggage hadn't gotten stolen, he could have gone on the sightseeing tour.

4 I probably wouldn't have missed my flight if I had come on time.

5 If they'd taken a few simple precautions, their luggage might not have gotten stolen.

UNIT 7

Linking sounds

Link plural noun endings to the first sound in the word that follows.

Superstitions about animals are very common. /supər'stɪʃənzəbout/

Some say rats leaving a ship will cause it to sink. /ræt'slivɪŋ/

Link third-person singular endings to the first sound in the word that follows.

A belief in a superstition often results in fear. /rɪ'zʌltsɪn/

> **Remember:** There are three different sounds for the endings of plural nouns and third-person singular verbs.
>
> | /z/ | /s/ | /ɪz/ |
> |---|---|---|
> | diamonds | results | promises |
> | superstitions | sharks | noises |
> | bottles | types | matches |
> | believes | beliefs | wishes |
> | dreams | sleeps | judges |

A ▶6:18 **Listen and practice.**

1 Superstitions about animals are very common.

2 Some say rats leaving a ship will cause it to sink.

3 A belief in a superstition often results in fear.

B ▶6:19 **Practice reading each sentence aloud, paying attention to the linking sounds you have learned. Listen to compare.*** (Note that your choices may differ from what you hear on the audio.)

1 A frog brings good luck to the house it enters.

2 Babies born with teeth become extremely selfish.

3 An itchy nose means you'll have a fight.

4 A lucky charm protects against the evil eye.

5 She keeps a large bowl of water near the front door.

6 Superstitions can be found in every culture.

7 A company claims to have invented a machine that allows people to talk with their pets.

8 Some fears are hard to overcome.

9 My sister believes in ghosts, avoids black cats, and carries a lucky charm in her pocket.

UNIT 8

Emphatic stress with auxiliary verbs

Use emphatic stress on an auxiliary verb to confirm or contradict.

A: Do you think Carrie Mulligan has a successful acting career?
B: I think so. She **IS** getting a lot of lead roles these days.

A: I wonder if I should take French lessons.
B: Great idea! I think you **SHOULD** learn French.

A: Have you eaten at the Blue Moon Café before?
B: Actually, I think I **HAVE** eaten there before.

A: Jan says you love coffee. Is that true?
B: Not at all. I really **DON'T** like coffee.

Remember: The auxiliary do needs to be added for emphatic stress in affirmative statements in the simple present or past tense.

A: Jan says you love coffee. Is that true?
B: Yes, it is. I really **DO** like coffee.

A ▶6:20 **Listen and practice.**

1 She **IS** getting a lot of lead roles these days.

2 I think you **SHOULD** learn French.

3 Actually, I think I **HAVE** eaten there before.

4 I really **DON'T** like coffee.

5 I really **DO** like coffee.

B ▶6:21 Practice responding to each speaker, using emphatic stress on the auxiliary verb. Listen to compare.*

1 "I think Olivia's a great cook."

RESPONSE: I agree. She does make great food.

2 "Your husband doesn't dance very well."

RESPONSE: That's true. He really doesn't dance well.

3 "Can you eat seafood?"

RESPONSE: Actually, I can't eat seafood. I'm allergic to it.

4 "Your cousins are hysterical!"

RESPONSE: I agree. They really do tell a lot of funny jokes.

5 "Ana's report is late again."

RESPONSE: Well, she does tend to procrastinate.

6 "Does Gary have a head for figures?"

RESPONSE: No. But he is taking a math class on Tuesday evenings.

7 "I think it's time to tell everyone you're going to quit."

RESPONSE: You're right. I should tell them sooner rather than later.

8 "Have you made up your mind yet?"

RESPONSE: No. But I have been thinking about it.

UNIT 9

Reading aloud

Because it's more difficult to understand language when it is read rather than spoken in conversation, read with a regular rhythm and use fewer sound reductions. If there's a title, state it separately with falling intonation. Pause at all punctuation. Separate sentences into thought groups, pausing after each. Pause slightly longer between sentences.

Envisioning the Future

In the 1960s, / only large institutions, / such as banks, / corporations, / and the military, / had computers. // They were expensive, / slow, / and very large– / requiring a special air-conditioned room– / and access to them was limited / to only a few people. // In the 1970s, / computer prices came down / and then small businesses began to use them. // Nevertheless, / in 1977, / the CEO and founder of Digital Equipment, / Kenneth Olsen, / predicted that computers would never be used in the home.

A ▶6:22 Listen to the selection. Then practice reading it aloud.

Envisioning the Future

In the 1960s, only large institutions, such as banks, corporations, and the military, had computers. They were expensive, slow, and very large—requiring a special air-conditioned room—and access to them was limited to only a few people. In the 1970s, computer prices came down and then small businesses began to use them. Nevertheless, in 1977, the CEO and founder of Digital Equipment, Kenneth Olsen, predicted that computers would never be used in the home.

B ▶6:23 Practice reading each selection aloud. Then listen to compare.* (Note that your choices may differ from what you hear on the audio.)

1 Birth of the Personal Computer

In the early 80s, Steve Jobs and Bill Gates introduced the personal computer—the Macintosh and the IBM PC, respectively—which made computing at home possible. In 1983, Jobs gave a speech about the future, in which he predicted that, for most people, a great deal of time would be spent interacting with personal computers. He also predicted that, within ten years, computers in the office and at home would be connected so people would be able to use them to communicate.

2 Predicting Social Media

In 1999, Gates predicted that small devices would be carried around by everyone so that they could get instant information and stay in touch with others. He also claimed that, by the early twenty-first century, Internet communities would have been formed, based on one's interests or to connect with friends and family.

Intonation of tag questions

When a tag question follows a statement to which a speaker anticipates agreement, both the statement and the tag question are said with falling intonation. The main stress in the tag question falls on the auxiliary verb and not on the pronoun. Note that there is generally no pause at the comma.

It's really shocking, isn't it?

They'll come up with a solution, won't they?

It's not really surprising, is it?

She didn't speak out against that project, did she?

It really makes you feel angry, doesn't it?

When the tag question represents a genuine question to which the speaker expects an answer, the statement is said with falling intonation, but the tag question is said with rising intonation.

It's really shocking, isn't it?

They'll come up with a solution, won't they?

It's not really surprising, is it?

She didn't speak out against that project, did she?

It really makes you feel angry, doesn't it?

A ▶6:24 **Listen and practice. (Each sentence is said two ways.)**

1 It's really shocking, isn't it?

2 It's not really surprising, is it?

3 It really makes you feel angry, doesn't it?

4 They'll come up with a solution, won't they?

5 She didn't speak out against that project, did she?

B ▶6:25 **Listen to the following tag questions. Check to indicate if each one anticipates agreement or expects an answer.**

	Anticipates agreement	Expects an answer
1 That's really appalling, isn't it?	☐	☐
2 He's worried about his children, isn't he?	☐	☐
3 It really makes you feel good, doesn't it?	☐	☐
4 It wasn't really true, was it?	☐	☐
5 They're going to do something about that problem, aren't they?	☐	☐
6 It's not really important, is it?	☐	☐
7 You heard that on TV, didn't you?	☐	☐
8 You'll support us, won't you?	☐	☐

▶6:25 **Now practice saying each tag question aloud and listen to compare.***

C ▶6:26 **Practice saying each tag question two ways, first to express anticipated agreement and then to express a genuine question. Listen to compare.***

1 It really makes you stop and think, doesn't it?

2 They're concerned about global warming, aren't they?

3 The president's economic policy is effective, isn't it?

4 The benefits of globalization are very clear, aren't they?

5 The benefits of globalization aren't very clear, are they?

6 There's no turning back, is there?

Test-Taking Skills Booster

The Test-Taking Skills Booster is optional. It provides practice in applying some key logical thinking and comprehension skills typically included in reading and listening tasks on standardized proficiency tests. Each unit contains one Reading Completion activity and one or more Listening Completion activities.

*Note that the practice activities in the Booster are not intended to test student achievement after each unit. Complete Achievement Tests for *Summit* can be found in the *Summit* ActiveTeach.

READING COMPLETION

Read the selection. Choose the word or phrase that best completes each statement.

Gender Roles

Until recently in the developed world, most married couples **(1)** ..... traditional roles, with the husband working outside the home and the wife taking care of the children and the house. Although many families still follow this tradition, those roles have become less iron-clad. A number of factors have contributed to this **(2)** ..... . **(3)** ..... , perhaps as a consequence of feminism, people have begun to believe that one's **(4)** ..... should not dictate one's role. **(5)** ..... , people feel they have "permission" to decide what they want to do in life. It's no longer **(6)** ..... for men to want to be the primary caregiver or homemaker. **(7)** ..... , many women would prefer to enter the working world instead of staying home. **(8)** ..... , a large number of women have achieved advanced academic and professional training, providing them with a significant earning potential.

On the other hand, factors other than personal choice have **(9)** ..... to the fluidity of gender roles. Life has become more expensive and it's **(10)** ..... for a family to exist on only one income, requiring married women to leave the home to earn money to help support the family. **(11)** ..... , the number of two-income households has grown exponentially. And despite the fact that women on average still earn less than men for the same job, their incomes have become an **(12)** ..... component of survival and prosperity in today's world. In similar fashion, a man's decision to stay home may not be voluntary. In the event he has lost his job, his decision to stay home might be one of necessity, not **(13)** ..... .

1	**A** rejected	**B** adopted	**C** gave	**D** needed
2	**A** change	**B** consequence	**C** continuation	**D** conflict
3	**A** Whereas	**B** While	**C** On the one hand	**D** On the other hand
4	**A** parents	**B** income	**C** gender	**D** age
5	**A** Despite this	**B** As a result	**C** Nevertheless	**D** Whereas
6	**A** beneficial	**B** advantageous	**C** harmful	**D** shameful
7	**A** Nevertheless	**B** Despite the fact	**C** By the same token	**D** First
8	**A** On the other hand	**B** Moreover	**C** For example	**D** Finally
9	**A** contradicted	**B** contributed	**C** coincided	**D** donated
10	**A** convenient	**B** difficult	**C** easy	**D** traditional
11	**A** Yet	**B** Even though	**C** Even if	**D** Consequently
12	**A** ordinary	**B** arbitrary	**C** unnecessary	**D** essential
13	**A** need	**B** habit	**C** choice	**D** logic

LISTENING COMPLETION

▶ 6:27 You will hear a conversation. Read the paragraph below. Then listen and complete each statement with the word or short phrase you hear in the conversation. Listen a second time to check your work.

The woman, Diane, is upset because she can't (1) .... Her husband is trying to help her, and he asks her (2) .... she saw it (3) .... She remembers that she used it (4) .... her friend Mark when she was (5) .... Her husband asks if she had been (6) .... when she texted Mark. Diane wants to know why that question is relevant, and her husband says that even though it's (7) .... to text while driving, the main reason he asked was to help her figure out when she (8) .... That question helps Diane remember that she had been downstairs (9) .... when she texted and that she had stuck (10) .... in the grocery bag.

READING COMPLETION

Read the selection. Choose the word or phrase that best completes each statement.

Where Values Come From

All of us live by a set of principles or beliefs that guide our actions and help us develop a sense of what is morally acceptable **(1)** ..... what is unacceptable behavior. But where do our values come from? According to psychologists, they develop throughout our lives and **(2)** ..... from a variety of sources, such as family, school, religious upbringing, the places we work in, **(3)** ..... as the media and music we watch and listen to.

For example, most of us learn from our parents to **(4)** ..... between right and wrong. When they read to us or tell us children's stories, we **(5)** ..... moral lessons about the consequences of good and bad behavior. **(6)** ..... we make mistakes or when we don't tell the truth, our parents correct us. Moreover, we learn from our parents' actions. Children **(7)** ..... how their parents relate to each other and handle social situations, and they always notice whether their parents are truthful or not.

(8) ..... , we are strongly affected by the views of our peers. Our friends, colleagues, and acquaintances "categorize" the people we know or who we hear about on the news—for example, who is unfriendly, who is generous, which politicians or celebrities are honest. Many people also believe their moral principles can be **(9)** ..... to their religious upbringing. Religion can provide a clear set of guidelines to live by that make it easier to distinguish between right and wrong.

1	**A** between	**B** from	**C** to	**D** about
2	**A** originate	**B** learn	**C** match	**D** populate
3	**A** known	**B** such	**C** as well	**D** as far
4	**A** activate	**B** distinguish	**C** enter	**D** educate
5	**A** absorb	**B** calculate	**C** inspire	**D** encourage
6	**A** Therefore	**B** Although	**C** Even if	**D** When
7	**A** observe	**B** disagree	**C** ignore	**D** compete
8	**A** Consequently	**B** As a result	**C** For instance	**D** Similarly
9	**A** described	**B** contributed	**C** attributed	**D** celebrated

LISTENING COMPLETION

▶6:28 **You will hear part of a report. Read the paragraph below. Then listen and complete each statement with the word or short phrase you hear in the report. Listen a second time to check your work.**

In the report, the speaker notes that celebrity philanthropists get lots of attention but also have their (1) .... For example, an aid worker complains that bringing celebrities in to do humanitarian work is more (2) .... it's worth. Why? Because celebrity philanthropists can be (3) .... and demanding. They also often do little to (4) .... the people they came to help. On the other hand, supporters note that some celebrity philanthropists (5) .... way and don't ask for special (6) .... Another criticism of celebrity philanthropists, however, is that they sometimes spread a (7) .... that places like Africa are hopeless and (8) .... Finally, some critics say celebrities (9) .... local humanitarian efforts and provide increased opportunities for (10) ....

READING COMPLETION

Read the selection. Choose the word or phrase that best completes each statement.

Avoiding Hearing Loss

Hearing plays a crucial role in all aspects of communication and learning. **(1)** ..... does even a small amount of hearing loss have a profound, negative effect on language development and comprehension, it **(2)** ..... affects the classroom learning of students who have difficulty hearing. **(3)** ..... deafness that occurs at birth or because of disease or injury, permanent **(4)** ..... to hearing can result from excessive exposure to noise. In fact, millions of people **(5)** ..... from this sort of hearing loss, called "noise-induced hearing loss." It is **(6)** ..... by damage to structures and / or nerve fibers in the inner ear. It can result from a one-time exposure to a very loud sound or from listening to loud sounds over an extended period of time. Unfortunately, noise-induced hearing loss cannot be medically or surgically **(7)** ..... .

So how can noise-induced hearing loss be **(8)** ..... ? In some cases it's impossible to avoid the **(9)** ..... exposure to one very loud sound, and some work environments are noisy. Nevertheless, there are many cases in which people can avoid voluntary exposure to loud sounds, and they **(10)** ..... . What are some steps anyone can take? Most importantly, identify the **(11)** ..... of loud sounds, such as lawnmowers, power tools, and music in your life. Next, adopt behaviors to protect hearing, such as avoiding or **(12)** ..... exposure to the loud sounds as much as you can. After that, make it a practice to automatically turn down the volume of music systems. Finally, when it's not feasible to avoid or **(13)** ..... loud sounds, use hearing protection devices. Such devices can reduce the noise to a safe level.

1	**A** Even though	**B** Not only	**C** If only	**D** Therefore
2	**A** yet	**B** in spite of this	**C** even if	**D** also
3	**A** Whenever	**B** Whereas	**C** Before	**D** Unlike
4	**A** aid	**B** damage	**C** benefits	**D** symptoms
5	**A** enjoy	**B** are helped	**C** result	**D** suffer
6	**A** aided	**B** caused	**C** benefitted	**D** cured
7	**A** caused	**B** corrected	**C** heard	**D** possible
8	**A** improved	**B** prevented	**C** treated	**D** confirmed
9	**A** fortunate	**B** accidental	**C** intentional	**D** obvious
10	**A** can	**B** might	**C** should	**D** do not
11	**A** effects	**B** sources	**C** problems	**D** consequences
12	**A** limiting	**B** combining	**C** making	**D** causing
13	**A** increase	**B** hope for	**C** create	**D** reduce

LISTENING COMPLETION

▶6:29 You will hear a report. Read the paragraph below. Then listen and complete each statement with the word or short phrase you hear in the report. Listen a second time to check your work.

Seol Ik Soo, a Korean (1) .... who was a passenger on a flight returning (2) .... South Korea (3) .... China, was daydreaming about his wife as the plane prepared (4) .... He and his wife had been married only (5) .... before and this was the first time they had been (6) .... Suddenly, he saw a ball of (7) .... in the cabin of the plane and the plane (8) .... Luckily, Seol escaped through a hole in the crashed plane. From outside of the plane he could hear other passengers calling (9) .... Instead of running away, Seol went back in to rescue others. No one knows exactly how many passengers Seol managed to carry out of the plane. There may have been (10) .... ten. After it was all over, Seol was asked how he had managed to behave so heroically and he responded that he's sure he couldn't have done it in his (11) ....

READING COMPLETION

Read the selection. Choose the word or phrase that best completes each statement.

Friendship

In the words of a famous song, friendship is "like a bridge over troubled water." In other words, you can always count on your friends' support when you need it the **(1)** ..... . Friends can tell when you're feeling **(2)** ..... , and they know whether or not you want to talk about it. They are thoughtful when it comes to your well-being, and they can **(3)** ..... according to your needs.

The truth is we need our friends to be dependable—through thick and thin. **(4)** ..... constantly trying to change you, good friends accept you as you are. And good friends roll with the punches. They get it that inside you're a good person with flaws, and that those shortcomings are part of who you are. **(5)** ..... ,

they know you make mistakes, and they forgive you for them, knowing you'll try to do better next time. And when people criticize you, friends stick up for you because even **(6)** ..... you're being difficult, friends are patient.

While you and your friends may have disagreements, you **(7)** ..... respect each other's opinions. Above all, you need to know that you can **(8)** ..... your friends with your secrets. If there's a problem between you, a friend will talk to you **(9)** ..... and not gossip about you with others. We can always count on our friends to be honest with us when others aren't. Friends don't keep things bottled up inside. Whenever there's an **(10)** ..... , they work things out together and move on.

	A	B	C	D
1	A heaviest	B most	C least	D nearest
2	A ready	B cold	C energetic	D blue
3	A criticize	B argue	C adjust	D learn
4	A Rather than	B Whereas	C Despite	D Before
5	A Moreover	B Otherwise	C Whether or not	D Unfortunately
6	A despite	B especially	C when	D so
7	A should	B never	C don't	D might
8	A help	B save	C trust	D lend
9	A formally	B casually	C importantly	D directly
10	A accident	B issue	C attribute	D examination

LISTENING COMPLETION

A ▶ 6:30 You will hear a description. Read the paragraph below. Then listen and complete each statement with the word or short phrase you hear in the description. Listen a second time to check your work.

The woman says she sometimes feels (1) .... because she's so (2) .... She says that when she puts things away, she then can't (3) .... She feels embarrassed to (4) .... because there's such a mess. So she asked her friend Alicia for help because Alicia's so (5) .... Alicia helped her (6) .... all her stuff to decide what was important and what she could (7) ....

B ▶ 6:31 You will hear a description. Read the paragraph below. Then listen and complete each statement with the word or short phrase you hear in the description. Listen a second time to check your work.

The woman is concerned about what she calls a problem with her (8) .... It's not a problem at (9) .... , but she worries when she gets really angry at her (10) .... and starts (11) .... at them. She believes that, after a bad day at work, she's just (12) .... it out on them. As a result, she took a workshop on (13) .... , where she learned that it's important to let off a little steam. So she took up (14) .... three days a week. When she feels angry, exercising helps her (15) .... what's making her mad.

READING COMPLETION

Read the selection. Choose the word or phrase that best completes each statement.

Laughter Yoga

The principle of Laughter Yoga is that you cannot be physically stressed and mentally relaxed at the same time. **(1)** ..... most forms of Yoga include body positions and exercises, Laughter Yoga is based on the physical activity of laughing, which relaxes the body and mind. Proponents of Laughter Yoga **(2)** ..... that it permits us to be more aware of the present **(3)** ..... dwelling on the past or worrying about the future. In short, it enables us to simply *be*.

Some **(4)** ..... that Laughter Yoga can be considered a new form of exercise. **(5)** ..... its proponents, it's a kind of internal jogging. Anyone can do it because, they say, everybody knows how to laugh. It is not necessary to tell jokes, have a sense of **(6)** ..... , or be happy in order to laugh. In fact, practitioners of Laughter Yoga are invited to "laugh for no reason," faking the laughter until it becomes real. It is **(7)** ..... that the physical action of laughing brings oxygen and certain body chemicals such as hormones to the body and the brain, thus fostering **(8)** ..... feelings and improving interpersonal skills. **(9)** ..... Laughter Yoga is practiced in groups, people leave each session laughing and feeling **(10)** ..... to each other. Believers in Laughter Yoga **(11)** ..... contend it can contribute to world peace. They say, "World peace first starts inside every one of us. We don't laugh because we are happy. We are happy because we laugh."

1	A Until	B While	C Whether	D If
2	A continue	B complain	C assert	D admit
3	A in addition to	B instead of	C in favor of	D along with
4	A tell	B ask	C claim	D wonder
5	A Even if	B Whenever	C Although	D According to
6	A anger	B humor	C happiness	D knowledge
7	A argued	B disputed	C required	D intended
8	A negative	B hopeless	C lucky	D positive
9	A Since	B All the same	C Even if	D Until
10	A separate	B connected	C different	D annoyed
11	A however	B nevertheless	C therefore	D besides

LISTENING COMPLETION

▶6:32 You will hear a story. Read the paragraph below. Then listen and complete each statement with the word or short phrase you hear in the story. Listen a second time to check your work.

The woman tells a story about her friend Mark, who loves to (1) .... Mark decided to play a joke on his friend John, who was very (2) .... and was always looking for (3) .... One day, Mark spoke to (4) .... of the Bargain Burger restaurant and asked her if she would (5) .... two very large burgers. The manager said "Sure," and Mark paid her for them (6) .... Mark explained that he would bring (7) .... for lunch and that the manager should (8) .... the huge burgers and put the regular low price on the check. When Mark and John finished eating, (9) .... and John was pleasantly surprised at the low price of the burgers. So the (10) .... John invited a couple of his friends to Bargain Burger for the huge hamburgers. But when the burgers came to the table, they were the ordinary tiny little ones, which made John (11) .... in front of his friends.

READING COMPLETION

Read the selection. Choose the word or phrase that best completes each statement.

Wi-Fi Safety

Staying connected anywhere is relatively easy today. We almost always have smartphones, tablets, or laptops at the ready. And **(1)** ..... the availability of free Wi-Fi everywhere—in hotels, cafés, stores, even in parks—we feel empowered to act as we do at home. For instance, we can do our online banking and make online purchases anywhere with **(2)** ..... . On the one hand, easy connectivity is a great **(3)** ..... . But on the other, wishful thinking can lull us into a false sense of **(4)** ..... . It's important to remember that **(5)** ..... at home, where our Internet connections are securely encrypted, free public Wi-Fi away from home is not.

What are some of the possible **(6)** ..... of using unencrypted Wi-Fi? First, a thief might be able to access your credit card information and make online or in-store purchases, leaving you to pay the bill. Many such purchases, however, especially if they don't conform to your usual buying pattern, **(7)** ..... the credit card company that the purchaser isn't you. Luckily, the company can cancel your card to stop any further **(8)** ..... from being made. **(9)** ..... , but perhaps more importantly, thieves can **(10)** ..... your usernames and passwords, enabling them to access your bank accounts and withdraw money. Finally, in the worst-case scenario, they can steal your identity, leaving you to **(11)** ..... it at great trouble to you. So how can you **(12)** ..... yourself? In summary, although free public Wi-Fi seems convenient, send personal information only to sites that are fully encrypted, and avoid using any mobile apps that **(13)** ..... personal or financial information.

#	A	B	C	D
1	A in spite of	B since	C in addition to	D due to
2	A aggravation	B difficulty	C cash	D ease
3	A advantage	B disadvantage	C importance	D problem
4	A disadvantage	B the future	C security	D anxiety
5	A like	B similarly	C unlike	D as well
6	A reasons	B consequences	C points of view	D possibilities
7	A indicate	B avoid	C alert	D accuse
8	A purchases	B decisions	C claims	D conflicts
9	A Secondly	B By the same token	C After	D Before
10	A provide	B recover	C return	D steal
11	A recover	B relate	C return	D resist
12	A affect	B promote	C remove	D protect
13	A provide	B require	C resist	D donate

LISTENING COMPLETION

▶ 6:33 You will hear part of a report. Read the paragraph below. Then listen and complete each statement with the word or short phrase you hear in the report. Listen a second time to check your work.

Consider this situation: You are waiting patiently for your bags at (1) .... You see other travelers pick up their bags, but still yours are nowhere in sight. There are fewer and fewer bags until finally (2) .... You wonder what happened to your bags and think perhaps they weren't transferred to your (3) .... when you changed planes. Or maybe the missing luggage was sent to (4) .... You go to the airline's (5) .... to file a claim and hope the bags will (6) .... and be delivered to (7) .... within a short time. If, on the other hand, the bags are permanently (8) .... or completely (9) .... , you will want to file a claim for damages. If you can document what you have lost, you will probably be reimbursed. But be aware that even if you have (10) .... to prove the value of items in your luggage, you won't receive (11) .... you originally paid for your property. But you will definitely receive something.

READING COMPLETION

Read the selection. Choose the word or phrase that best completes each statement.

Coping with Phobias

According to recent research, one in ten people worldwide has some kind of phobia or overwhelming (1) ..... . And even though phobias are (2) ..... , they are much more severe than the common garden-variety fear. But in what way?

For one thing, while most people can (3) ..... with most normal fears, a full-blown phobia is something people can't just put out of their mind. (4) ..... , phobics don't have much control over their phobias. As a result, they suffer from unpleasant physical and mental (5) ..... when confronted with what they fear. Such symptoms are similar to ones people experience when faced with real physical (6) ..... . (7) ..... , their heartbeat gets rapid, their throat goes dry, and their sweating increases. These unpleasant physical symptoms are intended to prepare people to (8) ..... harm in the face of real danger. However, the phobic, who isn't in any real physical danger, reacts in the same way. (9) ..... , phobics will go to great lengths to avoid what they fear and these extremely unpleasant physical responses. (10) ..... , there is hope for people with phobias despite their severity. In "cognitive behavioral therapy," or CBT, phobics are repeatedly (11) ..... to what causes the fear, which desensitizes them to it because nothing bad happens. If CBT doesn't work, "counter-conditioning" can teach patients to substitute a physical relaxation response when in the presence of what (12) ..... them. In summary, there is hope for phobics who get (13) ..... . The success rate of therapy is excellent.

	A	B	C	D
1	A danger	B anxiety	C relaxation	D need
2	A talents	B harmful	C fears	D certain
3	A appreciate	B come down	C cope	D notice
4	A Fortunately	B In other words	C Similarly	D Even so
5	A symptoms	B fears	C benefits	D emotions
6	A relief	B pleasure	C danger	D symptoms
7	A Even so	B For example	C However	D Moreover
8	A undergo	B avoid	C cause	D receive
9	A However	B Because	C In contrast	D Consequently
10	A For example	B While	C Unfortunately	D Fortunately
11	A exposed	B allowed	C reduced	D increased
12	A relaxes	B helps	C angers	D frightens
13	A success	B failure	C treatment	D ready

LISTENING COMPLETION

A ▶6:34 You will hear a conversation. Read the paragraph below. Then listen and complete each statement with the word or short phrase you hear in the conversation. Listen a second time to check your work.

The man is reading about a way (1) .... in a short time. But the woman is doubtful and says it sounds (2) .... He disagrees and explains the scheme: You get a list of (3) .... and then send (4) .... to the last person on the list. Then you add (5) .... to the list. When someone else gets that list, the money (6) .... rolling in. The woman says that this is such an (7) .... get-rich-quick scam.

B ▶6:35 You will hear a conversation. Read the paragraph below. Then listen and complete each statement with a word or short phrase you hear in the conversation. Listen a second time to check your work.

The woman says there's a company that has (8) .... for people to learn to speak a new language during the time when they're (9) .... She thinks it's absolutely (10) .... The man, on the other hand, says he wouldn't (11) .... that it's impossible. He says he heard that some (12) .... in a sleep-learning lab had (13) .... the basics of Russian in only one week.

READING COMPLETION

Read the selection. Choose the word or phrase that best completes each statement.

Can We Increase Our Intelligence?

In a general sense, intelligence can be defined as the ability to learn, understand, and apply knowledge or skills. While many experts have argued that one's IQ score simply cannot be **(1)** ..... , others claim that these abilities can be maximized by exercising the brain. In their opinion, certain activities, **(2)** ..... reading regularly, doing puzzles daily, or learning a new language, may in fact improve our thinking skills, capacity to remember, and general knowledge. Furthermore, they make the point that IQ tests don't provide an adequate **(3)** ..... of real intelligence. In fact, they measure how one's level of academic achievement can be predicted but do not measure creativity or "street smarts"—the ability to **(4)** ..... with everyday life. Likewise, they are **(5)** ..... to measure one's potential for growth. Some experts suggest that other aspects of intelligence be considered as well— emotional intelligence being one example.

Moreover, Harvard University's Howard Gardner proposed that psychologists and educators **(6)** ..... the existence of at least seven distinct areas of intelligence. Two of these, linguistic and mathematical, are currently measured to some degrees by IQ tests. **(7)** ..... , another two, interpersonal and intrapersonal, are measured by EQ tests. He also proposed including visual-spatial intelligence. In addition, Gardner recommended that two other aspects of intelligence be **(8)** ..... : musical and physical. Gardner considers each of these intelligences to be areas of human potential; **(9)** ..... , they can be developed and increased.

	A	B	C	D
1	believed	increased	provided	genetic
2	such as	from	for instance	to
3	tool	measurement	improvement	completion
4	measure	encounter	face	deal
5	unable	equipped	incomplete	designed
6	contribute	criticize	acknowledge	change
7	Similarly	As a result	Because of this	For instance
8	recognized	removed	presented	altered
9	otherwise	that is	even so	besides

LISTENING COMPLETION

▶ 6:36 You will hear part of a lecture. Read the paragraph below. Then listen and complete each statement with the word or short phrase you hear in the lecture. Listen a second time to check your work.

The lecturer says that a key argument in favor of (1) .... being the source of extreme intelligence is that most geniuses don't have extremely (2) .... ancestors. However, an argument in favor of the (3) .... view is that talented families do (4) .... They believe it shows that talent is (5) .... through genes. One living example that supports this (6) .... is the story of the (7) .... Srinivasa Ramanujan, who was raised in a (8) .... in India and had almost (9) .... in mathematics. In other words, he was (10) .... talent.

UNIT 9

READING COMPLETION

Read the selection. Choose the word or phrase that best completes each statement.

Protecting Wildlife and People's Livelihoods

Due to its **(1)** ..... rising population as well as unregulated development, Cambodia's wildlife habitats have been at risk. **(2)** ..... more and more poor, uneducated, and inexperienced farmers have taken up agriculture near the edges of Cambodia's shrinking forests, conflicts with Cambodia's wild Asian elephants have increased. An increasing number of hungry elephants have been searching for food near the edges of the forests. As a consequence, they have **(3)** ..... crops severely, forcing the farmers to kill the elephants in order to protect their livelihoods.

Tuy Sereivathana (known as Vathana), who grew up in the countryside, learned to respect both nature and the elephants. After choosing to study forestry at his university, he committed himself to the **(4)** ..... of Cambodia's natural resources and began working for the protection of the country's national parks. To begin

with, Vathana focused his attention on understanding the **(5)** ..... the Cambodian farmers were facing. As a result, he came to the **(6)** ..... that the farmers needed to know more about the elephants' migration patterns and how to apply practical solutions for protecting their farms.

First, he helped them build electric fences. Then, he **(7)** ..... them how to use hot chili peppers and other native plants that elephants don't like in order to discourage the animals from eating their crops. Moreover, he **(8)** ..... the farmers to organize themselves to help each other guard their farms at night and to use fireworks and make other loud noises to scare the elephants off. Most **(9)** ..... , he helped farmers improve their farming techniques so they would have no reason to go farther into the elephants' habitat.

	A	B	C	D
1	simply	respectfully	rapidly	likely
2	As	Provided that	Unless	Whether or not
3	lost	gathered	damaged	planted
4	ecology	conservation	habitat	education
5	opportunities	challenges	tools	families
6	realization	education	occupation	notification
7	asked	showed	indicated	developed
8	ordered	changed	corrected	advised
9	importantly	truthfully	quickly	interestingly

LISTENING COMPLETION

▶ 6:37 You will hear part of a report. Read the paragraph below. Then listen and complete each statement with the word or short phrase you hear in the report. Listen a second time to check your work.

Some experts believe the world's total population will increase through 2070. However, it will stabilize and will have (1) .... by that time. They also predict an (2) .... life expectancy and (3) .... birthrates. This will contribute to a (4) .... toward aging populations worldwide, particularly in (5) .... developed countries. According to newsweek.com, one in every six people will be (6) .... over sixty-five by 2050. In fact, there will be (7) .... seniors as children. However, in Africa, the population of children under eighteen years old will (8) .... These challenges will require more funding for children's (9) .... and (10) .... resources for seniors. In addition, more (11) .... will have to be produced for a growing population.

READING COMPLETION

Read the selection. Choose the word or phrase that best completes each statement.

The Other Side of the Story

Although globalization has promised to benefit everyone with an increase in worldwide wealth and prosperity, critics argue that there is **(1)** ..... a widening gap between the rich and the poor. While corporations in some developed countries have outsourced both manufacturing and customer service jobs to developing countries overseas, workers who have lost those jobs **(2)** ..... to make ends meet. On the other hand, India's economy has reaped the **(3)** ..... of globalization with the establishment of call centers, where English-speaking staff provide 24/7 technical support by phone and Internet to customers all over the world. So, more people in India have **(4)** ..... good jobs and a steady income.

Even so, critics of globalization argue that **(5)** ..... free trade has made the world so competitive that criminal activities have flourished. While child labor is illegal in many countries, its practice has increased to fill manufacturing **(6)** ..... for gold and textiles. Recent news reports have exposed the use of slavery on merchant ships, where workers are mistreated and forced to work without receiving any wages. Even worse, due to the fact that there is little international **(7)** ..... regulation, some developing countries are becoming dumping grounds for hazardous industrial waste. In other countries, increased development has brought with it uncontrolled pollution, **(8)** ..... threatens public health and contributes to global warming.

(9) ..... , economic opportunities made possible by globalization have also encouraged government corruption. Some argue that a global economy has helped drug cartels and terrorists move people and materials across borders more easily.

1	**A** either	**B** instead	**C** contrast	**D** neither
2	**A** struggle	**B** demonstrate	**C** apply	**D** interview
3	**A** changes	**B** unemployment	**C** challenges	**D** benefits
4	**A** obtained	**B** lost	**C** searched	**D** desired
5	**A** unwanted	**B** unregulated	**C** inadequate	**D** decreased
6	**A** locations	**B** resources	**C** opportunities	**D** demands
7	**A** environmental	**B** illegal	**C** recognized	**D** agreement
8	**A** which	**B** so that it	**C** since it	**D** and
9	**A** For instance	**B** Even so	**C** As a result	**D** Unfortunately

LISTENING COMPLETION

A ▶6:38 You will hear a report. Read the paragraph below. Then listen and complete each statement with the word or short phrase you hear in the report. Listen a second time to check your work.

The woman says that consumers in (1) .... have been catching up with consumers in (2) .... in purchasing nonessential luxury goods. However, there is concern that the increase in (3) .... of luxury goods will have a (4) .... on the environment. The director of research for Worldwatch warns that supplies of natural resources may (5) ....

B ▶6:39 You will hear a report. Read the paragraph below. Then listen and complete each statement with the word or short phrase you hear in the report. Listen a second time to check your work.

The man reports that a recent survey conducted in more than (6) .... countries shows that people continue to be concerned about (7) .... issues. Specifically, they worry about their country's (8) .... , deteriorating (9) .... , and the growing gap between the (10) .... However, most respondents didn't blame these concerns on (11) ....